THE ROAD TO MORAL CAPITALISM

THE ROAD TO MORAL CAPITALISM

STEPHEN B. YOUNG

道
德

"My only topics are benevolence and righteousness."

- Mencius

ISBN: 978-1-941768-23-5 ebook edition
ISBN: 978-1-941768-89-1 print edition

TABLE OF CONTENTS

道
德

INTRODUCTION

STEPHEN B. YOUNG

The collapse of global financial markets in the fall of 2008 was not just another equilibrium adjustment in capitalism. It exposed a fundamental weakness in the operations of free markets. In markets for financial products that were not closely regulated by the state to minimize speculation, pricing became inefficient and global economic resources were poorly allocated. Several trillion dollars were spent on investments that had no commensurate long term value, causing losses in real terms to many, many people and pushing the world economic into recession with job losses and business failures.

This book introduces the concept of why financial markets fail, what are the human forces that drive such failures, and what might be done to correct the moral aptitude of buyers and sellers. Implicit in this presentation of a failure of capitalism in a belief that a moral sense can be brought to bear in business and economic activity. It would be, of course, mixing apples and oranges, oil and water, at times. The claims of unenlightened self-interest, especially under conditions of speculation, are powerful and hard to offset. The voice of a longer term rationality, the prudence and foresight that arise from the moral mind, can be heard only with difficulty under those conditions. That is why the collapse of financial markets in 2008 was brought about by the most highly compensated and best educated American business professionals – graduates of MIT, Harvard Business School, Wharton, the University of Chicago business school and only a few other similar institutions of demanding intellectual achievement. But in the last analysis all the mathematical formulae, all the proprietary algorithms of trading desks, came to naught. The core valuation equations were wrong. Sub-prime mortgages and related CDOs and CDSs were over-valued given longer term realities. Mortgages issued to borrowers who were very likely to default are worth less than their face value. They are bad investments and a bad use of capital. But under the operational code of financial markets, billions of dollars were put into these instruments willy-nilly.

Great banking houses like Bear Stearns and Lehman Brothers collapsed. Other great and wealthy financial institutions on Wall Street – AIG, Citigroup – would have failed too if the public authorities, mostly the Federal Reserve Bank, had not given them billions in additional capital.

But the most important casualty of the 2008 collapse was not the bankrupt firms or all those who lost money, it was a conviction in the rationality of free markets. An ideology that had won many Nobel Prizes in economics died. Since the fall of 2008, few have commented on this particular death so it has not become notorious. But it is important nonetheless. It was a Gotterdamerung – a twilight of a once powerful God – Mammon in Christian New Testament terminology. The religious certainty of the Washington Consensus, of Neo-liberalism, can be no more. It was a Martin Luther moment of challenge and potential reformation in free market capitalism.

The opportunity before us is to re-think capitalism to avoid the rent-seeking exploitations and political abuses of state run economies on one side and the dislocations of free market mispricing on the other side.

We need an ideology of good human values – economic values that are stable and reward both workers and investors and moral values that respect the claims of customers, employees, investors, suppliers, communities, and the environment.

This book is a small step towards such a new theory of capitalism.

Stephen B. Young
St Paul, Minnesota
January 2013

道

德

Tao Te 25 in Running Script © 2014 by Weiwing Lu

CHAPTER ONE
CSR AND PUBLIC GOODS

A very helpful way to understand corporate social responsibility within capitalism is to think of it in structural/functional terms as a process for the private business enterprise that mediates the enterprise with its environment.

Private enterprise does not have modern society all to itself. There is government and there is, increasingly, civil society. Private enterprise seeks profit within the rules and regulations set down by government and ingests the social capital provided by civil society. Successful business enterprise in the post-industrial society of the 21st century needs an internal function that will mediate interactions among business, government, and civil society. Such mediation, I suggest, is the function of CSR and CSR managers.

I speak largely of "CSR" but sustainability management as well as ESG – environment, society and governance – or comprehensive risk management all point to the same strategic management function that promotes the wellbeing of the business firm in the future and so enhances its current capital valuation.

But what, exactly, does CSR mediate? CSR is not a production function delivering the goods and services of private enterprise, though it influences the substance of such outputs. It is not corporate governance precisely, though it shapes governance policies and procedures. It is not any of the traditional fields of study in business schools: human relations, operations, finance, marketing and sales, strategy and organization; though it intrudes into each of these practical disciplines.

Mediation is a process only. What does CSR have to say about the direction of mediation in any given decisional situation? How domineering should the company be towards government and civil society? How submissive? Be nice to its stakeholders? Care about the environment? Be a good citizen? Where are guidelines for such policies and decisions? Should the company be more forthcoming or less? Raise prices or lower them? Add costs or turn its back on external concerns and keep the cost of its goods and services as low as possible?

Mediation as a function is not a rule of conduct; it is not a set of ten commandments or a noble eightfold way that would apply under all circumstances as the definition of the right thing to do. It is rather a form of discourse ethics where issues have to be spotted, analyzed, and addressed.

So, then, what actually is the subject matter specific to CSR mediation?

I would like to suggest that there is a special character to CSR concerns within its task to mediate for the private enterprise with other social sectors.

Organizational outputs can be, and often are, considered as private goods or public goods.

Private goods are:

Private goods can be transferred in a market. They can be priced and exchanged. A loaf of bread is a private good; its owner can exclude others from using it, and once it has been consumed, it cannot be used again. Private goods are conveniently the subject of personal ownership; they admit to designation as "mine" or "yours" and come within the reach of having a title that permits an owner to exclude all others from possession, use and enjoyment. With ownership, we can exclude others. Also, with ownership people are in rivalry with one another to get their hands on the good or enjoy the service. For example, if one individual visits a doctor there is one less doctor's visit for everyone else, and it is possible to exclude others from visiting the doctor. This makes doctor visits a rivaled and excludable private good.

Public goods are:

any outcome that is open to all. Such an outcome is sharable; it is said to be non-rivalrous and non-excludable. It is hard to personally own and exchange public goods even though they can be enjoyed. A traffic light is a public good. One person can benefit in safely crossing a street and so can everyone else who passes by. But none of them owns the pole and light. Usually the government does. Non-rivalry means that consumption of the good by one individual does not reduce availability of the good for consumption by others. Non-excludability means that no one can be effectively excluded from using the good.

Breathing air does not significantly reduce the amount of air available to others, and people cannot be effectively excluded from using the air. This makes air a public good, albeit one that is economically trivial, since air is a free good.

A standard list of public goods would include: peace, rule of law, a system of property rights and enforcement of contracts, communications and transportation systems, including the internet, the Linux community of software, beauty, knowledge, lighthouses.

Paul A. Samuelson is usually credited as the first economist to develop the theory of public goods. In his classic 1954 paper The Pure Theory of Public Expenditure, he defined a public good, or as he called it in the paper a *"collective consumption good"*, *as follows: ...*

[goods] which all enjoy in common in the sense that each individual's con-sumption of such a good leads to no subtractions from any other individual's consumption of that good...

In the real world, there may be no such thing as an absolutely non-rivaled and non-excludable good; but economists think that some goods approximate the concept closely enough for the analysis to be economically useful.

One of the most basic of public goods is a state where individuals can enjoy their liberties, including use of property and the pursuit of happiness. This public good is protected by the rule that one person's freedom stops where it impinges on the equal freedom of others. (Declaration of Rights of Man and Citizen) Drawing the appropriate line between private right (which authorizes private initiatives) and limitations on that right to protect the rights of others is a messy process.

Where does my freedom to smoke end so that your liberty not to inhale second-hand smoke can be vindicated? Adam Smith in his lectures on jurisprudence called this intersection of private and public goods the problem of "police".

The production of public goods can also result in positive externalities which are not remunerated. If private organizations don't reap all the benefits of a public good which they have produced, their incentives to produce it voluntarily might be insufficient. Consumers can take advantage of such positive externalities or public goods without contributing sufficiently to their creation. This is called the free rider problem, or occasionally, the "easy rider problem" [1]

In the classic theory of the private firm, the business enterprise need not concern itself with public goods. It is to define its success or failure only with respect to the private goods or services it sells. Under this theory, as advocated with skill and passion by Milton Friedman and the Chicago School of economic thinking, if there are negative externalities spawned by the private sector creating a public concern, then it is up to government to step in and provide new, additional public goods in the form of regulation of private activity for the common good.

Thus, even in a theoretical world of purely private goods, there remains a problem along the border where something "public" arises to change the character of the private good into something of greater communal concern. The border must not only be defined, it must be defended on both sides. The private goods side seeks to push the border farther away from its core autonomy and the public goods side seeks to prevent harm from crossing the border and to encourage positive externalities to be produced and shipped out "abroad" for public consumption. Watching over the border and adjusting disputes between the two sides is the function of CSR.

We might note that both the collapse of credit markets in 2008 and BP's oil leak in the bed of the Gulf of Mexico are instances of private goods suddenly becoming more than just that, becoming of great concern to many publics.

But outputs cannot so easily be allocated to just two categories of private and public. Some services that produce a public good, education for example, can be well delivered by private enterprise without government direction or supervision. Consider Oxford University or Harvard College. But say, are financial services similarly suitable for private enterprise production or do they require supervision of their externalities? What are we to do with goods of a mixed character – leave them to markets or subject them to regulation? If a company is producing goods or services of a mixed character, it might then have to mediate between market realities and government regulations.

It may make more sense to think of a continuum of goods with completely private goods at one extreme and purely public goods at the other extreme. Next to fully private goods would come quasi-private goods and then a set of quasi-public goods before we get to purely public goods.

Quasi-private goods

Quasi-private goods arise when private goods or services throw off positive and negative externalities. The idea is a crossing of the border between a purely private good and something with a more public character. A positive externality occurs when some benefit can be enjoyed beyond the ties of privity attaching one owner to a subsequent owner. Thus, a work of art, though it can be owned and rival others may be excluded from seeing or appreciating it, casts positive benefits of beauty and understanding. Its beauty or social meaning can be more than just a personal possession. Education provided privately is a benefit to more that those who pay tuition to learn new knowledge and skills. It contributes to social capital and to the capacity of a family or a society to advance in politics and economics.

A way of thinking of the difference between absolutely pure private goods and quasi-public goods is that others take an interest in the creation or the effect of quasi-private goods. The concept applicable here is analogous to that of negligence in the common law. Under the tent of negligence, when one's actions implicate the wellbeing of others, a duty may arise to use caution in so acting so that others are not harmed. Brett, Master of Rolls and later Lord Esher, put the concept this way in the case of Heaven v. Pender (1883, 11Q.B.D. 503): "Whenever one person is by circumstances placed in such a position with regard to another that every one of ordinary sense who did think would at once recognize that if he did not use ordinary care and skill in his own conduct with regard to those circumstances he would cause danger of injury to the person or property of the other, a duty arises to use ordinary care and skill to avoid such danger." Much later, Lord Atkin offered a different version of this principle of responsibility for use of private property in Donoghue v. Stevenson (1932, A.C. 562): The rule that you are to love your neighbor becomes in law, you must not injure your neighbor; and the lawyer's question Who is my neighbor? receives a restricted reply. You must take reasonable care to avoid acts or omissions which you can reasonably foresee would be likely to injure your neighbor. Who, then in law is my neighbor? The answer seems to be – persons who are so closely and directly affected by my act that I ought reasonably to have them in contemplation as being so affected when I am directing my mind to the acts or omissions which are called into question."

A rather similar point was also made in the 1789 Declaration of Rights of Man and Citizen as follows in paragraph 4: Liberty consists in the power to do anything the does not injure others; accordingly, the exercise of the rights of each man has no limits except those that secure the enjoyment of these same rights to the other members of society.

Private goods lose some of their privileged autonomy when they assume a character that can or will impact a wider circle of circumstances.

Quasi-private goods and services retain the core features of private goods. They are the subject of rivalry and potential owners and users can be excluded from ownership and use. They can be priced and sold with title changing hands or beneficial enjoyment placed in another's possession. But unlike pure public goods, they are encumbered with impacts on others outside the connection of buyer and seller. They create externalities. Thus, those others who are impacted by the use of the good or service take an interest in how the good or service is financed, made, sold, delivered, and used.

CSR paradigms thus arise to mediate between the core privacy of the good or service and the legal autonomy of the company that provides it and the interests, claims and expectations of those who fall within the circumference of its externalities. CSR mediation can be analogized to avoiding negligence through prudent foresight.

A negative externality occurs when production and sale of a private good impinges on the enjoyment or well-being of others. Pollution of air and water from manufacturing is perhaps the classic case of a negative externality. As pollutants are discharged from private property into a public stream or river or penetrate into groundwater from which others draw their drinking water they create negative externalities for those who might suffer from such pollution. Littering, or not picking up after your dog on a sidewalk or a public park, are other examples of a negative externality.

The concept of negative externality slides into the distinction of being a "public bad". If enough people are negatively affected by behavior that undermines public health, the rule of law, public morals and decency, safety and security of persons and property, then it loses its entirely private character and becomes at least a quasi-private good, or perhaps even a quasi public good liable to regulation and control. Bad factory working conditions, for example, become quasi private goods and generate advocacy for remediation on the part of unions and socially concerned NGOs.

Banking and financial services are business that produce both positive and negative externalities. And so banking and the selling of securities are highly regulated. As are public health, drug manufacture and sale, insurance and agriculture.

Quasi-private goods also include those public goods which can be and are rendered private – ownership rights are created to exclude others and make them compete for use. This occurs in intellectual property when creativity, knowledge and technique which are conceptually accessible to all freely without dilution of their potential are placed under patent or copyright to prevent free use and to force pricing of access through a market.

A poem for example can be read by many people without reducing the consumption of that good by others; it is non-rivalrous. However, the individual who wrote the poem may decline to share it with others by not publishing it and keeping it as exclusively "his" or "hers". Similarly, the information in most patents can be used by any party without reducing consumption of that good by others. Copyrights and patents provide temporary monopolies, or, in the terminology of public goods, providing a legal mechanism to enforce excludability for a limited period of time.

Some quasi-private goods are called "club goods" for their use is restricted to members of a club, like a union or a country club or a co-operative. In this category are attendance at sporting events – football matches – and theaters. These goods are public for some for a price of admission but excludable to others. Sports teams are usually owned privately but emotionally are considered not as private property but as part of a community's emotional identity. In moments of team crisis, fans think they should have a say in the decisions of owners to, say, fire or hire a coach or to move the team to a different community.

Thus, we might say education or health care is a quasi-private good. Each brings non-excludable and non-rival benefits to a public but can be provided through private contract in a market place where a price is placed on access to the service. Communities are better off with higher educational achievements and higher standards of public health.

A good which is rivalrous but non-excludable is sometimes called a common pool resource. Such goods raise similar issues to public goods: the mirror to the public goods problem for this case is sometimes called the tragedy of the commons. For example, it is so difficult to enforce restrictions on deep sea fishing that the world's fish stocks can be seen as a non-excludable resource, but one which is finite and diminishing.

Quasi-public goods

Some outcomes are open to competition but no claims of ownership can prevent entry of competitors. Natural resources are such quasi-public goods. Their exploitation gives rise to the tragedy of the commons: each acquirer of the good over-consumes and destroys the underlying asset, which is finite and diminishing. Fish in the oceans and potable water are such diminishing assets that will inflict harm once they are depleted. With such quasi-public goods, pricing for current market consumption does not charge enough to encourage slow use for preservation of stocks and supplies.

With quasi-public goods, the priority claim of privacy and autonomy in decision-making around the making and use of the good or service attenuates even more than with quasi private goods. The scope or intensity of the externalities associated with the good or service is wider and deeper. So wide and so deep that something of a public interest can be said to have arisen. More than a few people external to the core production and exchange of the good or service care about its existential application in society, politics, the economy, and the environment.

Another version of quasi-public goods is goods and services produced by businesses "affected with a public interest." At the Common Law in traditional England, such business as hotels, ferries, common carriers, wharfs were held to higher standards of liability and responsibility because their customers had to rely to their detriment on the probity and caution of the owners. There was a general shared interest in personal safety to be enjoyed by numerous and unknowable future customers.

So, today for similar reasons, utilities, railways and airplanes are regulated by government to insure that the public interest in safety is vindicated by private parties.

Where a business has a monopoly or several businesses establish a cartel, government regulation steps in to prevent abuse of private power. When private capital is knowingly invested in such businesses, the private owners assume a responsibility to be good stewards of a public interest. Where private enterprise assumes the risk of market competition, it does not trespass into this zone of quasi-public goods.

Where private goods are created by intermingling private profit seeking with government powers to exclude rivals, rent seeking replaces market competition as the means of making money. Rent seeking, or crony capitalism, creates less new wealth and more social injustice and markets for private goods only. These private goods therefore actually become "public bads" because of the damage their production and sale does to the rule of law and the abuse of power so engendered. Such rent seeking transcends all justifications that tolerate private ordering through markets and so cannot benefit from the legitimacy of free market values. Such rent seeking merits restriction and elimination on the grounds it has a quasi public character (really a quasi public "bad") that is harmful to the community at large.

Protected national parks and wilderness areas are quasi-public goods. They are open to full exploitation as public property but

THE ROAD TO MORAL CAPITALISM

are placed in government ownership as a trust so that their use can be moderated and regulation through exclusion of some potential uses and users. One hiker on a trail does not prevent others from coming along to enjoy the same views and experiences. But at some point too many hikers, or drivers of ATV's, will indeed destroy the enjoyment value of the pristine physical setting. Airways for radio and television which, if unregulated would be public goods, are placed under government control for allocation to private businesses for exploitation.

With quasi-public goods, we may infer that the mediating function of CSR is more intense than in the case of quasi private goods. Any company confronting production and marketing decisions with respect to quasi public goods needs more than cost accounting and normal accounting controls to guide its decisions, especially at the level of the board of directors. Engagement with government, political actors, and NGOs is quite necessary in this realm where entrepreneurial activity intersects with the public interest.

Thus, the mediating role of CSR is strongest in the middle range of goods – where quasi-private and quasi-public goods are being offered. Here is where strategic CSR thinking and tactical CSR decision-making is of greatest value to a company. The need for CSR mediation is weakest at the extremes.

With fully private goods, we can expect market mechanisms of consumer and producer choice following price signals to rather adequately determine the quantity and quality of goods to be produced and sold. Here classical microeconomics holds intellectual sway.

At the other extreme, where government produced purely public goods, public authority legislates and regulates what will be provided, how it will be provided and at what cost. The function of private enterprise here is compliance with laws and regulations.

CSR enters in first on boundary issues: is this good purely private? Is it purely public so that private enterprise should be precluded from providing it? How large should the sphere of public goods publicly provided become? Should there be limits on what government should do? Is there a public good (usually a public bad) so intensely associated with the good that public concerns should be taken into account by private providers?

But most importantly, CSR comes to fore around issues raised by the production of quasi-private and quasi-public goods.

Production and sale of each kind of good or service – private, quasi-private, quasi-public, public – needs its own business model.

Private goods and services can be produced with the traditional micro-economic, price-setting model where supply and demand curves meet in free market exchanges and no attention need be paid to the costs or benefits of externalities. Here the principal driver of enterprise profits is cost control.

But, standards of internal governance, which do not reflect micro-economic considerations, and consideration for employees are none-the-less mandatory for sustained enterprise success even with respect to the production of only private goods and services. Here the American National Association of Corporate Directors and the OECD have provided guidelines for high standards of corporate governance in publicly traded enterprises.

And, of course, any business that loses sight of customer satisfaction will face increasing difficulties in earning satisfactory returns. So, even in the heart of autonomous ordering of enterprise decisions, concern for non-financial factors associated with certain stakeholder needs is still a necessary condition of business success.

These intangible CSR variables that live in a private firm's culture arise, in large part, from a concern for human dignity. Human dignity is both a positive and a negative externality of private ordering. How does our behavior affect the dignity of others? This is a standard of ethical consideration and moral right that applies to private persons, even when they engage in commercial and capitalist activities. It is a trump card overriding more self-centered and brutish behaviors and values. CSR considerations, therefore, have a role to play even in the heart of the most private of private enterprises. The autonomy of owners themselves is limited by claims arising from the need to validate human dignity.

The recently advocated oath of good conduct to graduates of MBA programs embraces a commitment to reflection on CSR approaches even in the most autonomous of private enterprises.

For quasi-private goods a more nuanced and complex business model is required. Driving down costs will not optimize firm profits as, in future periods, the costs of remediating negative externalities will more than off-set short-term profits and will compromise the firm's intangible assets supporting its brand equity and goodwill. Seeking quality is the preferred strategy for success in this range of goods and services. Assuming that a company's goods or services have a quasi-private character will induce the company to enhance customer loyalty and so avoid unexpected market shocks in its cost base or the demand curve for its outputs.

CSR management guides become applicable for these goods and services. Early intentional efforts to engage CSR perspectives in the management of private enterprises included the ISO 9000 standard for better quality and the ISO 14000 standard for reduction of externalities harmful to the environment.

Standards for non-cost based sourcing, production, and distribution are necessary supports for business decision-making. The quality movement's focus on quality and customer satisfaction is perhaps the best example of a CSR approach to producing this range of goods and services. The SA 8000 standards for factory working conditions is another such example. The Principles for Responsible Investing, associated with the United Nation's Global Compact, apply to quasi-private goods associated with portfolio investments. Other examples are industry codes such as the Coffee Community Common Code, The Wolfsburg Principles for banks, the Equator Principles for participation in World Bank projects, the ICC Code for Advertising and Marketing, the Electronics Code of Conduct, the code for extractive industries, the Jewelry Industry Code of Conduct, the Kimberley Process for certifying diamonds, etc., are other examples. An important and ongoing compliance component joins the CSR function at this point.

The Global Reporting Initiative, or GRI, provides a set of reportable data that surface points of concern over a firm's positive and negative externalities. GRI reports thus provide a basis for consideration of more astute CSR strategies on the firm's part.

With respect to quasi-public goods, adherence to standards, seeking quality, and sensitivity to externalities are necessary but not sufficient. In this environment, dialogue and negotiations with important constituencies and stakeholders may become necessary. Thus, a company needs to track the perceptions and needs of those quasi-publics, and real publics that voice concern or opposition to its business methods. As a matter of course the company too, most likely, will find it wise to maintain dialogue with government agencies and politicians to influence the introduction of laws, rules and regulations design to meet public interests and to moderate the impact on the firm of such regulatory requirements.

Here the CSR function expands to embrace very rigorous compliance and internal audit procedures and the role of legal counsel. The CSR function here is a very active one of express and overt mediation between the firm, government and civil society.

The business model most appropriate here is a hybrid one of market performance and regulatory compliance with cost requirements and imposed quality considerations. The model would be firms engaged in government contract work, say as a supplier of equipment to the military or to a space agency, or as administrator of government welfare programs in health and education. Profit comes from a negotiated margin provided for in a long term contract. A business in this environment takes on some of the characteristics of a regulated utility serving the public interest. It has lost a large degree of control over its costs, its production methods and its pricing to customers.

Governments also may easily contract for and subsidize quasi-public goods and services, such as education and loans for education.

The United Nation's Global Compact, which draws its principles from international treaties among governments and not from business dynamics, lists in its 10 principles examples of public goods or "bads" arising from important externalities. The point of the Global Compact is to remind companies that they should not degrade the quality of these public goods in their provision of market-based goods and services. By aligning itself with the Global Compact, a company therefore agrees to consider its business as one providing, to some extent, quasi-public goods.

Finally with pure public goods, I question whether a traditional free market business model is at all relevant. Such goods and services – justice, infrastructure, trustworthy currencies, vibrant social capital – are the responsibility first and foremost of public authorities. They are simply to be provided, not bought and sold. The Constitution of the United States in its preamble provides a noted list of such public goods: justice, domestic tranquility, the common defense, the general welfare, and the blessings of liberty. These are the goods that people seek by entering into allegiance with one another and through submission to a common public authority, a "res publica" of Roman heritage.

However, since some production function is inherent in the delivery of these goods and services, issues of quality and efficiency do arise. CSR plays a role with pure public goods in seeking ways for private firms to produce and deliver them as quasi-public goods under contract with public authority at lower cost or more efficiently than would be the case with publicly owned administrative bureaucracies.

The Caux Round Table Principles for Responsible Business provide a framework for CSR management in every environment – private goods, quasi-private goods, quasi-public goods and even with public goods. The CRT Principles set forth seven primary considerations for the impact of business decisions and the guidelines provide a structure for evaluating the interests of key stakeholders. Under the stakeholder constituency of community, intersection of the firm with pure public goods is considered.

CHAPTER TWO
THE SOCIAL ECOSYSTEM OF CSR: MEDIATING AMONG BUSINESSES, GOVERNMENT AND CIVIL SOCIETY

Corporate Social Responsibility (CSR) plays a vital, yet unheralded, role in mediation among the business sector, which creates private goods and so the wealth of nations, government, which provides for public goods, and civil society, which fosters and sustains social capital, which consists of all goods, public and private. Thus, CSR theory and practice has become necessary for the smooth functioning of any sophisticated, post-modern social ecosystem.

CSR guides what a firm produces in the way of private goods, quasi- private goods, quasi-public goods and public goods.

In the social ecosystem corporate social responsibility ("CSR") mediates between business, government, and civil society. As mediator, CSR provides both theory and practice. It is theory in that it provides principles, standards and benchmarks for business decision-making and it is practice in that it demands structures of action and implementation. In practice, CSR is the zone in which interactions between business and government, business and civil society, and among business, government and civil society exist and unfold in social reality.

The Caux Round Table has provided three interdependent sets of ethical principles, one for each of the three main social sectors – business, government, and civil society NGO organizations. Each sector requires interaction with the other two and, therefore, must look not only to its internal requirements for success, but to the needs and concerns of the other sectors as well. The Caux Round Table sets of principles can be found on its website at www.cauxroundtable.org.

CSR as a separate intellectual approach to business decision-making and as a set of best practices emerged in the mid 1990's. Its appeal grew as a response to concerns over how to control the negative externalities of capitalism after faith in government regulation of wealth creation collapsed with the fall of the Berlin Wall and the end of Communism. CSR was advanced by its first advocates as a process for the internalization into the business enterprise of social concerns and interests. As such, CSR fulfills a necessary role in modern, post-industrial society where the social processing falls under three distinct spheres of productive activity. First, government provides public goods, including the remediation and reduction of public "bads". Second, private enterprise or business produces material wealth for consumption. Third, values, norms, and other cultural standards are devised, set and advocated by civil society institutions from the family to the church and NGO activists.

The interaction of government, business and civil society with balance and harmony and without abuse of power is a state of social justice. The following chart helps us understand the interactions of these three primary sectors and therefore guides us to a more clear understanding of the role of CSR.

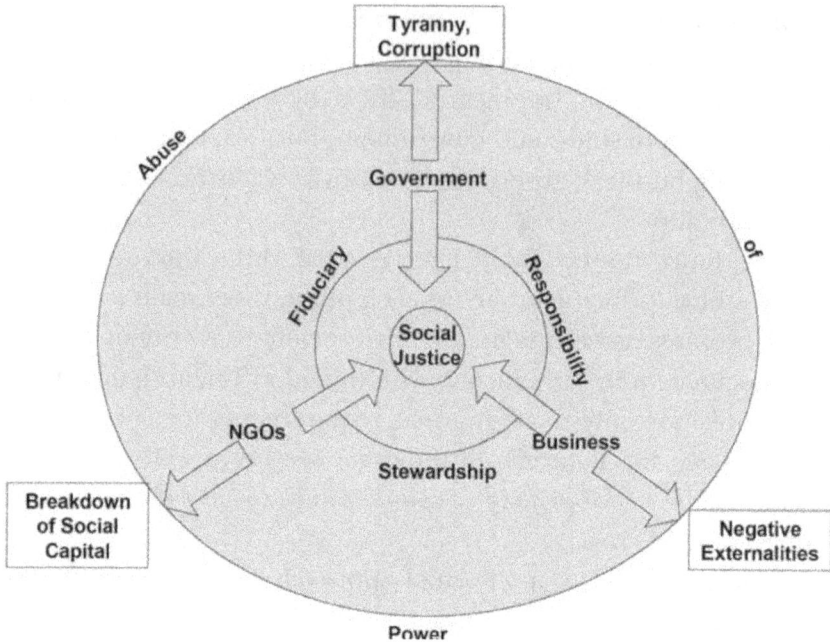

This chart presents the three sectors of modern society as dynamic forces that can tend towards social justice or, when they forget to use their powers as responsible fiduciary stewardship, towards conditions of injustice. When government oversteps the line and come to abuse its powers, there tyranny and corruption begin. When business oversteps that same line of unthinking concern for others, negative externalities are imposed on other parts of society, including of course the environment. When NGOs fail to meet the standards of responsible conduct, social capital erodes, undermining both good governance and responsible business practices.

CSR theory and practice keeps business within the zone of responsible fiduciary stewardship, moving the social contributions of business towards social justice.

The chart presents an ecosystem of interactions. Movements within each separate sector play off conditions and changes in the other sectors and, reciprocally, can set off changes in the other sectors. The ecosystem could be in equilibrium, or it could be in a dynamic process of change as flows of innovation move from one sector to the others and, then modified by other parts of the larger system, back into the sector of origin.

Thus, we can map Max Weber's famous theory of the role of the Protestant work ethic in the rise of capitalism. Change in the civil society sector – a new religious conviction – generated changes in business, which then brought about changes in government that in turn reinforced the key themes of Protestant ministry and taking action by individual covenant. More representative government, in turn, fostered the rule of law, protecting private property and enforcing contract rights, giving new impetus to the emerging capitalist tendencies in the business sector.

The Vectors of CSR Mediation

Now, CSR as a sub-system of the business sector on this chart mediates in several directions. First, it mediates the relationship between business and civil-society. Second it mediates aspects of the relationship between business and government. When the business/government relationship turns to statutory law and the administrative regulation of business, CSR within the business sector has been replaced by public functions of government and business has lost some degree of autonomy. One goal of CSR as a mediator for business is to sustain decision-making autonomy for the private sector. Frequently, as the reform response to the 2008 collapse of financial markets shows, the subordination of private business to more public regulation follows such a humiliating failure of CSR thinking in business. Where CSR does not put business ahead of the learning curve where public goods or quasi-public goods are concerned, business will lose its autonomy in market-based decision-making and become subject to public regulation and constraint.

Within business, CSR functions to monitor the relationships between enterprise and stakeholders: customers, employees, owners, other contributors of financial capital, suppliers, competitors, and communities. CSR most robustly understood sets performance goals for stakeholder relationships. Alignment of the enterprise with CSR strategies and management of stakeholder relationships within the moral compass of CSR strategies keeps private enterprise from abusing its powers.

The Forms of CSR Mediation

CSR operates in different modes. There is the mode of theory and analysis; there is the mode of standards; there is the implementation mode of practices; there is the mode of NGO engagement for CSR purposes; there is the mode of CSR evolution within companies.

CSR theories invoke the competencies of academics, consultants and NGO activities. CSR practices are the organizational expression of such theories and other normative realities.

These modes of CSR are contextualized by laws that establish market dynamics and by the supply and demand functions of markets themselves. With respect to markets, CSR both influences prices and, conversely, responds to price signals.

CSR Theory

CSR theory arises from many sources of thinking about ethics and business. Most anciently are the wisdom traditions of many religions. Human spiritual needs set forth moral norms on the good life and on the role of virtue. One thinks perhaps most readily of the Golden Rule, known in various analogous forms to most major religious traditions. Or, the gospel saying of Jesus Christ on not trying to serve both "God and Mammon".

In this religious sphere we find the advocacy of Confucius on virtues of propriety and righteousness, the teachings of Buddhism on the illusory essence of material possessions, and the guidance of Qur'an that humans are to be servants of God (khalifah) seeking to bring benefits to his creation and not to take from others for the self.

Appearing in a quasi-religious format, we can trace CSR concerns for minimizing the negative externalities of business to social disdain for the vulgar, the unrefined bourgeois arrievist, and the crassness of mercantile greed and the profits of financial usury.

Early socialism in England and France, Dickens' savage stereotype of Ebenezer Scrooge before his spiritual conversion, romantic poets and early bohemians, and church based campaigns for moral reformation all contained more than a hint of aristocratic disdain of mere truck and barter as the best way to make a life. From a more secular perspective, nineteenth century and later efforts to invoke state power in restraint of free enterprise provided themes for subsequent CSR normative advocacy. Consumer protection, unionization, anti-trust prohibitions, regulation of charges and fees, disclosure of information about securities invoked law to push certain negative social consequences of business back into the internal workings of enterprise.

During the 1980's in the United States, the discipline of business ethics emerged in leading business schools to provide a moral formal theory for the integration of these social concerns into core business decision-making. The academic enterprise of business ethics was primarily Kantian, searching for over-arching normative standards by which to restrain the more traditional short-sighted focus on profit as the criterion for measurement of business success. The discipline of business ethics, therefore, pitted itself in figurative mortal combat against the far more quantitative disciplines of finance and accounting.

In a famous response to the initial demand for business ethics, Professor Milton Friedman and his colleagues in the University of Chicago Economics Department and law school argued, in essence, that the only moral obligation of a business was to make a profit. Concern for management of externalities was the business of government. If certain lines of business activity were found objectionable, then the proper remedy was to regulate against them in hindsight. In terms of the above chart, the Milton Friedman approach was to seal off the sector of business as much as possible from penetration by civil society and from government. The undertaking of this stance was to minimize CSR engagement and maximize private sector autonomy. This stance turned to market pricing mechanisms to produce optimum social outcomes from business.

The Kantian approach, however, proposed the stakeholder theory of enterprise. In short, the theory of the firm was revised into a more complex system. The enterprise was to be seen not as a legal entity closed to outsiders under its own economic sovereignty resting on its own financial capital with command and control of its employees and in adversarial relationships with customers, suppliers and investors. The new stakeholder theory of the firm proposed that any large firm was really more of a de-facto partnership of investors, customers, employees, managers and suppliers, with more junior partners in the community and a circle of dependents that included the environment and competitors.

Environment activism starting in the 1970's provided additional intellectual support for a CSR approach both as company actions came under review and criticism and as the importance of environment sustainability was more persuasively advocated.

Parallel to this was the creation of social responsible investing in the United States, where companies were screened for, in the minds of some, unwholesome activities such as doing business in South Africa under conditions of Apartheid, making weapons or liquor, producing nuclear power, polluting, complicity in human rights violations, etc. These concerns for impacts on stakeholders measured not in financial, but in moral terms, created an heightened consciousness of doing business with regard for non-financial metrics. CSR emerged as an explicit theory during the 1990s in the European Union.

However, none of these approaches rested the case for CSR on financial analysis.

At the end of the day, if CSR does not embrace financial drives it will not rest securely within the business sector, but will be only intrusions imposed from the other two sectors. Thus, CSR theory needs to find a home in financial analysis in order to mediate successfully the intersections of business with civil society and government.

Financial Value Based CSR Theory

To overcome past limitations imposed by partially developed theories of CSR, I suggest that valuation analysis from investment theory be adopted for CSR purposes. In this way, CSR variables, which are primarily non-financial, can be integrated into mainstream approaches to doing business as the rational for certain important best practices. Using this approach to thinking about CSR and to practicing CSR equips CSR practitioners to optimize the mediating functions of CSR in the context of profitable business, just public governance, and a robust civil society.

Valuation theory uses as a principal theoretical approach to maximizing the economic value of an enterprise an estimation of future earnings, discounted back to the present as a net figure of potential profits. Then, the net figure is multiplied by an amount that represents the opportunity cost of buying that stream of future income. A high multiplier indicates a belief that the quality of the future income is good, that the probability of its actually being earned in the future is high while a low multiplier indicates doubt about the future earning capacity of the firm. A high multiplier justifies paying a high price for the company; a low multiplier, conversely, a low price.

Such valuation analysis includes estimates of risk in two places: first in estimating the probability that prospective future income will be actually received; and, second, in selecting the multiplier that determines the total value of the enterprise. In the first case, high risk reduces the present net value of future returns and in the second case high risk lowers the multiplier.

In most every case, the components of risk are the intangible relationships of the firm with its stakeholders: future customer loyalty, future brand equity; future access to capital, future productivity, creativity, loyalty of employees; future conditions of government regulation, etc. These stakeholder relationships constitute the core of CSR concerns. Stakeholder relationships are the action arms of CSR mediation between a firm and its socio-political environment. Best CSR practices lead directly to better, more profitable, less risky, more sustainable relationships with stakeholders. Using best CSR practices, therefore, reduces enterprise risk and so raises current and future valuations.

In my 2004 book Moral Capitalism, I also proposed a theory of the firm that breaks the concept of firm capital into 5 separate components: reputation capital, social capital, financial capital, human capital and physical capital. Each source of capital is necessary for continued firm success. Each form of capital is bound up in stakeholder relationships.

Reputational capital and brand equity depend on customer preferences, employee quality, and management strategic planning.

Social capital depends on firm culture, core values of leadership, quality of management, and internal human relations functions. From the outside, the social capital of a firm depends on the social capital – education, work ethic, corruption or the lack, physical infrastructure, health and sanitation – of the society in which the firm must recruit, manage, buy and sell.

Human capital depends on employees – productivity, loyalty, attitudes and morale.

Finance capital is a derivative function of reputational capital, social capital and human capital. And physical capital is acquired with financial capital.

Thus, stakeholder relationships drive any firm' ability to raise capital and so to function on a sustainable basis. In the 2008 collapse of financial markets, Bear Stearns and Lehman Brothers ran out of reputational capital before they ran out of working capital. But their inability to access working capital at the end was a direct result of loss of confidence in their business model on the part of potential creditors. And, their loss of reputational capital arose from a degraded social capital where a culture of excessive risk taking, short term borrowings, high leverage to cover trading speculation, and large bonuses for senior managers lead to illusions of profitability.

At this level of theory, CSR provides mediation of the relations between business, on the one hand, and government and civil society, on the other, by giving business the conceptual and planning apparatus to incorporate in a timely and rational fashion the relevant concerns of the two other sectors.

It should also be noted that CSR theory is a place of conceptual mediation among the three sectors. The ideas and perspectives, suggestions and conclusions, which shape the evolution of CSR theory and form its intellectual structure, meet at an open intersection of the three sectors. Business, civil society – through academics and NGOs in particular – and government – both bureaucrats and politicians, launch points of CSR thinking which can be appropriated, considered and refined by the other sectors. CSR thinking is not a monopoly of business people.

What is proposed by civil society is qualified by business experience and requirements; and what business proposes as its goals and objectives is qualified by advocates from civil society and by those in or seeking public office.

CSR Standards

At the conceptual level of standards which are the first step in moving from theory to results on the ground, there are a number of well-recognized models.

The CERES Principles for the protection of the environment were published in 1989 in response to the oil spill occasioned by the ship Exxon Valdez of the coast of Alaska.

The first comprehensive set of principles for business proposed by business leaders were was the Caux Round Table Principles for Business of 1994.

The Caux Round Table Principles were introduced to the Office of UN Secretary General Kofi Annan in 1998. In 1999 Secretary General Annan announced the need for a set of standards to improve the outcomes of globalization. In 2000 the United Nations proposed a Global Compact for the voluntary ratification by private firms, labor unions, and NGOs. The 9, now 10, principles of the Global Compact were derived directly from international agreements among governments: the conventions on human rights, the international labor convention, the Rio Declaration on the environment, and, most recently, the UN Convention Against Corruption.

The OECD proposed guidelines for multinational companies and standards for corporate governance. The National Association of Corporate Directors in the United States has proposed 10 standards for good corporate governance. Social Accountability International created the SA8000 set of detailed workplace conditions as requirements for responsible factories out of a concern to protect workers in manufacturing plants around the world.

A number of industry codes of practice, among others, have been proposed and adopted as part of the contemporary CSR movement:

- The Wolfsburg Principles for banks to expose illegal financial transactions supporting terrorism, drug trafficking, and corruption of public officials. (http://www.wolfsberg-principles.com/)
- The Equator Principles for environmental and social impact analysis of World Bank projects. (http://www.equator-principles.com/)
- The Principles for Responsible Investing (http://www.unpri.org/)
- A code of conduct for extractive industries (http://www.international-alert.org/pdf/conflict_sensitive_business_practice_section_1.pdf)
- The Coffee Industry Code of Conduct (http://www2.gtz.de/dokumente/bib/06-1059.pdf)
- The Kimberly process for certifying the origins of diamonds (http://www.kimberleyprocess.com/)
- The electronic industry code of conduct (http://www.eicc.info/EICC%20CODE.htm)
- The jewelry industry code of conduct (http://www.responsiblejewellery.com/downloads/crjp_code_of_practices.pdf)

These principles and codes provide decision-making guidance and highlight priority considerations that private companies need to include in their market-driven calculations of investments and expenditures. Such principles and codes take non-financial concerns, goals and objectives of concern to various sets of direct or indirect stakeholders and require that they be factored in to for-profit decision-making. This integration of stakeholder concerns with internal rate of return calculations by business is a mediation function of CSR.

CSR Practices

At the level of practice, CSR provides mediation between business and the sectors of government and civil society in shaping concrete actions that impact business, government and civil society. Using CSR practices, business may act to improve its stakeholder relationships. It may cooperate with government or NGOs to find solutions to environmental, cultural, or social problems. It may engage with stakeholders in non-market forums to learn of their needs and concerns. Under CSR business will consider its products and services to minimize negative externalities and find appropriate opportunities for value pricing in specialized niche markets.

Using best CSR practices, business will selectively obtain from government and civil society optimum support for its operations.

Next, CSR practices will guide allocation of funds by business through charitable commitments to the arts, education, culture and social needs meeting the financial requirements of civil society and NGOs.

A key CSR practice is the company code of conduct or statement of core values. The related CSR best practice is to align company strategic planning, key performance indicators, and rewards for successful performance with its core values. ENRON is now a famous example of a company which had an admirable company code from the perspective of CSR theory but which dishonored those values in practice. On the other hand, Johnson & Johnson in its recall of Tylenol gave us a famous example of a company that lived up to its credo even at a substantial short-term financial cost.

Key to the implementation of CSR principles, standards and codes of conduct is the commitment of the company's leadership to alignment with core values. In public companies, this must be the board of directors. In private companies it is more the owners who have direct authority over the decisions of the firm. In the public company, the board has the ultimate responsibility for setting and enforcing company values, starting with its selection of a chief executive officer. It is then the responsibility of the chief executive to lead based on those core values and to manage by ensuring the overflow of those values down through the ranks of the organization.

CSR practices emphasize the task of the executive as execution of values as the "glue" that holds the voluntary cooperative structure of a private firm together. The chief executive must be more than a boss or a facilitator of teams and managers; he or she must lead from vision and values.

In this role as values leader, the CEO serving an enlightened board of directors is directly concerned with the interfaces between the company and the society. Mangers may focus primarily on concerns internal to the company but leaders must be vigilant to know what is going on in the wider environment on which the company depends for its profits. Such management of these interfaces is a mediation function for business with government and civil society.

Another level of CSR practice is compliance and risk management within the business enterprise. Compliance is necessary to insure alignment of actions with core values and stated rules and policies. Comprehensive risk management alerts business leaders to frictions between business and the other sectors. Mismanagement of stakeholder relationships, including environmental footprints, creates difficulties and possible losses for business. Thus, risk management must embrace non-financial contingencies as well as more narrowly focused market based mistakes in pricing and the offering of in appropriate products and services.

The collapse of major banking houses in the financial crisis of 2008 revealed in dramatic and surprising fashion the consequences of poor risk management. Banks for example in Canada, Australia, Thailand and Singapore were less affected by the financial crisis due to different risk management practices.

The Caux Round Table provides its Arcturus risk assessment process to enable better comprehensive risk management.

Finally, within the realm of best CSR practices is reporting. Both government and civil society are less trusting of business and less comfortable in meeting business needs when business is secretive and opaque. Reporting of results – both financial and non-financial – is an important mediation function by which business can maximize its claims on the other two sectors. Triple-bottom line reports, sustainability reports, or "people, planet, and profits" reports have been commonplace among large multinational companies as the reporting format that includes important non-financial information. The Global Reporting Initiative provides a framework for reporting of data on the environmental and social footprints of business.

Within the business sector, consultants from accountants, risk management experts, CSR professionals, and those who help research and write CSR reports provide human resources for the implementation of best CSR practices.

CSR expressed within Civil Society

While CSR practices are limited to implementation within the business sector, CSR theory can be helpfully enhanced by contributions from civil society. Academics within business schools through teachings, publication and participation in workshops and conferences have provided and continue to provide thought leadership about CSR theory, principles and practices. Journals such as the Journal of Business Ethics and Business Ethics Quarterly feed ideas and concerns into the public domain. Conferences and workshops promote discussions and review of research data with the participation of thought leaders from all three sectors. Professional organizations of academics like ISBEE, International Society for Business, Ethics and Economics, and EABIS – European Association for Business In Society, host important conferences. CSR and ethics centers at the University of Santa Clara, at Bentley College, the Boston College Center for Corporate Citizenship, or the Doughty Center for Corporate Responsibility at Cranfield University in the UK, sustain continued conversations about CSR theory and best practices. For profit efforts such as Ethical Corporation Magazine bring more attention to CSR concerns and management alternatives.

In the United Kingdom the All Parliamentary Committee on CSR provides a link between academic views, business perspectives, and parliamentary discussions of business as a social sector.

NGOs such as the Caux Round Table, CSR Europe, Accountability 21, The Aspen Institute Program for Business and Society, CSR Wire, Business for Social Responsibility, the OCEG, the Business Civic Leadership Center of the US Chamber of Commerce, the Committee Encouraging Corporate Philanthropy, the Institute of Business Ethics in London, Business in the Community in London, Social Accountability International, ALIARSE in Mexico, the Global Reporting Initiative, the office of the UN Global Compact, among others, circulate ideas and best practices among business executives and managers.

道德

甲午年作於于荼湖州

Tao Te 35 in Running Script © 2014 by Weiming Lu

CHAPTER THREE
CONTRIBUTION OF
MARKETS – PRICING

A vital lesson taught by the collapse of Wall Street in 2008 is that markets don't always get prices right. Or at least, markets don't get them "right" in the sense that the information provided by current prices may mislead in some important ways.

I recommend that you read as quickly as you can the new book by Justin Fox entitled The Myth of the Rational Market. Now, please understand, Fox's style is a bit journalistic and choppy – he is a writer on business and economic for Time – and his sequencing is a bit fast and loose. But he has give generalists an approachable intellectual history of the ideas and theorems which dominate modern global capitalism.

Interestingly, they and their creators are all American.

One can quickly see in Fox the development of those practices – managed by "quants" in financial analysis using complex formulas on pricing and risk – which led directly to the asset bubble around sub-prime mortgages, CDOs and CDSs and the resulting meltdown of Wall Street and the collapse of great investment banking houses.

One obvious conclusion is that concerns for business ethics and corporate social responsibility never entered into those calculations.

Another obvious conclusion is that until such intangible standards of good practice are included in the math for financial decision-making, capitalism is at risk of being manipulated by financial objectives and trading practices.

Fox presents the current state of financial theory as at a dead end: the brilliance of the technical analysis has been betrayed by market practices which did not conform to the theory. Market prices, it turns out, are not reliable measures of real present value. Nor are they, and this is old news, efficient predictors of future market prices. The old paradigm has failed and no new one has emerged.

The 1965 promise of efficient markets was that "In an efficient market, the actions of the many competing participants should cause the actual price of a security to wander randomly about its intrinsic value."

Fox notes that "stock prices do contain lots of information. ... Yet mixed up amid the information in security prices is an awful lot of emotion, error, and noise."

Fox concludes in line with the concerns of business ethics and CSR advocates that therefore "managers of publicly traded companies should insulate themselves and their employees from day-to-day or even month-to-month stock price fluctuations."

Asset Pricing and Asset Bubbles

The asset bubble and ensuing bust swirling around the Duc de Saint Simon in France during 1719 and 1720 arose from the selling of shares in the Mississippi Company. The project was the brainchild of a Scotsman, John Law, who proposed his scheme to the Regent of France as a way to earn money for the government. Sales of the stock were very successful; share prices rose to absurd heights; millions were made by those who bought early and sold early; losses, when they came with the collapse of the company, withered the entire economy of France, coming to roost most heavily on those who could least afford the cost.

Saint Simon, a landed aristocrat, never bought shares even when pressured by his friend the Regent to take up thousands for the cash equivalent of a pretty song. Saint Simon didn't believe in the inherent value of paper assets.

He wrote in his diary:

One day M. le Duc d'Orleans (the Regent of France during the minority of Louis XV) made an appointment to meet me at Saint-Cloud, so as to take the air after he had been working there, and we both sat on the balustrade before the Orangery, looking down the slope of the woods towards Les Goulottes (fountains). He spoke again of the Mississippi Bank, urging me to accept stock from Law. I refused once more, but he continued to press me, producing one argument after another, until at last he grew angry, saying that it was mere vanity to refuse what the King offered (all was done in his name), when so many other persons of my rank and condition urgently desired it. I said that such a refusal would be stupid and impertinent, as well as conceited, and was not my way. Therefore, as he was so pressing, I would explain my true reasons. Not since the reign of King Midas had I heard of anyone who turn all he touched into gold, and I did not think that even Law had this talent. All his ability was, I believed, no more than clever trickery, a brilliant exhibition of juggling, a robbing of Peter to pay Paul, by which some people became rich at the expense of others. Sooner or later, I declared, it would be seen for what it was; enormous numbers would be made bankrupt, and then how, and to whom, would restitution be made? I added that I abhorred the idea of touching other people's money, and that nothing on earth could persuade me to do so now, not even at second hand.

M. le Duc d'Orleans was at a loss how to answer.

At a later point in his Memoirs as the Mississippi Company was desperately writhing in its death spiral, the Duc de Saint Simon commented:

It had become necessary to substitute something real for the mirage of the Mississippi, converting to a new trading company the Indies Bank, capable of guaranteeing the exchange of 600 million in banknotes and have profits of tobacco monopoly and numerous other vast sources of revenues, but even so it was still unable to meet the demand for payments of its notes and this despite all the measures taken to lower their value which, incidentally, had ruined great numbers of the people by reduction of their savings.

All this known as of 1719 and still we had to suffer globally from Wall Street's unsustainable issuance of subprime mortgages and CDOs derived therefrom.

Why can't this great reoccurring flaw in capital markets be permanently corrected?

Is it all because of a greed that lies forever chained to the beating heart of capitalism and, from time to time, makes financial fools of us all?

Or, as I am coming to think, is it more a question of systematic distortion of pricing under certain conditions, leading to mis-pricing that opens the door of markets to "irrational exuberance" and supporting avarice for immediate cash profits.

My argument is the following:

First, when asset bubbles occur, the strategic good sense normally encouraged by microeconomic supply and demand curves does not operate. Under conventional supply and demand interactions, the marginal utility of additional amounts of supply is worth less and less. At some point it therefore becomes unprofitable to produce more of the good or service and so supply contracts and a market equilibrium at a sustainable value is reached between demand and supply. No asset bubble occurs. There is no "irrational exuberance" driving prices ever higher and higher.

Under these circumstances, the price/supply curve slopes downward to the right on the graph where supply is the horizontal axis and price is the vertical axis. But when asset bubbles build up, the supply curve slopes very differently. It slopes upward to the right. As price increases, so does supply, without any deterrent effect set in motion by declining marginal utility of additional units of the asset brought to market. This supply curve accurately represents the "irrational' belief of buyers that more of the good or service deserves higher and higher prices. There is no diminishing demand curve to intersect with the supply curve at a point of sustainable equilibrium. Demand grows; supply responds; and prices keep going up. Each increment of the good or the service seems to have added value attached to it, at least in the eyes of potential buyers.

Everybody is happy; the nominal price value of the asset class keeps growing higher and higher as more and more assets are brought to market to enjoy higher and higher returns – like shares in the Mississippi Company or, in the subprime mortgage bubble, new houses built to take advantage of easy credit. There is no regulation of self-interest by price that cautions producers to keep more product off the market. There is no automatic governor on the engine to keep it from spinning out of control.

Markets for contract rights – shares, loans, mortgages, CDOs – are especially susceptible to such upward sloping supply curves. As prices paid by willing investors rise, more opportunities to buy the contracts are brought to market by creative sellers. Each additional opportunity to invest in these promises for future returns continues to have the same (or greater) utility to buyers than the previous opportunity. The marginal cost of bringing more contracts to the market is almost zero –mostly payment for secretarial formalisms. It was thus very easy for John Law and his Mississippi Company to issue more shares; very easy for Enron to create more special purpose entities with which to manage reported earnings, and very easy for banks to issue both more sub-prime mortgages and CDOs.

But rising prices for assets can only be supported by rising supplies of money with which to buy them. Here is where the price of credit seems to become dysfunctional. In a bubble, as the price of the asset rises, the supply of credit expands as well. Another supply curve sloping upward to the right. Under conditions of "irrational exuberance" official bank interest rates do not rise with the amount of credit being made available as you would think. More and more credit is made available to buyers when bubbles are growing. The buyers, using mostly borrowed money, pass the resulting cash on to sellers.

The dynamic expanding the supply of credit for subprime mortgages was the proliferation of CDO sales. Global capital markets bought up CDOs and the cash from those sales was passed back to the originators of subprime mortgages, who then lent the money out on more subprime mortgages, which kept buyers in the market for houses at ever rising prices.

In the dot.com/telecom bubble of the late 1990's, stock prices of these companies had been kept high by the arrival of day-traders in the market, using their equity plus borrowed funds to take advantage of rising prices for stocks.

As the risk/return tradeoff inherent in the extension of credit would have it, you would think, that as more and more credit is extended, the most reliable debtors would be taken care of first, so that later extensions of credit should carry more risk, and therefore be harder to sell. One might say that the marginal utility of additional credit carries higher and higher risk for the usefulness of the money lent.

The market for credit should stabilize at the point where investors providing new credits at the margins where new lending is offered and accepted begin to question if the returns and the security they are promised will support the risks they are to undertake. At that point of decreasing returns to credit, lending investors will demand so much for use of their money, that providers of the underlying assets will balk at the price demanded for credit and the market will slowly stabilize around sustainable prices of assets.

But in bubble environments, pricing does not reliably lead to sustainable asset valuations. Rising prices bring on speculation and then growing speculation brings on yet higher prices until buyer's remorse finally sets in at the margin, new supply is not taken up, and the market suddenly collapses.

Normally as the supply of credit expands, the price charged for increments of credit rises. The normal curve here is one sloping upward to the right. But when an asset bubble is underway, the curve is more flat; as the supply of credit expands, the price for credit does not rise substantially. Credit becomes, relatively speaking, cheaper than it should be. The gap between the thoughtful price for credit (high) and the actual price for credit (low) exposes the market to risk of future collapse.

One reason for this odd pricing of credit is the financial security seemingly provided by rising asset prices. The nominal higher and higher values of the asset offered for sale by the bubble market provide a vision of security protecting the money borrowed to own the asset. The owner/borrower feels confident that he or she can sell the asset at a moment's notice to repay the debt and the investor/lender feels confident that the asset can be acquired from the owner and sold if necessary to repay the debt.

But when the market collapses, asset values collapse and the credit appears in truth as having been essentially unsecured. It has long been said prudentially that lending too much money to an enterprise makes one take the risks of an equity investor – in for a dollar of risk as well as for the actual dime lent on security.

As asset bubbles expand, another gap in prices emerges to undermine the sustainability of nominal asset values. Under thoughtful analysis, the value of an asset should stay reasonably steady or decline some as more and more assets are brought to market. The value/supply curve is then largely level or sloping downward to the right. This assessment of value is largely sustainable.

But, in a bubble, the value of the asset rises and rises ever higher as more and more assets come to market. The value/supply curve slopes upward to the right. The growing divergence between the thoughtful curve and the "irrationally exuberant" curve is the gap between sustainability (thoughtful valuations) and collapse (irrational valuations). At some point, the gap between the two valuations becomes so large that it can't be ignored. Upon the discovery that "irrational" valuations are at risk, nominal asset prices start to drop towards the level of sustainability and the market collapses.

Mis-pricing drives financial markets first to excess and then to collapse. Greed may sustain the mis-pricing and its resulting bubble, but mis-pricing gives to greed its sometime power to trump thoughtful analysis of risk and sound valuations.

Discouraging mis-pricing of both assets and credit would seem to be essential to improving the level of economic justice provided by free capital markets to all participants, but especially to the less well capitalized ones.

If we could better understand the mechanics of how mis-pricing begins in any cycle of excessive accumulation of assets, especially the contract right assets favored by financial markets, we might be able to better eliminate such erroneous pricing signals. Better pricing would tip the odds away from speculators towards genuine value investors.

Two factors, it seems to me, contribute to the onset and the maintenance of mis-pricing.

First is the fact that most providers of contract rights (equity securities, debt obligations, derivatives, etc.) take a fee out of the deal on the sale of the right and leave town so to speak. They have no incentive to price accurately for the sustainable long run. They price to sell in the market at the time. They feed speculation and they feed off of speculation.

Second, and related to the way in which originators of contract rights get paid, is the fact that those who originate contracts rights to sell in financial markets very frequently assume no long-term ownership risk for sustaining the value of the asset. These originators do not retain an interest either in the tradable contract right sold to investors or in the underlying asset, if there is one, which supports the right to future income that is sold to the investor via the contract.

If the fees charged for selling contract rights became less and less profitable as the market for such securities grew, or if ownership responsibilities became more and more unavoidable as the risk of market collapse accumulates, then market-wise, enlightened self-interest would find ways to dampen speculation and to protect asset values.

Getting Asset Prices Right

Markets are unforgiving; they expose truth and drive out chaff. As the Tao Te Ching says of Heaven itself, markets "treat all things as straw dogs". They have no emotions, shedding no tears for losers and taking no pride in winners, for today's winner may be tomorrow's loser. And, markets refuse to subsidize idealisms. Over time, free markets reject fraud, abandon products that have no sound purpose or accommodating price, and undermine false or misleading valuations.

That Bear Sterns with balance sheet assets worth $80 per share was sold for $2 (later renegotiated for $10 per share) that Lehman Brothers with billions in assets nonetheless went bankrupt, wiping out owner's equity, and that Enron as an enterprise was gone within months of revelation regarding its true debt obligations and real income flows, testify to the cruel discipline of markets at work.

True, markets create liquidity and asset bubbles; but then they turn and destroy them if they are bubbles. Bubbles can't last forever. Only well-supported valuations are sustainable.

It is better, I think, to say that market makers create bubbles and also that market makers break bubbles. Perhaps market makers are more irresponsible in making than in breaking bubbles for the breaking can only occur if bubbles have been created. And, the breaking gets us back closer to the reality of sustainable values, a salutary step towards truth.

But, in the breaking of bubbles, people get hurt as we see happen all around us in the continued destruction of wealth and value flowing from the sub-prime mortgage/CDO/credit default swap bubble and bust of the past 5 years.

Asset bubbles undermine the public good provided by financial markets. They move prices to an unsustainable extreme so that the market gets frothy with the provision of private goods that have lost connection with long-term realities. When that connection attenuates, negative externalities begin to accumulate to break out at some future time when the bubble bursts. Upon the burst, the happening of negative consequences – the collapse of asset values, the loss of wealth and income, the onset of economic decline – suddenly coat the heretofore private goods with a public character, making them quasi-public goods.

Thus it is said that during the run up of the bubble gains were privatized while, upon the burst, losses are socialized in order to minimize the harm to public goods such as economic wellbeing for the society as a whole.

The valuations at play in the market have become unreliable. The information they provides is now seen as false. Prices will thereafter drop until valuations become more acceptable. The bubble stretches credulity about valuations ("irrational exuberance" some call it) until confidence is lost and the search for "quality" and security begins.

So, in some sense the recession suffered by America and other economies hit by the 2008 collapse of the bubble in financial assets is necessary and just. It is correcting past mis-pricing. Only, the pain of correction does not fall fairly on those who made the mistakes in the first place. They have most likely taken the money and run. Prices go down, wealth is un-created, and the economy contracts. People lose jobs; families suffer.

The lesson of this current financial retraction is perhaps keener still. It may be telling us that the share of global cash flows appropriated by the financial services industry in general was excessive and unsustainable. The value of mortgage brokers, investment banks, and insurance companies like AIG, depended on their making hay while the cash was flowing. High fees, charges for all kinds of intermediation, huge bonuses, were converted into capital values. But such substantial and systematic extraction of commissions from the economy could not last if the financial intermediaries collectively were not providing real value-added to investors and players in the real economy.

And, perhaps the failed Wall Street intermediaries were not contributing enough to justify their returns. So, losing them – in the long run – is just treating them like "straw dogs" - useless playthings that will burn and disappear.

Some coldness is required to let companies and their fortunes decline and fade away as casualties of poor risk management and imprudent forethought.

The un-creation of value is not what we want from free markets and capitalism. We should hold the system and its leaders to the powerful capitalist standard of wealth creation on a grand scale so that the positive synergies of investment and production will flow throughout the economy improving lives for all.

Thus a proper measurement of value creation can guide successful CSR mediation at the intersection of business, government and civil society. The first Principle of the Caux Round Table Principles for Business sets this standard: the purpose of a business is to create wealth, not destroy it. Other CRT Principles and stakeholder considerations add ethical obligations to the manner in which such wealth is to be created and its benefits distributed.

I would assert that the titans of financial intermediation which took the lead in building the investment bubble in sub-prime mortgages and subordinate contracts did not live up to this CRT ethical principle. Had they done so, the bubble would have been smaller and so its bursting would have caused less harm to society and far fewer financial losses to investors and owners.

The value that counts most is the capital value of a firm – a balance sheet concept. Profits – or losses – are mile-markers on the way to a more valuable firm. Owners seek an increase in the capital value of their holdings. But many assets of a firm today are intangible. Things like brand equity, customer loyalty, development of cutting edge intellectual property, low cost of credit, etc. contribute directly to a firm's value. Enhancing these intangible assets requires engagement with the stakeholders – customers, employees, suppliers, creditors, etc. – that contribute to the firm's future success. CSR mediation focuses directly on stakeholders and so contributes to a firm's capital value. If a firm's valuation is increasing, it is a prima facia indication that the firm is doing well in its mediation function with its environment.

If the CRT Principles for Responsible Business are to be assiduously implemented, there should be no bubbles at all – not ever - just a sustainable rise in valuations as a rising tide floats all boats. Such a sustainable rise would rest on sound, real value-adding, business activities of tangible, non-illusory benefit to stakeholders.

The better meaning of CSR is one that links the justification of business enterprise to the deepest, sustaining sources of human well-being in addition to the creation of material wealth and the satisfaction of consumer wants; in a profound and necessary way, business enterprise provides sustenance for human dignity and moral achievement and this function of business needs to be recognized in theories of the firm and of free market institutions; this deeper meaning of responsibility should not be restricted to business enterprises; a concern for the common good, including global perspectives, provides such a link.

Such concern requires the acceptance of responsibility. It is the obligation of actors always to consider the effects of their acts and omissions over a relevantly practicable scope of time and space; human actions embed themselves in history, forming conditions for the future which, on the one hand, may become disturbing realities or, on the other, the basis for social cooperation based on mutual respect and trust. Because they are setting such destinies in motion, actors should be prudent in their initiatives out of regard for others yet to come on the scene.

It is the obligation of all actors to invest in the forms of social and human capital that foster societal cooperation for mutual advantage. Those who create, possess, or use wealth must realize that the right to property carries responsibility. Numerous actors contribute to the capital value of an enterprise and, therefore, those who own or manage this wealth must take into account the interests of these stakeholders in their decision making; this realization makes adoption of this more deeply grounded understanding of CSR more important.

A new level of disengagement, resignation, and discouragement due to perceptions of disempowerment in the face of a highly complex and intellectually fragmented globalized world is wide spread in the early years of the 21st Century. This trend is particularly disturbing because it prevents the emergence of those shared conceptions that inspire us to act for the common good; this trend has been amplified by "short-termism" and opportunism on the part of political and business leaders; however, greed and selfishness on the part of individuals contributes seriously to this avoidance of responsibility for the common good. A Moral Capitalism requires no less.

Total Credit Market Debt as a % of GDP

3/31/2008 Debt = $49.614 Trillion
3/31/2008 GDP = $14.196 Trillion = 349.5%

CHAPTER FOUR
WHY DID WALL STREET COLLAPSE IN 2008? AMERICAN VALUES CHANGED!

This chart from the US Federal Reserve System is all you need to have to understand why Wall Street collapsed in 2008. In short, there was too much debt in financial markets. From 1980 to March

2008, total credit market debt of the United States as a percent of GDP rose from 150% to 350%.

The concomitant economic trend would be how much money Americans saved over those years to offset their increasing debt. Starting in 1980, American savings rates declined as noted in the following chart:

Series: PSAVERT, Personal Saving Rate

View Data | Download Data | Notify Me of Updates | Add to My Data List | Vintage Series in ALFRED

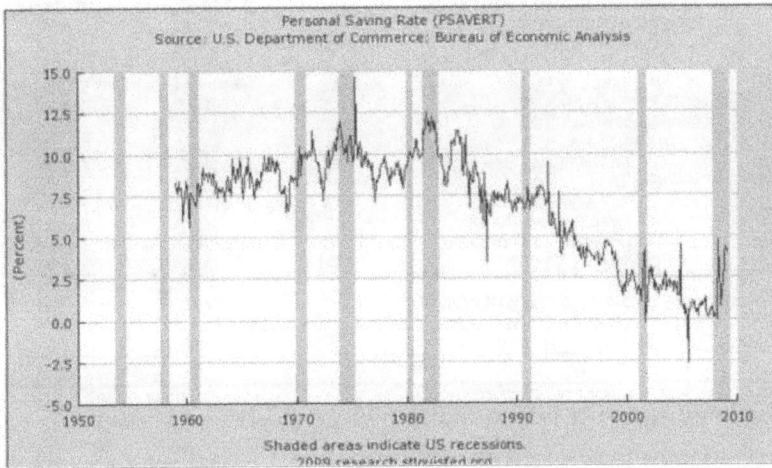

Personal Saving Rate (PSAVERT)
Source: U.S. Department of Commerce: Bureau of Economic Analysis

Shaded areas indicate US recessions.

Fully engaging in the growth of capital market debt, major American banks and investment banking houses bought derivative contracts in amounts far in excess of their capital reserves as reported in the chart below provided by the Controller of the Currency.

RANK	BANK NAME	STATE	TOTAL ASSETS	TOTAL DERIVATIVES
1	JPMORGAN CHASE BANK NA	OH	$1,746,242	$87,362,672
2	BANK OF AMERICA NA	NC	1,471,631	38,304,564
3	CITIBANK NATIONAL ASSN	NV	1,231,154	31,887,069
4	GOLDMAN SACHS BANK USA	UT	162,474	30,229,614
5	HSBC BANK USA NATIONAL ASSN	VA	181,620	3,713,075
6	WACHOVIA BANK NATIONAL ASSN	NC	635,476	3,664,823
7	WELLS FARGO BANK NA	SD	538,958	1,494,745
8	BANK OF NEW YORK MELLON	NY	195,164	1,125,889
9	STATE STREET BANK&TRUST CO	MA	171,228	731,180
10	SUNTRUST BANK	GA	185,099	255,942
11	PNC BANK NATIONAL ASSN	PA	140,777	141,291
12	NORTHERN TRUST CO	IL	70,434	128,376
13	KEYBANK NATIONAL ASSN	OH	101,869	122,560
14	NATIONAL CITY BANK	OH	146,058	117,785
15	U S BANK NATIONAL ASSN	OH	261,776	105,626
16	REGIONS BANK	AL	142,084	97,421
17	MERRILL LYNCH BANK USA	UT	61,810	88,520
18	BRANCH BANKING&TRUST CO	NC	147,484	77,250
19	FIFTH THIRD BANK	OH	69,460	70,418
20	RBS CITIZENS NATIONAL ASSN	RI	129,491	51,238
21	UBS BANK USA	UT	30,495	37,167
22	UNION BANK NATIONAL ASSN	CA	69,737	37,087
23	MORGAN STANLEY BANK NA	UT	58,058	36,561
24	DEUTSCHE BANK TR CO AMERICAS	NY	50,801	31,437
25	HUNTINGTON NATIONAL BANK	OH	53,548	25,162
TOP 25 COMMERCIAL BANKS & TCs WITH DERIVATIVES			$8,052,925	$199,938,274
OTHER COMMERCIAL BANKS & TCs WITH DERIVATIVES			2,761,938	443,333
TOTAL COMMERCIAL BANKS & TCs WITH DERIVATIVES			10,814,862	200,381,607

In keeping with accumulating huge positions in derivatives, American banks went from holding risks to trading risks. They went into debt in order to buy financial instruments to sell to others, not lending their own money but using the funds of others. This gave leading American banks and investment banking houses historically high debt to equity ratios as the following chart reveals:

Company	On-book assets (A)	Intangibles (B)	Tangible Assets (C) = (A) - (B)	Equity (D)	Preferred (E)	Tangible Common Equity (F) = (D) - (B) - (E)	Leverage Ratio (G) = (C) / (F)
Citigroup	$2,050	$63	$1,987	$126	$27	$36	56
Bank of America	$1,831	$91	$1,740	$161	$24	$46	38
JP Morgan Chase	$2,252	$69	$2,183	$146	$8	$69	32
Wells Fargo (ex-Wachovia)	$622	$14	$609	$47	$1	$33	19
Goldman Sachs	$1,082	$10	$1,071	$46	$3	$32	33
Morgan Stanley	$987	$4	$983	$36	$1	$31	32
GE	$830	$99	$731	$112	$0	$14	54
TOTAL	$9,654	$349	$9,305	$674	$66	$260	36

$ in billions   OptionARMageddon.com

Why did this happen?

Simply put: American culture changed. The appetite for debt grew and grew. Older, more conservative preferences for thrift and pay-as-you go evaporated. Americans accelerated the timing of gratification from a distant future to the present. Regulatory and legal constraints were changed to follow the dominant cultural predisposition. Under the Republican Administrations of Ronald Reagan, George H. W. Bush, and George W. Bush and the Democrat Administration of Bill Clinton, regulatory controls were eased on capital markets.

As American culture changed and Wall Street followed the new, more self-centered and self-seeking trends, Wall Street firms never installed a CSR mediation capacity to balance private wealth seeking with its quasi-private, quasi-public, and public good counterparts. Wall Street took to heart that finance was only about private wealth accumulation so that serious concern for leverage and risk evaporated. Wall Street forgot that finance has important public goods associated with its success. Having a sound system of financial intermediation is foundational for successful economic growth and national development.

In a telling moment of social truth, in 1983 when President Reagan struck his compromise with Democrat Speaker of the House of Representatives, Tip O'Neil and won O'Neil's assent to lower taxes and the principle of supply side economics, Reagan had to accept O'Neil's demand for higher government spending. Both men got what they wanted and the country paid for lower taxes coupled with higher spending through debt.

The collapse of Wall Street in the fall of 2008 was caused by selling too much debt supported by too little real value. The gap between the nominal face values of houses, mortgages, CDOs and CDSs and their sustainable, long term value became wider and wider after 2003 as more and more debt was purchased by investors in those homes and financial instruments. When the gap became too wide, nominal prices collapsed and market value was destroyed. Investors fled credit markets, looking for more secure places to put their money and the liquidity needed to lubricate global capitalism's daily transactions disappeared as a result.

The grandiose rise in the level of American debt sold had other supporting causes as well as a change in preferences for borrowing. Risk of price collapse was not accurately calculated and predicted by Wall Street traders and dealers in financial instruments. The industry looked only to the near term where profits could be made. As CitiGroup CEO Chuck Prince said: "As long as they play the music, you get up and dance." Sophisticated mathematical algorithms did not include the right data to properly calculate contingencies.

Chaos theory would have been more appropriate than the models used by risk managers. Chaos theory presumes that in every complex system, small and unexpected variations at the margin or unpredicted shocks from the outside can send the system spinning into, well, chaos.

A third support for the astounding rise in debt was a blind trust in professionals and experts. Those with degrees in finance; those working for famous banks and investment banking houses like JP Morgan Chase or Lehman Brothers; those who were making lots of money were trusted and imitated. As often happens in the run up of asset bubbles, those on the inside gained authority and others deferred to their judgment.

Yet, one doubts that the use of complex mathematics and deference to Wall Street insiders alone could have changed America's taste for debt. Something else was no doubt at work.

Dramatic changes in behaviors such as commitments to unheard of levels of debt, I suggest, most likely reflect changes in deep cultural predispositions. To understand the behaviors, it is comfortable to look at the supporting values.

In 1980 the generation known as the "Baby Boomers" took over American culture. The leading edge of Boomers turned 35 that year. They were moving up as consumers, workers, voters, writers, managers, doctors and lawyers. Large in number and with significant disposable incomes, it is easy to understand why Baby Boomer preferences drove the American economy.

Culture as a Driver of Social Action

But before we analyze what changes the Baby Boomers brought to American Culture, let's step back and consider why culture should be taken seriously as a driver of behaviors and social outcomes.

There are of course powerful intellectual traditions that argue for the marginal role of culture as a cause of great events. Values, it is said, are superficial, reflecting more the power of underlying material wants and needs than conditioning those more kinetic sources of human action. Herbert Spencer, for example, argued in his sociology that human are fundamentally still part of the animal kingdom, without a controlling moral sense and so fitted most for competition and brutish rivalries. His insights gave rise to the social philosophy of Social Darwinism. Karl Marx famously looked to economic conditions and class perspectives as determining values and political institutions. His Dialectical Materialism allegedly provided a more profound understanding of history than did the stated goals and objectives of kings and generals, courtiers and priests. Friedrich Nietzsche challenged any value as subjective and possessing only a limited command of truth. He triumphed the will to power as moving the course of human civilization. Also analyzing action on the level of the individual, Sigmund Freud postulated that the realm of value – the super ego – and the conscious attempt to align acts with values – the ego – were of lesser consequence than the deep, hidden from most self awareness, fears, suspicions, and lusts housed in the Id.

From perspectives of sociology, economics, philosophy and psychology there are good arguments as to why we should not overrate the role of values and culture in our lives. Thus, to accurately fix responsibility for the 2008 collapse of Wall Street and the resulting global economic recession, we should be overly concerned with fundamental American cultural values.

On the other hand, the suggestions of contemporary German philosopher Jurgen Habermas give us good reasons to value the role of values.[2] Habermas presents several observations about human experience which either intuition or common sense can appreciate and can affirm as being more true than not. First, Habermas observes that part of human experience takes place in a realm of internal conceptual construction which he calls the realm of normativity. Normativity is internal to an individual mind and revolves around our capacity for mental processing of thoughts, images, feelings, impressions and insights. Normativity is the home for reason; it is what the Chinese Daoists called the "discriminating" mind that falls short of the true Dao of eternal cosmic purpose. Normativity is also the home for conceptualizations, for the framing of understanding and the ordering of perceptions.

Pure normativity has no presence in the material world. It can only enter the world of space and time through human action which seeks to align conditions with a normative template. Normativity and dreams are close cousins as to their presence in the world. They are both very real to those minds that house them.

Second, on a very different level of reality, Habermas points out that humans, like all embodied creatures, live in a world of matter and fact. This reality Habermas calls facticity. It is corporeal and substantial; it can be measured, tasted, touched and described. It is history and politics and economics. It is society into which people are born, where they live their lives with lungs that breath and hearts that pump, and from which they pass when death comes.

Thirdly, and for me most importantly, it follows from Habermas' postulates on normativity and facticity, that human persons live in both realms simultaneously. We have a normative aspect to our lives while we live in circumstances of facticity. Accordingly, in the human person, normativity can be imposed on facticity through action while facticity can shape normativity through thought and emotion.

To assume that values, which live in the realm of normativity, are of lesser importance than more rude passions and impulses comes close to affirming that facticity must, on balance, drive normativity. Indeed, our passions and impulses, needs and desires, do seem quite closely connected to our experiences in the realm of facticity – hunger, sex, power, security, etc.

And yet, because of the power of human action, the asserted dominance of facticity over normativity cannot be absolute. Normativity shapes and guides actions, from the most abstract and general kinds of ideas and insights down to more and more specific principles, rules, categories, goals and objectives. In Aristotelian terms, normativity – not facticity - gives rise to our sense of proper ends, our teleology.

Out of our moral sense we use normativity to make sense of and manipulate facticity for our own purposes.

A material consideration to have in mind when we consider the power of the moral sense in our daily lives, or, to put it another way, the importance of normativity in shaping our lives and social interactions, is the capacity of our minds for moral thinking. As creatures living in the circumstances of facticity, are we structured to operate easily and successfully at the level of moral thinking and corresponding action?

Four contemporary sciences – cognitive neuroscience, behavioral genetics, evolutionary psychology, and evolutionary biology – present evidence that the human person is very much a moral being not subject to the pulls of instincts and immediate gratification of physical needs. In short, these sciences are proving that the human brain contains as internal architecture that positions our species to live productively in social settings.[3]

Different parts of our brain coordinate different responses. We are, therefore, not subject to any one set of stimuli or reaction predispositions. The cerebral cortex handles decision-making and ethical dilemmas; in the limbic system, the hippocampus masters memory and mental maps, the amygdale processes emotions, especially fear and aggression; and the hypothalamus processes sexual desire and other emotions; the basal ganglia and the cerebellum modify and coordinate movement of the body.

Evolutionary psychology and biology now argue that natural selection led early humans to form loyalty groups for purposes of survival. Thus, people are prepared to trust other people.[4] Traits that build collective enterprise such as reciprocity and generosity are common to people.[5] Bonding and social connection release oxcytocin, a neurotransmitter, from the hypothalamus. Oxcytocin, dopamine and serotonin are released by the brain into the blood stream and produce warming and calming effects. Mirror neurons found in the premotor cortex, inferior and posterior parietal lobes, the superior temporal sulcus and the insula areas of the brain – areas that are associated with an ability to sense and understand someone else's feelings and emotions, allow us to develop social skills and social networks.[6] In short, human beings seem to have an innate moral sense that governs their lives in community.[7]

The presence of normativity as a mental capacity gives credence to the approach of German sociologist Max Weber in coming to understand constructed economic systems. His thesis as to the origins of capitalism demonstrates the potential power of normativity. Weber pointed out that capitalism as a self-sustaining system of investment in production and wealth creation first arose in the Calvinist cultures of Holland, Scotland and England and in the British colonies in North America. It did not, for example, arise in the Catholic cultures of Europe, nor in Asia or India or African or within Islam. Weber in his noted study The Protestant Ethic and the Spirit of Capitalism then tried to turn an association of one particular economic system with a peculiar set of religious beliefs and practices into an explanation of one by the other, the economic system by the religion

The particular dynamics imposed on believers by Calvinist normativity as presented by Weber may not provide for everyone a fully adequate explanation of nascent capitalist practices and investment in productive firms. However, the connection of Calvinism with the only communities that birthed modern capitalism provides a persuasive rational for believing in some connective tissue between normativity and facticity.

A second set of historical connections between culture and capitalism is provided by Francis Fukuyama in his book Trust.[8] Fukuyama notes the coincidence between cultures that have high levels of trust among their members and sustained, superior achievement in business and commerce. In these communities, behaviors that inspire investment and reciprocity respond to cultural preferences and reflect patterns of express, conformist, socialization in line with such values.

Following in Fukuyama's steps, Lawrence Harrison and Samuel Huntington edited a series of essays on the power of culture with the title Culture Matters; How values shape human progress.[9] Writers such as David Landes and Michael Porter bring arguments to bear from observations of economic development that culture makes almost all the difference in explaining which communities grow rich and which do not. Porter notes that economic development flows directly from rapid and sustain growth in productivity. To change productivity requires achievement in knowledge, investment, insight and innovation – which respond to cultural dynamics of purpose and meaning in how to lead one's life. Human capital must be mobilized to take advantage of natural endowments and commercial opportunity.

Taking another approach that similarly leads to appreciation of the importance of norms and culture, Peter Berger and Thomas Luckmann argued in an influential treatise that reality as we come to know it is socially constructed.[10] If this is true, then variables of human perception and thinking – activity largely at the level of normativity – would seem prior in shaping our relationship to the physical world than the manipulations of that world itself. Facticity is shaped for us by our cognitions about it. Mediation between facticity, especially the hardness of institutions, and normativity say Berger and Luckmann is accomplished by language. "Language provides the fundamental superimposition of logic on the objectivated world."[11] Language is a human capability that bridges the normative and the factual, confirming the human ability to rise above deterministic naturally occurrences and shape environments through purposeful action. Language allows experiences with faciticity to be incorporated into knowledge. And knowledge guides the application of human interventions in the realm of facticity. Knowledge as it becomes more and more theoretical, detaches itself from particulars of facticity to become more and more pure concept.

Berger and Luckmann stress the need of human communities to legitimate institutions. Symbolic universes at a high level of normativity provide the highest level of integration for discrepant meanings arising from everyday life much closer to facticity.[12] A person's identity, that source of psychological determinism that keeps one functional in the midst of facticity, is ultimately legitimated by placing it in the context of a symbolic universe. That is why, perhaps, our normative propositions are so important to our sense of self and personal security and why we defend them at high risk from endangerment. Conflicts of principle, arguments over legitimation, threats to identity are cultural conflicts rarely subject to quick and easy compromise. On the other hand, sharing of material wealth to end a dispute, tactical collaboration in pursuit of a specific objective, and differences of taste are more easily adjusted amicably without rancor and bitterness.

Next, we can speculate on the inter-relationship of normativity and facticity with a thought experiment: which is more likely to be predictive of a person's future action – his or her values and beliefs or his or her factual circumstances? Generally, if we know a person's emotional dispositions, likes and dislikes, fears and desires, patterns of association with good and bad, we can predict rather well their life style choices. Otherwise, the disciplines of political polling and focus group studies for product marketing would be a waste of time and money.

Cultures have stable normative preferences and patterns which are reflected in social customs – mores the Romans called them – otherwise they would not be cultures with identity and style. Institutions – familial, religious, social, political and economic – play their important role in sustaining cultural priorities to be sure. But institutions deviations from higher priority cultural preferences are usually forestalled and rejected when cultures are in psychic equilibrium with their environment. Cultures provide individuals and institutions with legitimacy and, in turn, individuals and institutions conform to the cultural expectations that elevate them above mere random happenstance or coercively imposed subjection to the will of others.

Who were the Baby Boomers?

American behaviors with respect to the use of debt did dramatically change after 1980. Why? Attitudes towards debt and responsibility changed and so institutional arrangements adapted to new preferences.

Baby Boomers brought to the forefront of American consumerism new tastes and trends. This generation was born between 1946 and 1965. Most of them were the children of the soldiers who fought World War II for the United States and their wives. These parents of Baby Boomers had themselves grown up as children during the great depression.

Baby Boomers were special; they were indulged and they grew up to be different. They were the first generation of Americans to fully embrace a new culture and ethic of being "teenagers". The teenager in the America of the 1950's was a new social status – neither child nor adult. The teenager was more independent and autonomous than a child, no longer under parental direction, but was not yet responsible for mature undertakings of marriage, parental disciplining, career, civic service, or prudent financial planning.

The teenager's freedoms and indulgences were a luxury as yet unknown to traditional human societies where wealth was limited to the very few. Teenager culture grew up with the suburbanization of America and the rise of a middle-class of wage-earners, home owners and consumers.

Teenagers from a psycho-social perspective of being neither within a formal family structure nor in a position of adult responsibility to others are perfectly suited to the expression of a through going modernism. They have unencumbered selves with floating ego identities. They are "other directed" as David Reisman defined that personality profile in his book The Lonely Crowd.

The Other Directed Personality

David Riesman described his book The Lonely Crowd as a study of social character and the ways in which different social character types, once they are formed at the knee of society, are then deployed in the work, play, politics, and childrearing activities of society.[13] Social character, Riesman says, is that part of individual character which is shared among significant social groups and both arises from their salient identity traits and gives to their collective identity its uniqueness in contrast with other social groups. With social character, a cultural phenomenon, outer force is replaced with inner compulsion or desire to channel human energy in particular ways preferred by that social collectivity.[14] Through the operations of social character, society, Riesman argues, ensures some degree of conformity from the individuals who make it up. Such conformity is built into the child and then encouraged or frustrated in later adult experience.

So for the generation of Baby Boomers, their childhood experiences in the late 1940's, 1950's and early 1960's disposed them to more immediate gratification and autonomy of ego than had been the case in previous generations of Americans. In more common terms, Baby Boomers were raised as "spoiled brats" given cash allowances and considerable leisure for their own enjoyment. They were largely raised by their parents without any serious inner orientation to responsibility or to systematic conformity to traditional adult roles, either within the family or in the workplace.

Riesman believed that industrial America with a large and growing middle class and increasingly thriving consumer markets no longer needed a limited set of character types; differentiation of character was now possible. Thus, he noted parents began to raise children. Internalized, disciplined pursuit of clear goals would limit a child's flexibility to adapt to new modes of personal expression and interaction. "Inhibited from presenting their children with sharply silhouetted images of self and society, parents in our era can only equip the child to do his best, whatever that may turn out to be." Riesman wrote.[15]

He continued: "Increasingly in doubt as to how to bring up their children, parents turn to other contemporaries for advice; they also look to the mass media, and ...they turn, in effect, in effect to the children themselves. ...The other-directed child faces ... the problem of defining what making good means. He finds that both the definition and the evaluation of himself depends on the company he keeps: first on his schoolmates and teachers; later on peers and superiors. .... Approval itself, irrespective of content, becomes also the only unequivocal good in this situation: one makes good when one is approved of. Thus all power, not merely some power, is in the hands of the actual or imaginary approving group."[16]

The well socialized, "other directed" American becomes highly sensitive to the swings of fashion with a surrender of any claim to independence of judgment and taste and a learned mastery of the art of consumerism. Safety in this new social environment comes from skilful manipulation of consumer preferences and expression of peer values.[17] This opens the teenager to a work of immediate gratification and blocks the doors of decision-making to saving for some future acquisition. In 2012 Bloomberg-Business Week reported that only 1% of young Americans saved the allowances they receive from their families.

Thus we come to the emergence of the teenager – an older child or a young adult – who seeks approval from peers and takes for self-reference the norms and practices of an approving group other than parents, though for some teenagers parents are still respected and honored. One sees this dynamic presented in the 1954 film Rebel Without A Cause where James Dean rebels against what and for what even he is not too sure of. One thing is certain, though, his friends are more important to him in all ways than his parents.

Also, taken as a truth is that he has no vision of himself as an adult citizen making a contribution to his society. The J.D. Salinger novel of the same era, Catcher in the Rye, similarly presented a teenager too aware of his angst to be a child but not mature enough to be at ease in society.[18]

As Riesman describes the normal practices of "other directed" Americans, he unknowingly prescribes core traits of Baby Boomers: eating food becomes both more casual and more inventive; sex becomes a consumptive good fit for a daytime agenda and equal to the importance of work for the happy individual as moral shame and inhibitions are lost or submerged; dress becomes casual – evening dress disappears and men no longer change for dinner; civic participation declines as people conclude they can do nothing to change politics and they seek to become sycophants on the "inside" learning through connections and gossip what the trend-setters are doing and saying; people become cynical about institutions and laws; glamour takes over to combat indifference and apathy; "captains of consumption" take over social leadership from "captains of industry"; there are no leaders as everyone seeks, not power, but adjustment.

The "other directed" social character Riesman delineates in 1950 becomes the template for the teenagers who emerge as trend setters and consumers 5 years later and who gain dispositive cultural influence in America as the Baby Boomers. Character, the Greeks argued, is fate. The social character of the Baby Boomers brought changes to American culture and so shaped its history.

In 1976, as the Baby Boomers were making their mark on American culture and history, the sociologist Daniel Bell wrote his dystopic book The Cultural Contradictions of Capitalism. For Bell, culture is realm of symbolic forms and the arena of expressive symbolism.[19] Bell, therefore, places his analysis of America in the realm of Normativity as that term is presented to us by Habermas. Bell finds his contemporary culture to be prodigal, promiscuous, dominated by an anti-rational, anti-intellectual temper where the self is taken as the touchstone of cultural judgments.[20] The culture that

Bell describes is the very same one Riesman located as the normative production of other-directed individuals.

Bell calls this cultural temper modernism – a self-willed effort to remain in the forefront of advanced consciousness.[21] This temper leads to an absolute imperiousness of the self says Bell, a meglomania that made an infinity of the self, throwing off all constraints and fears of failure. Impulse and pleasure alone become real and life-affirming. How much this sounds like a teenage party without end.

Bell positions this modernism as a replacement of the bourgeois world view that produced capitalism, a world view that was rational, sober, unheroic and anti-tragic, where order was superior to impulse. Here Bell is noting the triumph of Baby Boomer preferences over the more inner-directed patterns of their parents. He writes of the evolution of Weber's Protestant Ethics into the "psychedelic bazaar, noting that the Protestant Ethic and the Puritan temper had been reduced to "pale ideologies".[22]

Bell blames economic forces such as the rise of mass production, consumer marketing, and that "revolution in moral habit" installment selling.[23] Savings was the heart of the Puritan ethical wrote Bell. Lose that and all moorings are lost and a selfish will to power dominates markets. This abandonment of Puritanism and the Protestant Ethic left capitalism, he asserted, with no moral or transcendent ethic. In the ensuing hedonistic life, there will be a loss of will and fortitude.[24]

In 1991, as the debt culture was well on its way to dominance of the American economy, Richard Brookhiser echoed Daniel Bell's anxieties about a change in American values in a more journalistic book entitled The Way of the WASP.[25] The letters WASP stand for "White, Anglo-Saxon, Protestants", in short the carriers of the Protestant Ethic who were also the biological descendents of the Puritans and other immigrants to the United States from England, Scotland and Wales. Brookhiser describes the core character of WASPs in ways which echo Riesman's "inner directed" social type and Bell's concept of bourgeois values. WASPs, says Brookhiser, were raised to value conscience, anti-sensuality, industry, use, success and civic-mindedness.

Conscience shapes behavior; conscience directs us to work; work depends on finding and enhancing useful things; sensuality is a diversion from work and is frowned upon by strict conscience; industry leads to success; conscience also directs the successful to civic-mindedness to benefit society. This was the Way of the WASP which had made America great and respected. It was also a cultural system that not everyone appreciated.

When the WASPs lost their children to teenagerism and other-direction, as a class they lost all sense of strategic direction. Brookhiser blames what he calls "modernism" for this subversion of WASP character and leadership.[26] For him, "modernism" is primarily a political ideology from the left that saw inner directed lives as plagued with neurosis and capitalist society dependent on exploitation of the vulnerable and the lower orders. WASPs, concludes Brookhiser, could not tame this "modernism". It destroyed them as surely as did Oedipus his royal father.

The Hipster

Brookhiser's surmise was not mistaken. He overlooked Norman Mailer's seminal article of 1957 in Dissent entitled provocatively "The White Negro".[27] Here Mailer called for a cultural revolution through which to overthrow the ruling American cultural and political order. Mailer's partisans would not be the workers and peasants of classical Marxism but newly uninhibited White males (predominantly WASPs) who would be transformed into "psychopaths" through adoption of behaviors and values associated with Negro males.

The realism of his cultural agenda was being provided by the rise of rock and roll among young White Americans, led by Elvis Presley who borrowed his lyrics and sensual dance style from Negro singers. In the wedding of the white and the black, Mailer observed "it was the Negro who brought the cultural dowry."

Mailer pointed out that if White American males were to focus on sex and other sensual indulgence, on immediate gratification, and were to refuse intellectual discipline, they would not be fit to maintain an establishment. America would change.

Mailer's hero – the anti-hero for followers of the Protestant Ethic – he called the "hipster" who was infantile in his psychology but when such infantilism was a sign of the times. The "hipster" existed without roots, set out on an uncharted journey into the rebellious imperatives of the self. The "hipster" seeks to escape boredom and conformity, to live rather in only the present, "in that enormous present which is without past or future, memory or planned intention." Mailer asserted that the source of the Hip was the Negro, who had been living on the margin for two centuries. Whatever made the Hipster feel good was the good.

The Negro, according to Mailer, stayed alive in lives of constant humility or every-threatening danger by following the need of his body. The Negro could not afford the sophisticated inhibitions of civilization and so he kept for his survival the art of the primitive, living in the enormous present and relinquishing the pleasures of the mind for the pleasures of the body. Psychopathology, asserted Mailer, was most prevalent with the Negro for "hated from the outside and therefore hating himself, the Negro was forced into the position of exploring all those moral wildernesses of civilized life which the Square automatically condemns as delinquent or evil or immature or morbid or self-destructive or corrupt."

Mailer prophesied that "the psychopath may indeed be the perverted and dangerous front-runner of a new kind of personality which could become the central expression of human nature before the twentieth century is over" Writing as if he were David Riesman describing other-directed Americans, Mailer said insightfully that "Hip sees the context as generally dominating the man, dominating him because his character is less significant than the context in which he must function." Mailer added: "Character being thus seen as perpetually ambivalent and dynamic enters then into an absolute relativity where there are no truths other than the isolated truths of what each observer feels at each instant of his existence."

In the enormous present, where truth is only present sensuality, why not prefer materialism with debt pushing the cost of pleasure out into the future over the moralism of a demanding work ethic? The culture of the Hip, of the "White Negro", would lead to a very different society in America than what had gone before.

Mailer estimated that the number of self-conscious Hipsters in America was "probably not more than one hundred thousand" but their importance was in their elitism, not in their numbers. They were an elite, wrote Mailer in 1957, "with the potential ruthless-ness of an elite and a language most adolescents can understand instinctively for the hipsters' intense view of existence matches their experience and their desire to rebel."

Mailer was remarkably prescient. It was the Hipsters and their cultural progeny that lead the avant-guard counter-culture move-ment of drugs, sex and rock and roll in the 1960's, the movement in protest over the Vietnam War, the re-definitions of gender around women's roles and expressive and career opportunities, the advo-cacy of multi-culturalism and affirmative social, political and eco-nomic advancement for non-WASP ethnic minorities. The small in-crowd of hipsters became a power national elite in politics (tak-ing over the Democratic Party in the Robert Kennedy and George McGovern presidential campaigns of 1968 and 1972), in society, and in culture.

The Intelligensia

Riesman pointed out in his Lonely Crowd analysis of other-directed personalities how they looked more and more to teachers and the media for normative content and relevant trends around which to act with momentary confidence in the preservation of self. For their part, teachers in high schools, colleges and graduate pro-fessional schools, and successful media writers, editors, publishers, filmmakers, and movie producers and directors more and more internalized a new symbolic sense of meaning and importance. As they become more and more "other directed", they adopted the philosophical psychology of rationalism that was shaped by the European Enlightenment.

Thinkers such as Jean Jacques Rousseau, Diderot, Voltaire, Immanuel Kant, challenged received norms and practices based on custom or revealed religion. Following the lead of Descartes, these writers put the origin of normativity in the individual human mind. For them, subjectivity and its twin individual isolation and alienation from society could be avoided because the operations of reason would link different people to a common truth. Rousseau famously wrote that "man is born free but everywhere he is in chains." By this he meant that each person had reason freely to lead him or her as an autonomous person subject to no authority and yet, society and culture had conspired to prevent that reason from using the full scope of its powers to liberate the individual from constraint. For Rousseau whatever was wrong with the world could be set right through human action set on a proper course by reason and will. Rousseau's dream of such liberating and progressive normative flexibility undergirds many a modern adventure with romance, reform, and indefatigable self-expression.

There were two consequences of this understanding that would come to practical fruition in the life-worlds of the American Baby Boomers. First was subjectivity divorced from any truth value. Reason, it seems, is not such a reliable cultural adhesive after all. In the subjective approach to normativity, all is possible, nothing is certain and flexibility is key to survival in a live always on the edge of emotional and intellectual chaos. When such subjectivity prevails, there is no present sense of the past and no conviction about the future. What is left is Mailer's "enormous present".

Second, social governance by rationality leads to political and economic hierarchies of professionals and experts and to cultural dominance by skilled self-promoting trend setters. In politics, those trained in public policy take over from politicians; in companies specialized technocrats in finance, human relations, management science, law, accounting are retained for their expertise; in culture we arrive at the Andy Warhol moment when everyone will have his or her "15 minutes of fame".

One consequence of professionalism is to dis-empower all who are not professionally educated. Professionalism promotes excessive risk-aversion among ordinary people and those not in position of technocratic authority; in other words, most everyone. Increased risk-aversion reinforces dispositions to defer to others in matters of judgment, taste and decision-making. Bureaucracies, which organize experts into production structures, gain prestige and power over families and other small social units of cooperation.

Max Weber conceptualized this form of social organization as an "ideal type" when he described three kinds of legitimate authority.[28] He wrote of authority which rested on rational, not interpersonal grounds, where the validity of claims to normative precedence rest on a belief in the "legality" of patterns of rules and the right of those elevated to power under such rules to make decisions and issue commands. Weber elaborated that "obedience is owed to the legally established impersonal order. It extends to the persons exercising the authority of office under it only by virtue of the formal legality of their commands and only within the scope of authority of office."[29] Such a system of collective social organization runs by abstract rules; people are fungible, subordinate to the functional needs of the system at any moment. To have a role in the system, a person must have a specific sphere of competence relevant to a set of obligations to perform functions that have been marked off as part of a systematic division of labor. Within that sphere of competence, the person has authority but not beyond it. The job makes the person.

In such a world, persons of vision, determination, and deeply felt passions are risks. They are not needed. Persons nicely other directed and so smoothly adjustable will fit in so much better with other people in the system and will more easily play their part as a good, reliable member of the team. Genius, with its uncontrollable bursts of creativity, insight and creative destruction of the status quo, is rival to reason. Genius is intuitive, right-brained, undisciplined and is centered in strong individuals. Enlightenment reason prefers order and specialization of function. It is much more comfortable with mediocrity and lack of inspiring leadership.

The educational socialization of Baby Boomers, then, focused on their joining the ranks of professionals. This training provided a secure economic foundation for their other-directedness wedding culture, personality and social power into one cohesive system.

The contemporary writer John Saul was no admirer of Enlightenment reason[30]. He saw its dark side. One of his insights most germane to the culture of Baby Boomers was that those who rise up in a system of rational administration really do so by a form of obsequious conformity. They are courtiers always seeking to please those above them. Only a fully formed "other-directed" personally can sustain success in such a system. The professional expert must also be in tune with the peer group and its preferences. They need expertise to perform their functions, yes, but their approach to gaining power lies in a different realm of personal competence. In the rational state, power is everything.[31] The unencumbered self fits in very nicely in such a schema.

Saul observes cynically that "a class of courtiers has never transformed itself into a responsible elite."[32]

The modern technocrat and the royal courtier both had a talent for manipulation, clever in the presentation of facts, contemptuous of public debate and the opinions of lesser lights, and obsequious behavior always making the superior look good. It is never the job of the courtier to announce that the emperor is wearing no clothes not is it the function of technocrats to challenge the norms and practices of the moment.

The distinctions drawn by Riesman, Bell, Brookhiser and Mailer between two ways of being in contemporary America importantly resonate with the systems theory of Talcott Parsons, a follower of Max Weber who attempted an integrated field theory of social systems. Parsons, in particular, wanted to understand in a predictable way the courses of human action.[33] He and his colleagues postulated five dichotomies according to which action sequences can be categorized. One dimension is that of affectivity – from the sensuality of immediate gratification to the distance of evaluation and the possible renunciation of action. A second dimension is that of orientation to self or to collective. The third dimension is from the universal to the particular. The fourth dimension is intensity of seeking to achieve a chosen social outcome, where acceptance of the status quo is the alternative to achievement. The final dimension is engagement with a possible action – should the actor narrow the meaning what is at stake or broaden it to far and diffuse horizons?[34]

Roughly speaking, the other-directed adolescent or teenager in approaching action will be disposed (1) to seek sensual immediate gratification, (2) pursuit of private interests regardless of its direct bearing on the interests of others, (3) use general categories homogenous for all individuals to think about actions, (4) focus on the currently presented aspects of objects, persons and events rather than on their performance value, and (5) to see life where everything varies by context and there are few limits to the contexts that become relevant to the actor.

To the converse, the inner-directed or more traditional American personality type would (1) avoid immediate gratification through evaluative discipline, (2) accept responsibility to community, (3) focus on the inherent qualities of the objects, people or events at hand, (4) give priority to actual or expected performances, and (5) accept a limited significance of an object, person or event that are related to a range of practical outcomes.

The disposition to action that is sensually affective, oriented to self, general in its range of values, accepting of relativistic meanings, and diffuse in its preferences seems rightly correlated with the inner-directed or adolescent person.

The alternative disposition to action that is judgmental and disciplined, accepting of responsibility, craft-like in using the environment, bent on achievement, and specific in application of talent and energy seems more properly correlated with a work ethic appropriate to successful capitalist endeavor.

The first set of orientations to action are most often located in pre-capitalist cultures and the second set is often ascribed to societies in the process of industrialization.

But America has moved into a post-industrial order. Might it, therefore, now be appropriate for a re-emergence of less disciplined personality types – Mailer's Hipsters and Riesman's other-directed hedonists?

Post Industrial America

By 1980 when the American cultural affinity for debt began to accelerate, Baby Boomers were reaching their middle years in an economy that had become post-industrial. New relations of production and distribution were more compatible with untraditional styles of work and personal interaction.[35] In pre-industrial societies, the labor force is engaged overwhelmingly in the extractive industries: mining, fishing, forestry, agriculture. Life there is primarily a game against nature as Bell puts it.[36] Industrial societies thrive on goods producing economies. Life, as Bell says, becomes a game against fabricated nature. People co-opt natural sources of energy and raw materials to make things that nature never did. The machine predominates and civilization is time bound, technical and rational. Energy and machines transform the nature of work and mass production becomes possible to create what Adam Smith called "the wealth of nations

Then comes post-industrial society, which is based on services. Life here, Bell posits, is a game among persons. What counts is not raw labor power, or energy and machines, but information. The person central to the post-industrial society is the professional, equipped by education and training to provide the quality of life – health, education, amusement, recreation, the arts – demanded by consumers in post-industrial cultures.[37]

Right after 1900 seven out of ten American workers were engaged in the production of goods. By 1960, six out of ten were in services. By 1980, the proportion would be seven out of 10. In 1974 only 33 percent of Americans completed high school; by 1973 the proportion was 85 percent. Admissions to colleges and graduate schools rose dramatically after World War II as access to elite opportunities was democratized across American society. The University became the center of establishment culture. Blue collar jobs lost out to white collar occupations. America became a white collar society by the 1980s. The number of workers organized in private sector labor unions dropped precipitously. Participation in the trade union movement reached its all time high in 1970.

In his book White Collar of 1951, C. Wright Mills had already pointed out that a white-collar economy was a personality market in which each person sold himself or herself in order to impress another and get ahead.[38]

Post industrial society was enriched and deepened by the information technology (PCs) and communications revolutions (internet and cell phones) of the 1990's. There was no turning back to an era of limited possibilities.

The economic opportunities provided by postindustrial society, married to the unencumbered self promoted by Rousseau-ist rationalism which is hosted by an other-directed personality structure, created a new American paradigm of social justice for the Baby Boomers to enjoy and exploit.

A Survey of American Cultural History

David Riesman's dichotomy between inner and other directed persons aligned with two opposing ideals in American history. One came from John Calvin and the other from Rousseau. John Calvin enthusiastically advocated a life of Christian vocation based on scrupulous following of Biblical teachings. Rousseau abandoned his Calvinist family as a young boy to follow a more self-focused calling. The Puritans came to Britain's colonies in New England to live out their Calvinism with more freedom and rigor than they could in England. Their mission as put by John Winthrop upon his 1630 arrival in Boston harbor was to "build a city upon a hill" to which the eyes of the world would turn in admiration and emulation. The Puritan project was to build a New Jerusalem, living as saints in a covenanted relationship with their God and keeping to his ways and instructions. In return for such steadfast service, he would, they believed provide them with success and protection through his blessings.[39]

This Protestant ethic, a life-long journey towards holiness with a priesthood of Godly accomplishment held out for every believer, provided certainty and inner-direction for its adherents. Protestant Christian belief in the permanence of sin demanded as a response strenuous inner personal discipline and self-control. One's salvation hopes depended, not on the opinion of others, but on the rigor of self-restraint and focused application to responsibility. Core to the personality admired by these first Americans was an active moral sense, of the kind promoted by Adam Smith in his treatise on The Theory of the Moral Sentiments and presumed by John Locke in his advocacy of republican government as a public trust.

The American Revolution, the Declaration of Independence, the form of the Federal Constitution, the arguments of the Federalist Papers, the appeals of George Washington in his presidential addresses, all flowed out of the thinking of John Locke and other English Whigs, who upheld the Calvinist tradition in English politics.

But there was another ideal presented as well. Both Thomas Paine and Thomas Jefferson envisioned American without the aid of Calvinist determinism. They rather looked to Rousseau and other French writers for wisdom. Neither Paine nor Jefferson had much affinity for the Puritan concern for sin and the need to overcome its stain on our characters. Neither Paine nor Jefferson worried over the need to develop a moral sense. As with Rousseau, they took all persons as born entitled to freedom and prosperity. Justice was a birthright; life was for enjoyment, not for paying one's way with responsibilities and sacrifices. Each self was unencumbered and free to follow its own will as tempered by its own reason. Americans, from this perspective, were returned to Eden before the fall of Adam and Eve.

America as a New Eden looked with favor on nature and the wonders of a great continent free of man-made sin and human oppression. The hopes of Thoreau writing about Walden Pond; the enthusiasm of Emerson breaking with Calvinist dogma and promoting self-reliance in communion with the Over-soul present throughout creation; the endless excitement of Walt Whitman over all things and all happenings; the paintings of the Hudson River School; all defined a stance of American exceptionalism in being free from sin and constraint.

Abolition of slavery pitted those who sought the New Jerusalem against those happy in the New Eden. Jefferson, for example, had written in his Notes on the State of Virginia (a report written to promote his reputation with French intellectuals) that Negroes from Africa were not of sufficient quality to deserve the New Eden. Native Americans, on the other hand, wrote Jefferson could aspire to admission as they were Noble Savages in the best Rousseauist tradition and contained the purity of the finest human instincts.[40] Southern culture had originated not with Puritans but with Anglican and Catholic settlers from the southwest of England; families who had fought for the Stuart Kings against the Calvinists. Southern families found comfort in lives of ease and indulgence supported by slaves.

Northern Calvinists sought to eliminate slavery. There could be no compromise on such an issue of fundamental right and wrong and the Civil War ensued. Abraham Lincoln drew upon the compelling normative themes of building a city upon a hill to rally Americans to the intermingled causes of preserving the Union and ending slavery. After the Union victory, America as a New Jerusalem took on added credence.

But after the Civil War, change came, ushered in by vast economic success and stunning material prosperity on a national scale.

Americans could become complacent that God had rewarded them for their fidelity so that wealth became evidence of entitlement to more wealth. One's moral stature could be measured in monetary terms. Social Darwinism, the harsh and divisive analysis of Herbert Spencer, fused with Calvinist notions of belonging to an elect circle of winners to ground a pro-business, pro-capitalist political party. The shiny ideals of the New Jerusalem were starting to tarnish from materialist oxidation.

Opposing the Social Darwinists were the Progressives and advocates of the Social Gospel. Both Progressives and Social Gospel thinkers picked up the theme of America as a New Eden. No one, they argued, should be excluded from prosperity; all were entitled - both those born to citizenship and immigrants. Government was called upon to redress inequities and unjust accumulations of wealth. Democratic Presidential Candidate William Jennings Bryan cried out that the Republicans should not "crucify mankind upon a cross of gold." The wealthy were called to charity and good works to care for the poor and the unfortunate.

As President, the Democrat Woodrow Wilson responded to the imperative of the New Eden with progressive legislation to restrain a brute capitalism and to the demands of the New Jerusalem with entry into a war to save democracy.

Wilson's Republican successors presided over a bountiful economy in the 1920's where material entitlements became more and more realistic. A political slogan was "two chickens in every pot". The Jazz Age and Flappers gave a prelude to Norman Mailer's hipster as a cultural icon. Novels by F. Scott Fitzgerald (This Side of Paradise; The Great Gatsby) looked at the workings of an entitlement society where work was less important than play and people didn't have to grow up into adults. Sinclair Lewis wrote disparagingly of small town morals and constraints and the hypocrisy of Protestant fundamentalism (Main Street, Babbitt, Elmer Gantry). Fundamentalism as a new religious movement arose attempting to replace the older Calvinist practices seeking the New Jerusalem. But Fundamentalism was more based on Baptist dedication to individual salvation than on Calvinist stewardship.

The irrational exuberance of the 1920's culminated in an asset bubble on Wall Street and a crash in stock market values. Poor polices on the part of central banks send the world into a great depression. In America Franklin Roosevelt was elected President to protect Americans from the failures of capitalism. Government as the provider of entitlements gained stature as the income tax was increased to pay for a wide range of government services and social security for the elderly was adopted. In his first inaugural address, Roosevelt excoriated those whose irresponsibility had cause such harm to ordinary people, saying "the rulers of the exchange of mankind's goods have failed, through their own stubbornness and their own incompetence, have admitted their failure and abdicated. ... They know only the rules of a generation of self-seekers. They have no vision and where there is no vision, the people perish. The money changers have fled from their high seats in the temple of our civilization. We may now restore that temple to the ancient truths. ... Happiness lies not in the mere possession of money; it lies in the joy of achievement, in the thrill of creative effort. The joy and moral stimulation of work no longer must be forgotten in the mad chase of evanescent profits."[41]

Here, Roosevelt, elected to confirm America as the New Eden, harks back to older standards more resonate with the New Jerusalem. Visions of normativity only slowly fade into irrelevance through social evolution. In 1961 the young Democrat President John F. Kennedy would also echo older notions when he said "My fellow Americans, ask not what your country can do for you; ask rather what you can do for your country."[42]

As the Baby Boomers found their generational voice in the 1960's after Kennedy's assassination and the 1965 victory of the Civil Rights Movement under Lyndon Johnson, a culture war emerged. On the one hand were Boomer demands to enjoy the New Eden as an entitlement open to all perspectives of utility and preference and on the other were defenders of a more traditional sense of America as a New Jerusalem. The Vietnam War first opened up the cultural divide. The educated elite among the Boomers resisted the war as an imposition on their life styles and found ways to avoid military service. President Nixon deftly ended massive protests over the war by ending the draft and turning America to a military of professional soldiers volunteering for a career in the armed services.

Defeat of American purposes in Vietnam exposed the older American ideal of responsibility for others and service over self as the Rotarians pledge to ridicule and rejection. If seeking the New Jerusalem had lost appeal, then what was wrong with enjoyment in a New Eden?

The Roosevelt New Deal paradigm lasted until 1980 with the election of Ronald Reagan as a "conservative" bent on reducing the size of government and lowering taxes. The attractions of living in a New Eden had become so compelling and so widespread that Reagan could not govern as a traditional Calvinist. His conservatism conformed to the premises of the New Eden that all Americans were deserving and entitled. Reagan's promise was that it was "morning in America again" where the sun shined on rich and poor alike and all could be for the best in the best of all possible countries. His was a sunny optimism in which few traces of dour Calvinism could be found.

But following the post-civil war blend of Social Darwinism and Calvinism, Reagan's normative vision of entitlement focused, not on government patronage, but on private wealth. For Reagan, Americans were entitled to their wealth and their personal freedoms, protected from the intrusion of government regulation and supervision.

For the social conservatives of Reagan's coalition – the "Leave me Alone" coalition - New Eden is a place of individual autonomy without regulation on behalf of others or the common good.

For the others, the Hipsters of Mailer's fancy who fully engaged with Rousseau's premise about the absence of sin and the appeal of professional accomplishment, Reagan's vision was a heresy. These, the progressives in the Democrat Party, say government as delivering the New Eden to deserving individuals and identity groups. They sought high taxes and activist government.

Reagan managed to square the circle when he accepted lower taxes with higher expenditures for certain constituencies at the price of growing government debt. This pattern continued under his successors George H. W. Bush, Willliam Clinton, and George W. Bush, though President Clinton was fortunate enough to be president during years of substantial economic growth and declining government borrowing.

Debt was the common denominator between the conservative side of the New Eden and its progressive side.

Baby Boomers, both conservative and progressive, living out their orientations of character and enjoying today's entitlements set the stage for the asset bubble caused by sub-prime lending and the resulting financial collapse of 2008.

道德

CHAPTER FIVE

MORAL CAPITALISM AND THE GREAT
FINANCIAL MELTDOWN OF 2008

What the world knew as "Wall Street" died from suicide in the fall of 2008. Manhattan's great investment banks are gone. The last two – Goldman Sachs and Morgan Stanley – converted themselves into banks, submitting to more intrusive government regulation in return for more secure sources of capital.

Communism couldn't kill this Wall Street; capitalism, however, did. Adam Smith won out over Karl Marx.

This "Wall Street" died at its own hands in a form of negligent suicide. It lived by the sword of extreme market capitalism and died by that same sword. It overdosed on toxic behaviors as did celebrities John Beluchi, Jimi Hendrix, Janis Joplin, and Jim Morrison.

The epitaph, I suppose, for "Wall Street's" mighty rise and astonishing fall should be "Sic Transit Gloria Mundi" – "thus passeth worldly glory".

Street talk for what killed Wall Street's investment bank titans is that it was "greed" that did them in. As in a Greek tragedy, excess and hubris worked through a cycle of boom and bust to humble even the best and the brightest. It's an old story, really, new in its techniques of subprime mortgages, CDOs, and credit default swaps, but very old in its moral fundamentals.

But I don't think it was greed precisely that was the cause of the losses and bankruptcies.

Greed – understood as seeking a profit, as pursuing one's interest in business transactions – has not always been so terribly dysfunctional and hurtful to the common good. Indeed most of our modern life was devised, produced, distributed and sold by capitalist behaviors and motivations. There was a baby in Wall Street's bathwater to be sure.

Goldman Sachs, Morgan Stanley, Merrill Lynch, Bear Sterns and their predecessors brought companies to life by raising capital for them. America's growth and resulting economic wellbeing rested on robust capital markets. Without them there would have been no railroads, steel mills, General Motors, Ford, Boeing, Microsoft, or all the other Fortune 1,000 and smaller companies that ever sold stock or debt securities to finance their businesses.

Imprudent decisions on the part of US and European investment banks, banks, mortgage brokers, insurance companies, and consumers - all seeking profitable advantage - have brought the global financial network that sustains global capitalism to crisis. It is the greatest crisis of capitalism since the great depression of the 1930's.

Great American financial houses – even Lehman Brothers that survived the Great Depression of the 1930s - are no more; banks in America and Europe have been propped up by governments - even to the extent of deposit guarantees; and massive amounts of liquidity have been injected into the financial system by the US Federal Reserve System and other central banks.

This is not business as usual. Trillions of dollars in private wealth has been destroyed in a matter of weeks, some of it never to be regained. And governments have been forced to step in to protect the economically vulnerable where markets have failed.

Yet, ironically, inadequate regulation and government policies also contributed in various ways to risks being negligently addressed by financial markets, thereby paving the way for the current crisis.

Beyond dealing with the immediate crisis, the critical task will be to address the underlying causes through reforms to restore trust and confidence in financial markets. Functioning and sound financial institutions, despite their current failure to meet their fundamental responsibilities, remains of first importance for supporting a successful free market economy. Credit is now scarce and capitalism cannot properly function without it.

The triggers to this crisis were centered on a lack of: prudence in the extension of credit; rigor in valuations; and of transparency in management. For example, major banks extended credit and assumed obligations on contracts that were inherently over-valued. When the over-valuation became apparent, bank capital was inadequate to support the corresponding liabilities. This was compounded by the mis-pricing of risk via the bundling and sale of debt through collateralized debt securities and via complex derivative based credit default swaps. These failures reflected profound shortcomings in private sector governance both as prescribed and as applied. In short, risk was not appropriately managed; it was not even properly understood both by those creating it and by those bound to mitigate it.

Driving this lack of prudent management was a dysfunctional and shortsighted system of incentives and personal remuneration.

Compensation of senior executives, traders and fund managers was built on greed and self interest and was decoupled from long-term wealth creation. Compensation based on fees earned and other incentive-based benchmarks blinded otherwise intelligent managers to the long-term dire consequences of their decisions. Rewards rose with excessive risk taking and was provided in ways that has largely shielded senior corporate officers and fund managers from liability for their decisions.

As a result, the best interests of customers, owners, employees and communities have been systematically overlooked. Decision-makers, driven by short-term interests, paid too little to no attention to managing risk accumulation.

Short-term speculation dominated, with part of the market enriching itself by betting on and contributing to the destruction of wealth via short-selling. Not only did the regulators fail to halt the growth in systemic risk, some of the contributing market activity and behavior was allowed to remain unregulated.

This global financial crisis has further exacerbated the very low levels of trust which the global community places in business. The fact that the profits were in effect privatized to those who created the crisis through excessive rewards, and the losses are now being socialized to taxpayers has further outraged the community. Though justly perhaps, the shareholders of the 'failed' financial institutions responsible for the crisis have lost most of their ownership wealth.

This is not the first time that market capitalism has so failed. Less than a decade ago, global markets lived through the bust of the dot-com and telecom bubble in equities and the accounting scandals of Enron and World-Com. Before that, world financial markets were upset by currency collapses in Thailand, Malaysia, Indonesia and Russia. And before that, the United States lived through the savings and loan/junk bond bubble and bust.

More fundamentally, the current crisis represents the latest, albeit the most severe, fallout from the systemic erosion within the corporate world of the importance of ethics and responsibility in business decision-making. Ideological commitments to laissez-faire free market fundamentalism, social darwinism philosophies, and shareholder primacy at the expense of other stakeholders, have divorced business leadership from standards of good faith, wise stewardship and care for the public interest.

As a result, capitalism's immune system of market discipline fails every so often and the cancer of "irrational exuberance", greed and narrow self interest metastasizes. The object of reform, obviously, should be either to eliminate this deep cancer within capitalism once and for all or to boost society's market immune system of accurate pricing, risk management and valuation transparency in order to keep the cancer in longterm remission.

At the core of all these market shortcomings were the boards of directors of the corporations involved. They were not sufficiently encased in an environment of accountability and transparency and ultimate accountability. The market failure, therefore, was ultimately a failure of governance.

So what went wrong? When did this "Wall Street" of once sound investment banking houses start walking on the wild side towards perdition?

The short answer is too much leverage – too much debt. Lehman Brothers, as an example, was leveraged 30 to 1 when it failed. When its chickens came home to roost in questions about how it was going to pay off its debt as the market turned sour, Lehman had insufficient capital of its own to be credibly self-reliant in down markets.

This answer raises a further question: why the need for so much leverage?

The answer to this question gets us closer to the culprit. Lehman wanted to buy securities and other tradable assets to resell them for a profit. It borrowed money to buy assets. It was not raising capital for other companies and taking a fee for the service. That was the traditional role for investment banks. No, Lehman had become a big trader on its own account as well. Lehman and the other investment banks were buying and selling any number of assets – short sales, currencies, options, puts and calls, stocks, bonds, many sorts of derivatives – to speculate on price movements.

When done well, such trading earned huge returns and permitted lavish bonuses and life styles on the part of its owners and employees.

The point to note is that trading is not real investing. It is playing in the space left open by other buyers and sellers. Trading is short term; it is not designed to hold rights to the income or the capital appreciation of companies over the long haul. The time frame for trading is "right now".

Trading is not a special, distinct part of capitalism with its genius for engineering modern economic growth. Trading has been with us since the dawn of time. Markets predate capitalism by millennia. Capitalism is a recent evolution in human social practices, substantially starting in Holland and England only in the 1600's.

In the ancient Chinese state of Qi before the time of Confucius, there was a famous Prime Minister, Quan Zi. His lord, Duke Huan, loved purple cloth but grew annoyed when the price for such beautiful cloth rose too high even for him. A shrewd judge of human nature, Quan Zi advised his Duke as follows: since the dye used to make the cloth purple left a smell, the next time someone approached the Duke wearing purple clothes, the Duke should hold his nose as if the smell was repugnant to him. The Duke did so and all the courtiers, suddenly fearful of offending the Duke by wearing purple, sold all their purple clothes. The price of purple cloth in the markets of Qi immediately dropped. Quan Zi bought up all the purple cloth for a song and gave it to his now very happy Lord.

Such trading in markets has a long history throughout human history. But capitalism seeks patient capital to invest over the long haul in companies that need the cash for working capital, wages, raw materials, plant, equipment, etc. For capitalism to succeed, the right kind of investment capital markets is very necessary. But it must be a market that attracts investment, not speculation. A market in speculation is a casino. From the beginning of capitalism, old trading habits were brought over to finance and trade the new possibilities created by the new, emerging economic system. But trading habits loosed inside capitalism have been disruptive.

Trading and investing thrive on different and inconsistent incentives. Traders like to take a fee from every trade; investors look to dividends and the sale of appreciated ownership shares as a company becomes successful in its business for their returns.

Trading is akin to speculation: you pay money for a chance to win. You don't always win so your winnings over time need to compensate for your losses and the risks associated with the gambles taken. Trading and speculation are inherently short term and limited in their consideration of consequences. Their spirit is at odds with the motivations and perseverance needed to grow a business.

Capital markets exist to accommodate traders and trading in financial instruments. Investment capital is raised by selling equity and debt contracts. We can't, as far as I can tell, eliminate trading from capitalism. Providers of capital and companies need the liquidity which the ability to sell into a robust market of buyers permits; trading sets prices, which give vital information on values and trends, successes and failures.

But the goose that lays the golden eggs is not one that lives on trading alone. Firms need patient capital – investors, not speculators renting stock for a while in order to profit from market movements. Speculators can easily divert management's attention away from long term strategies to short term manipulations of stock prices.

The most important role of financial intermediaries is to provide capital; therefore, short term trading in capital contracts should be subordinate to the mission of finding ways to raise money for companies so that they can create jobs, products and services – and, in consequence, the precious commodity of real economic growth.

We might want to consider having different kinds of markets – one for trading and one for investing, or pricing arrangements that add to the purchase price of the trade as the risk associated with each new, incremental trade gets bigger and bigger. If risk were properly priced, the demand for financial instruments would contract as risk conditions change adversely given the growth of excessive supply. Too much supply financed with debt leads to a boom, which sets us up for the ensuing bust.

But, this strategy would require taking into account up front all the external consequences – both positive and negative – for consumers, society, workers, lenders, investors, suppliers, government – that will flow from the activities funded by the extension of credit.

Not for the Very First Time

The recent global crisis in the financial markets of modern capitalism is merely the latest in a series of malfunctions in the integration of financial markets with the real economy.

Each malfunction follows the same pricing sequence: investors bid up prices for legal contracts to earn future cash returns; the value of the goods secured by the contracts increases starting an asset bubble; seeing rising prices, more investors buy the contracts to secure for themselves a share of the coming returns; cash is borrowed to purchase the contracts, or they are bought on credit – in either case debt obligations rapidly increase dramatically; the value of the future benefits under contract become irrationally divorced from the fundamental, inherent, or realistic market value of such benefits; the bubble bursts and the debtors are ruined; the value of the contracts and the underlying assets deflates to a reasonable price and markets start to work normally once again – until the next bubble in asset prices cycle starts.

The first of these malfunctions in capitalism was the tulip mania in Holland around 1620. That was followed by a huge bubble in France in shares of the Mississippi Company, and about the same time a bubble in the stock of the South Sea Company in London. During the 19th century a series of bubbles grew and burst every decade or so in the United States. The biggest such asset bubble was in company shares during the 1920's. That asset bubble cycle burst in October 1929 and brought on the great depression of the 1930's.

Then, in the United States, there was an asset bubble and bust around the purchase of "junk bonds" and investments in savings and loan associations in the 1980's and the sale and purchase of dot-com/telecom stocks in the late 1990's.

The current financial crisis, though a very large and serious one, started innocently enough in 2001 and 2002. Mortgage lenders in the United States noticed that sub-prime borrowers responsibly paid their loans as if they were good credit risks but at a higher rate of interest. Their mortgages offered higher returns for lower risk and money began to flow into that part of the housing market.

Housing prices started to rise; low interest rates as set by the Federal Reserve System meant that the cost of borrowing was low. Borrowing to invest in real property where prices were rising made great economic sense. An asset bubble began to build. To fund more loans, mortgage lenders sold off their loans, keeping a fee, and used the proceeds to make more loans. The buyers of the sub-prime loans sold by the originators looked to the home owners for regular payment of interest and principle.

Then sophisticated financial houses began to sell "collateral debt obligations" or CDOs. CDOs were sold to investors around the world and the proceeds were used to buy packages of sub-prime loans and other assets. The payment streams flowing from the home-owners were divided in many ways through "packaging" of rights to the income from many small loans into separate securities. Different levels of risk and return were thus constructed and sold.

To enhance the value of the CDOs, issuers would pay a fee to obtain a guarantee of payment by the underlying home owners and other obligors. These guarantees were called Credit Default Swaps and over US$40 trillion dollars of such guarantees were made by companies that really had no prospect of making good on their guarantees if the market ever went sour.

With the invention and a sale of CDOs backed by credit default swaps, billions of dollars from global financial markets flooded the US sub-prime mortgage market. As a result, the value assigned by global investors through the issuance of debt to support prices in that market was far in excess of any realistic, long-term, fundamental value that could be assigned to the underlying assets. That fundamental value was sustained by what level of income would be readily available to fund some level of debt. That level was much lower than the amount that had been lent by investors. Something had to give.

As the bubble grew, the risks of failure and default grew as well. By 2003 all the good credit "sub-prime" borrowers had been serviced and so new borrowers were increasingly at risk of default. Mortgage brokers and originators of mortgages began to get creative in order to make more loans. Sound lending practices went out the window; fraud was committed in making loans where there was no reasonable expectation of repayment by the borrower. Income reported by the borrower was falsified; payment terms were easy up front to become onerous in the future if conditions changes.

The gap between real risk and market-perceived risk grew and grew with real risk rising and market-perceived risk level or even declining as prices for house and real estate continued to rise. In 2007 the bubble began to lose momentum; reality finally caught up with market-perceptions; housing prices stopped increasing and began to fall; defaults in mortgage payments began to accelerate; rating agencies downgraded outstanding CDOs.

First came the collapse of two Bear Stearns hedge funds that had borrowed too much money for investment in assets that were suddenly losing value. Then came the collapse of Bear Sterns itself. Then major banks and investment banking houses had to write down billions of value to better align the values of their CDO and related holdings to the newly emerging values of what could be expected in actual payment on the underlying mortgages and the value of the collateral supporting those mortgage loans. This caused the capital accounts of those banks and investment banks to shrink, which caused their lenders to reduce lines of credit. That, in turn, caused the collapse of Lehman Brothers, the sale of Merrill Lynch and the conversion of Goldman Sachs and Morgan Stanley into commercial banks.

The flight to quality on the part of lenders reduced liquidity in global financial markets which brought crisis to Fortis, the banks in Iceland, to UBS, and many other global firms. In the United States, even lending to great corporations through the purchase of their short term commercial paper for cash dried up. AIG, an insurance company with over US$1 trillion in assets but a guarantor on many CDOs, was at risk of not being able to borrow short-term funds.

Without credit capitalism cannot thrive. The financial markets penetrate the "real" markets of production of goods and services. One can't function well without the other. To rescue capitalist production, financial markets had to be restored to confidence and trading viability in loans and investments of money.

Thus, governments had to step in and find ways to provide confidence in repayment by borrowers so that credit would flow. This the United States Treasure and Federal Reserve System did in massive ways – providing over US$7 trillion in loans to banks, investment banks, and even corporations by buying low value assets and corporate commercial paper and in providing other guarantees of payment by private firms. In addition, the US Congress approved spending US$700 billion in government funds to buy bad mortgages from banks and to increase their capital accounts through government purchases of their stock.

As a result of such government intervention in the United States and the European Union, financial markets stabilized – but, as a consequence of this malfunction of capital markets, jobs were lost, values dropped, real economic activity retrenched, consumer spending froze and government expenses went up. The world entered a recessionary environment.

What Went Wrong?

Simply put: two things went wrong. First, risk was imprudently assessed and managed and, second, valuations were poorly analyzed. The two processes – risk assessment and valuation – are inter-related. Risk assessment shapes the parameters of valuation and valuation takes into account future risks. In short, the higher the future risk, the lower the present, or "real", or "fundamental" value of an asset.

In the early stages of the current crisis, risk was not improperly assessed and values of sub-prime mortgages and CDOs based upon the promise of their future payments were reasonable. But, not paying close attention to rising risk levels as asset prices rise and setting higher and higher present cash values on assets such as houses, sub-prime mortgages, and CDOs, are the acts of poor judgment that created the bubble.

What drove the poor judgment? Greed and shortsightedness – the curse of financial markets. To some extent, financial markets are always driven by speculation – betting not on underlying enterprise but on perceptions held by others of where prices will go. Speculators and traders don't care what the long-term future is and they don't care what real values are. They just want to play off what other people think values are. If market players think sub-prime mortgages have value, brokers will sell them what they want to buy, take a fee, and walk away leaving all future risk with the buyer.

Financial markets, therefore, have a bias towards short-sighted profit taking when successful capitalism needs far-sighted "patient" capital. This is the continuing contradiction between financial markets and the good of responsible capitalism.

The Caux Round Table Approach

Overcoming the functionality of greed and short-term self-interest is the goal of those who promote responsible decision-making in business. And a daunting task they have.

The Caux Round Table published a set of ethical principles for business in 1994, the first such set of principles for guidance of global business and the only set of such principles yet designed by experienced business leaders.

The current massive disruption of financial markets initially brought on by the collapse of the sub-prime mortgage market in the United States provides an opportunity to assess the relevance of the CRT Principles for Business.

If they had been followed, are there reasonable grounds to believe that the crisis could have been avoided, or at least mitigated in scope and intensity?

I think the answer is, yes, the CRT Principles might have made a difference had they been infused in strategic and tactical decisions on the part of those financial institutions which contributed to the current crisis.

First, let us consider the implications of the first CRT Principle for Business:

"The value of a business to society is the wealth and employment it creates and the marketable products and services it provides to consumers at a reasonable price commensurate with quality. To create such value, a business must maintain its own economic health and viability ..."

Since the crisis is about the failure of major financial houses and banks such as Bear Sterns and Lehman Brothers, the sale of others such as Merrill Lynch and Washington Mutual, and the government rescue of Freddie Mac, Fannie Mae, AIG, Fortis, and others, we can quite quickly conclude that these companies failed to meet the ethical requirement of maintaining their own economic health and viability.

Their decision-making was wrong-headed in the accumulation of too much debt and in setting imprudent values on certain financial assets such as sub-prime home mortgages and CDOs. In their collapse, these firms caused a contraction of markets, thus erasing wealth and employment in violation of what the CRT advocates as the primary obligation of business firms.

Second, the current crisis was caused by a failure to provide quality products at a price commensurate with their inherent worth.

Sub-prime mortgages were priced inappropriately for many borrowers. Excessive and imprudent borrowings were offered to home owners. In the many cases where credit standards were waived or overlooked lenders and mortgage brokers knew or should have known as professionals that the borrowers were highly likely to default if economic conditions changed.

Borrowers were effectively sold defective financial products. Such mortgages were also sold in excessive quantities, creating an asset bubble that gave rise to perverse incentives on the part of home buyers to assume unreasonable risks of future default and foreclosure.

Similarly, the terms of many CDOs sold were not of the value that was represented to buyers. They carried more risk than was reasonable for the investment goals of those who purchased them. They were also issued in excessive amounts that undermined their long-term value.

This requirement to serve customers with respect for their needs is reinforced in Section 3 of the CRT Principles for Business with the requirement that businesses "provide their customers with the highest quality products and services consistent with their requirements."

The first CRT Principle also holds that:

"Businesses have a role to play in improving the lives of all their customers, employees, and shareholders by sharing with them the wealth they have created."

Here has been the greatest harm done by those who created the unsustainable markets in sub-prime mortgages and CDOs – they destroyed wealth and made worse the lives of many customers, employees, owners, creditors and communities.

Principle No. Three of the CRT Principles holds that:

"... businesses should recognize that sincerity, candor, truthfulness, the keeping of promises, and transparency contribute not only to their own credibility and stability but also to the smoothness and efficiency of business transactions, particularly on the international level."

The current crisis in financial markets was caused by a lack of sufficient transparency in CDOs valuations which eventually undermined the smoothness and efficiency of international marke ts for credit and liquidity.

Principle No. Four of the CRT Principles holds that:

"[Businesses] should recognize that some behavior, though legal, may still have adverse consequences."

It appears that in general, the provision of the financial products that gave rise to the crisis was legal. No laws were violated in lending to sub-prime borrowers or securitizing those mortgages and selling off interests in them through CDOs and in providing guarantees of payment through credit default swaps. Individuals here and there are being investigated for fraud in the sale of such products, but the products themselves were legitimate in concept. What went wrong was selling them to excess on unsustainable terms. That behavior, though legal, had adverse consequences that should have been foreseen and avoided.

With respect to their owners, those responsible for the credit crisis failed to meet other responsibilities set forth in the CRT Principles for Business. For example, they failed to "apply professional and diligent management" and to "conserve, protect and increase the owner's/investors assets". These failures lay at the heart of the dynamic that caused the crisis. There was strategically poor judgment exercised in the development of these markets. Risk was exacerbated to the point of destabilization; it was not properly foreseen or managed.

And, finally, those who caused this crisis failed to meet the CRT standard of enhancing community environments and standards of living. Where homes go into default when mortgages can't be paid, communities suffer disinvestment and even blight as home prices fall and homes are abandoned to the lenders.

Had the boards of directors and senior managers of Bear Sterns, Lehman Brothers, Merrill Lynch, Citibank, Morgan Stanley, Goldman Sachs, Washington Mutual, Freddie Mac, Fannie Mae, and others who thrived for a while off the issuance of sub-prime mortgages and CDOs taken their CRT responsibilities more seriously – and insisted on products and sales strategies consistent with those practices – there would have been less risk injected into the global financial system and less provision of unsustainable financial products.

I argued in my 2004 book Moral Capitalism that "Directors and corporate officers are hired to be agents not just for their fidelity but also for their skill. Their responsibility is to guard against high risk and imprudent courses of action."

I also emphasized there the intertwining of interdependencies and the need for trust in transactions. Capitalism breeds interdependencies through the specialization of function and the division of labor. Reliance and trust are essential for capitalism to thrive. Destruction of either leads to trouble in markets. People lose confidence and withhold their ideas, labor, and capital from productive exchange. The economy then contracts. That is what is happening now. The current crisis is really only a crisis of confidence; trust has been lost.

But how do you restore trust when it has been abused?

The principles of Moral Capitalism hold that "where mistrust prevails, people fear entering into dependency relationships. Mistrust always raises the risks of enterprise. Who would invest where risks are excessive and returns uncertain?"

This dynamic explains the collapse of value in Bear Sterns, Lehman Brothers, AIG and Washington Mutual and the sale of Merrill Lynch – they had billions of dollars of assets on their books but no one wanted to buy their shares. The value of Bear Sterns was $80 per share on the books, but only $2 per share in the market and that price only with a government promise to assume billions of dollars in bad assets to make the residual business more valuable as a going concern. Lehman Brothers went bankrupt and its owners could not realize the value of the company's book assets as no one wanted to buy those assets encumbered as they were by debt and uncertainty.

The principles of Moral Capitalism note the sometimes negative effect of desire for money. "The interest of owners and investors in making money introduces a challenge to moral capitalism. Money is easily idolized, provoking heresy by turning us away from the things of God to the things of Mammon. There are times when we may sell our souls to gain what money promises in way of power and license. This is especially true in today's culture of consumerism, where we have sanctified appetite over character."

Financial crises can be prevented if the Caux Round Table ethical Principles for Business become guidance for companies in the financial services industry. Standards of corporate social responsibility, measuring and monitoring the actual risks to stakeholders of business decisions as to product and price, will moderate the attractiveness of greed and short-term selfishness.

A very important thesis about how to create the wealth of nations holds that certain cultural preconditions shape the scope and intensity of capitalist success. When these preconditions are in effect, wealth is created; when they are missing, wealth is, relatively speaking, scarce and hard to create. The social nature of capitalism as a system demands an appropriate cultural context. Some values as carried into market and investment behaviors promote robust capitalism; other values don't. The CRT Principles for Responsible Business are those very needed cultural preconditions for success wealth creation. Social capital thus is a public good of fundamental importance if a society is to raise its living standards and give its members longer and better lives.

The key point calling for social capital seems to be that individuals on their own can't create much wealth. Sellers need buyers and buyers need sellers, for example. A business without customers is a failure.

If we extend that insight to the full range of capitalist endeavors, we arrive at conditions of social complexity and multiple inter-dependencies among investors, employees at senior, middle and lower levels of command and control, regulators, suppliers, researchers, customers at the high end and customers looking for bargains, and so on.

This observation honors the seminal insights of Max Weber, who a century ago, identified the rise of capitalism as an economic system new and unique in human history, with the social arrangements legitimated and encouraged by Calvinist religious beliefs. Weber argued that a peculiar set of values flowing from Calvinist convictions that individual salvation depended upon one's diligent and faithful application of one's talents to the calling that God had provided here on earth. Calvinist values and practices such as frugality, discipline, confidence in the future, trust in others of the same faith, stepping up to personal responsibility in one's relationship with God, feeling certain of one's salvation as a good and reliable person, thought Weber, all contributed to opportunities for investment in enterprise, reliable contracts, and high savings.

This Puritan "work ethic", on the one hand, increased the financial capital available for investment in enterprise and, on the other, enhanced confidence that such investment would not be abused or wasted by its recipients.

Calvinism created a synergy and mutual satisfaction between entrepreneurs and investors to kick-start modern industrialization in the late 16th, 17th, 18th centuries in Holland, England, Scotland and the British colonies in North America such as Boston, New York and Philadelphia.

While many have questioned Weber's attempt to link particular aspects of Calvinist beliefs and practices to nacent capitalism, few can deny the coincidence of capitalism's first emergence only in Calvinist societies. What Calvinism gave to the world was a special kind of social capital that made possible new economic undertakings and investment relationships.

Now, if recent practices on Wall Street associated with sub-prime mortgages, mortgage backed securities, CDOs, and CDSs produced a loss in 2008 of some US$50 trillion in asset values, one would have to question how successful such Wall Street capitalism was in creating new wealth. Did it have the values and practices that Max Weber found necessary for sustained, successful wealth creation?

More than triggering such losses, some of which will be restored as markets recover from the collapse, Wall Street's meltdown last year also caused the collapse of Bear Stearns and Lehman Brothers, along with the conversion of New York's remaining investment banks into more traditional depository institutions. The American government, through its Treasury and Federal Reserve System, assumed many trillions of dollars of financial obligations to keep banking and financial intermediation markets open and operating. At one point, the Federal Reserve was purchasing the commercial paper of American companies due to failure of the private market for such debt. This was an unprecedented failure of private sector decision making. Something had gone very wrong with free market financial capitalism.

Wall Street's marketing of the financial instruments causing the asset bubble and resulting collapse was not beneficial for anyone in the long run and so such marketing could not be sustained. This episode of financial intermediation was a failure from every point of view once "irrational exuberance" took over those markets. What happened during the bubble and its collapse should not be considered genuine capitalism but only speculation over the conversion value of present contract rights into future income or capital gains.

If the connection between habits of mind and corresponding actions and successful capitalism is to hold true, it must be that Wall Street lost some of its social capital as a prelude to this most recent round of irrational asset valuations.

The corollary argument to Weber's thesis on a smaller scale appropriate to these financial market transactions would be that the kind of social capital needed for capitalist achievement was missing from Wall Street in recent years. And, moreover, that loss of social capital caused, or at least contributed to, the collapse of asset values in the crash of 2008.

Where was the erosion of social capital on Wall Street prior to the financial crisis of 2008?

Let us consider first a generic model of the social capital relevant to capitalist wealth creation.

There are of course innumerable varieties of social capital, each with different modalities of values and behaviors and each promoting different outcomes. The social capital that supported Egyptian Pharaohs and supported their construction of pyramids and temples was most likely different from the social capital that sustained Native American tribes in their pueblos, teepees and long houses.

The virtuous behaviors that Weber marked as sponsoring capitalist endeavors flowed from a social capital value set that had certain special characteristics.

First, this Calvinist social capital supported longer time horizons for financial investment in others. Investment in more than trading on a village market day was brought to the fore of business thinking. One could partner in the productive capacity of others and so earn a return. Expectations of rewards were stable and realistic. Such people worked at their trades in a reliable fashion so that they became good credit risks and trustworthy stewards of moneys invested in their undertakings. Their word was their bond. There were clear laws and just enforcement so that promises and contracts became accurate predictions of future events. Having a reliance interest in the success of others was justified. People were patient and delayed gratification in order to invest today for a return tomorrow. Financial intermediation was enhanced; money capital could be accumulated for use in joint enterprises.

All these reliable behaviors lowered risks and so interest rates. Stable and lower interest rates promoted the use of long-term credit and equity investments. Borrowers were more willing to take on the risks of repayment and owners saw advantage in accepting equity investments and later sharing of their profits. Investment of time and money in production and delivery of goods and service, with the power through finance to leverage greater production of more and better goods and services in order to meet new needs, made good sense. The future would be better and capitalist business began to contribute to progress and modernity.

Second, the social capital of frugality, hard work for its own sake, and delayed gratification caused savings to grow. Money was accumulated to invest in the new, trustworthy opportunities.

Third, this Calvinist social capital placed a priority on learning, education and the introduction of new mechanics and technologies. It was comfortable with secular approaches and did not disdain the material world of chemistry, physics and biology.

Fourth, people acculturated to such conditions are more thoughtful about the consequences of their actions on others. Externalities are brought home to the actor through an ethic of pride in one's work and over one's contribution to community as a honorable citizen in good standing. The social construct under Calvinism is one of reciprocal mutuality in doing one's best; it is not a Hobbesian, dog-eat-dog, world of rabid selfishness, mistrust, and rip-offs.

Now, the opposite of these behaviors and commitments, we can infer, would most likely not lead to wealth creation.

Social patterns where people focus on the immediate and will not commit now to benefits to be received much later and where they have no patience and do not trust the word and reliability of others, will promote higher levels of risk. Where risk is higher, the rates charged for interest and the minimum returns expected on equity funds invested will also be correspondingly higher. The cost of doing business will be much higher. There will be fewer transactions as a rule. Savings will be rejected in favor of current consumption. People will seek cash money to use its power over those who are perceived to be and, in fact, are not trustworthy or reliable. Stewardship responsibilities will go begging for lack of honest fiduciaries to accept them.

Where lower standards of responsibility are accepted, there will be lower standards of care in general. Risks will be pushed off on others as much as possible. It will take more courage to enter into contractual transactions with third parties. New participants will hesitate to join in market activity. Where they do enter into transactions, taking short-term advantage will be very much on their minds. Economic growth will stagnate.

Starting in 1980, Americans in general moved from a high savings culture to a high debt culture as the Baby Boomers came into full maturity and provided dominant cultural leadership for the nation. New norms and behaviors came to the fore in many parts of American society. Assuming responsibility in civil society organizations, in politics, in anything outside one's family, circle of friends, or professional tasks linked to immediate personal remuneration occurred less and less. Robert Putnam noted this trend in his seminal book Bowling Alone. Even in family life, parental responsibilities were sloughed off to the other spouse, to day care providers or to schools. Divorce became very common. Schools and television were looked upon as the primary means of socializing children. Seniors were encouraged to live out their last years on their own in retirement homes and facilities.

Wall Street and its practices were not immune from this cultural evolution.

As a result, the social capital embraced and accumulated by Wall Street shifted in its nature and its proclivities. Calvinism lost and Boomerism won. For example, time horizons became shorter. Short term thinking became the norm. People lost loyalty to employers as they kept on constant lookout for new jobs with higher pay. Legal formalities replaced a personal standard of care for the well-being of clients and customers. Using more and more debt to fund consumption and more pleasurable life styles demonstrated the power of short-termism among Americans. Delayed gratification was disparaged by Baby Boomers.

People looked more and more for higher short term returns. Few invested equity in companies for the long haul. Investment preferences changed to "renting stocks" to profit from market speculation rather than owning them in order to realize long-term capital appreciation from the company's profits and retained earnings. Leverage to permit more and more "renting" of stocks and other investment vehicles became king. This way higher returns could be enjoyed through the short-term use of other people's money. The banking system converted from well-capitalized institutions that held risk to maturity to ones that merely traded risks back and forth for fees and spreads.

Investment banks went public and so lost the long-term perspective and caution that goes with partnership structures where the personal assets of the owners were always at stake in the risk level associated with firm activity. Professional mangers took over from owners as the drivers of firm strategies. Trading desks grew more powerful within the investment banks as their trading profits came to dominate firm income and the culture of traders took over from the older, more white-shoe culture of cultivating long term client loyalties and connections.

Short-term rewards encouraged engagement with the speculative side of financial markets. In every market, speculation is at work. Some traders look only to the desires and understandings of others as the key to pricing; long term fundamentals are of little concern to these market makers. Calvinist preferences for real investment where bit by bit eaten away by the cancer of immediate speculative indulgence.

Personal responsibility for investment decisions was replaced with reliance on portfolio theory and mathematical algorithms. The Black-Scholes formula for calculating value when no market for a contract claim existed and the "chasing" of Alpha returns by institutional money managers were the most famous examples of this new intellectual environment on Wall Street. Companies were judged for better or worse on whether they "made the numbers" predicted by professional estimators. Trust in a company's leadership was replaced with a more mechanical formulation of what constituted success.

This reliance on analysis provided a boost to hubris which was the doorway into "irrational exuberance"; the hubris was that intellectual ingenuity knew no faults and needed no bounds. Calvinism had been much more skeptical of human rationality and had kept its followers much more grounded in God's real order of creation.

The chase for higher returns – more fees and commissions – correlated with a decline in general levels of trust and commitment. Fund managers knew that to take risks and not earn returns within a peer group average would lead to the loss of money under their management. Herd thinking about where to invest became acceptable as it was "normative" within peer groups and necessary to chase speculative purchases and sales in the immediate time horizon.

Executive compensation was more and more linked to short term results, especially at senior levels where strategic commitments were made and cultural norms were adopted within firms for replication at lower levels of corporate hierarchies. Money results, not fiduciary quality, drove the decisions of many CEOs in all industries, not just Jack Welsh at General Electric.

Wall Street became captive to playing with other people's money on a gigantic scale. Savings and reserves in exporting countries like China and the funds accumulating in pension funds, sovereign wealth funds, and hedge funds was there for the taking, or rather, the borrowing. Access to funds came through the sale of instruments that promised high returns.

Debt and short-term investing – largely tradable instruments to boot - took over from traditional equity as the criterion for financing capitalism; leverage ratios of banks and investment banks went to historic highs; structured financial instruments – mortgage backed securities and CDOs – were produced to fit new market demands for using short term leverage and trading in contract rights. Pricing of these rights according to mathematics further removed markets from underlying realities. CDSs were invented to provide risk reduction in lieu of tradition equity and capital reserves. Sadly, since many CDSs were only backed by legal documentation and not real money, the risk reduction they provided was illusory. Most CDSs used pledges that had no reliable commitment behind them to give them any genuine "credit". Counterparty risk eventually caused the credit system to freeze in the fall of 2008 and so become useless.

An asset bubble in financial instruments was thus easily assembled by Wall Street firms and experts. And they took their inventions to global markets. The factors that grow asset bubbles are inimical to genuine capitalism that produces the "wealth of nations". When Wall Street produces such financial houses of cards, its capitalist social capital is thin at best.

To improve the outcomes of financial intermediation, then, the social capital accumulation of financial centers like Wall Street needs scrutiny and attention.

If we want to restore robust creation of real wealth which can be enjoyed for many years and which can lead to creation of further wealth on the part of others – workers and investors alike, then we must - as the first item of such business - look to the values embodied in our financial firms.

CHAPTER SIX
IS THERE AN AGENCY PROBLEM?

I want to call your attention, as we turn from crisis management to building more viable global institutions of financial intermediation, to a sophisticated cynicism that opposes more resolute commitment to business ethics and corporate social responsibility. I am not referring to the common mistrust of private enterprise on the grounds that working for personal profit is inconsistent with securing a greater good for society. This is the perennial tension posed by philosophers and religious leaders between the claims of virtue and the attractions of self-interest. Rather, I am referring to a more academically polished elaboration of that argument which is called "the agency problem."

Briefly put, the "agency problem" is said to be an inherent dysfunction in all principal/agent relationships, a dysfunction so powerful that such relationships can never fully achieve their stated objectives.

The "agency problem" exists on the agent side of the relationship: agents can't be trusted to be diligent or faithful to their principals. Agents, it is said, are always out for themselves and are constitutionally unable to put loyalty and service to their principals above their self-interest.

Thus, any business structure that relies on agency will always be a substantial risk to a principal, putting principals on their guard and forcing them to use tactics of fear and greed to keep their agents responsible. Self-interest is set to control self-interest. The social philosophy that explains the Agency Problem is Social Darwinism, a notion that people have no moral sense and that life is a war of all against all where only the most fit survive. From this perspective, there is no need to mediate with any other person or social force, only to seek ways of subjecting them to our will and power. It is kill or be killed, eat or be eaten, with truncated concepts of win/win engagements based on greed or fear, no room for fiduciary duties, no genuine sustaining mutuality of interests, no trust in others at all.

Modern financial theory, the theory of rational markets and statistical calculation of risk that promoted and justified Wall Street's over leveraging and creating the asset bubble that popped in the fall of 2008, adopts, affirms, and trumpets the Agency Problem as a natural law that cannot be ignored or overcome. But if there is an Agency Problem, if people can't be trusted to imbibe social capital, then there is no hope for a moral, responsible, sustainable capitalism.

The problem with this approach, however, is that the remedy feeds the disease.

Using self-interest to overcome self-interest has its limitations.

As long as we believe that the "agency problem" exists and is insurmountable, we have placed before us a conceptual roadblock to corporate social responsibility. Business enterprise is indeed little more than a complex network of principal/agent relationships, established by various forms of express and implied contracts. Owners of corporations are principals to the boards of directors who manage them; senior company officers are agents of the boards and the companies; all employees are agents of their employers; banks, insurance agents, accountants, investment managers, lawyers are all agents to some degree for others. If the "agency problem" exists, then every relationship in this network is infected with the risks of negligence and betrayal. Social Darwinism or dog-eat-dog wariness would seem to be the only rational approach to a life in such an environment. It would be foolish, or worse, to expect such an environment to ever promote responsibility to the common good. The cause of corporate social responsibility or business ethics is then rather hopeless in the world of real enterprise and finance.

Advocates of corporate social responsibility must, therefore, reject the intractability of the Agency Problem and rather presume something other than as an immutable fact of business life. Corporate social responsibility, corporate philanthropy, corporate citizenship, all ask of business and business decision-makers a showing of responsibility to others. Usually the responsibility of business is stated as having respect for the interests of stakeholders: customers, employees, owners, creditors, suppliers, competitors, and communities, including the environment.

The problem of faithless agents

If we want a more moral capitalism, we have to solve the "agency problem" or, at a minimum, contain its virulence. Modern capitalism generates wealth through specialization of function and division of labor. This fact was Adam Smith's great insight into the nature and origin of the "wealth of nations" as he called it. But, as labor is more and more specialized, each component sub-unit of the economic system becomes more and more dependent on all the other parts. In today's world of high technology, dependency on specialized machines and the skills of professional experts is higher than ever in human history.

For example, our modern world is also completely subservient to reliable flows of electricity. When the electric grid breaks down, our lives come to a jarring end to normalcy. The Turkish Airlines plane that crashed short of the runway at Schiphol Airport outside of Amsterdam did so because its altimeter was faulty. Nine people died as a consequence of the pilots' relying on a mechanical device for guidance in landing. We do not know what caused the Air France Airbus 330 to fall from mid-air to the Atlantic Ocean on its flight from Brazil, but everyone aboard was totally dependent on the machinery of that aircraft working as it should and on the pilots for skill in using that machinery.

Without trust in and reliance on those we cannot control, our economy cannot function. We are all in some sense principals dependent on others; thus we need reliable agents.

If the "agency problem" is all powerful and all pervasive, then modern capitalism is constant at risk of failure because the dependency relationships that flow from specialization are prone to intentional or negligent abuse on the part of those who thus dishonor the reliance and trust placed on their competence and their integrity.

A market place of lying sellers and conniving buyers will never grow very prosperous. When faith and trust evaporate, so does capitalist wealth. The current meltdown of global financial markets is a good case in point.

But, the seriousness of the "agency problem" has been overstated. If it were truly dominant in the business world, modern capitalism with all its relationships of interdependency and mutual benefits would not have emerged to produce the wealth that we enjoy today – even in these months of a serious global recession. Thus, we can infer that there are some countervailing forces that constantly nibble away at the "agency problem".

What can we do about faithless or negligent agents?

The problem is not a new one. In the Judeo-Christian tradition, the prophet Samuel warned the leaders of tribes of Israel not to put their faith in kings, for, as he predicted, kings would turn against their trust and abuse power for their own selfish advantage. Later, Jesus stated that one could not serve both God and Mammon.

The Common Law of England over the centuries fashioned many legal responses to minimize the effects of the "agency problem". These rules and practices constitute what is called the law of fiduciary duties. Also, the English courts of Equity contributed to fiduciary law with their own set of procedures and requirements designed to remedy abuse of legal power and prevent fraud and oppression in the marketplace.

The basic device used by the Common Law to minimize the effects of the "agency problem" was to define what was expected from agents as duties to their principals and give principals specific remedies for breach of those duties. This was a practical approach that sought to structure incentives so that agents would be more inclined to stick to the punctilio of their responsibilities and principals would be induced to assume the risk of trusting agents. Other words used in the Common Law to resolve the agency problem were fiduciary, trust, and beneficiary of the fiduciary trust. The fiduciary or the keeper of the trust was, in effect, the agent and the beneficiary was, in effect, the principal.

First, the agent was burdened with duties of loyalty and due care. When the self-interest of the agent was suspected of causing harm to the principal, the burden of proving loyalty was placed on the agent. The agent had the burden of coming forward with sufficient evidence to prove his or her loyalty. With respect to negligence on the part of the agent, the principal had the burden of proof but could hold the agent accountable when an objective standard of care had not been observed in management of the business consigned to the agent.

The Common Law thus turned the relationship of principal/ agent into a status for the agent. Agency was an office; so was being a partner, a trustee, a corporate director, etc. With office came specific responsibilities. Failure of performance was transformed from a difference of private opinion between agent and principal over the quality of performance into a notorious setting of public expectations. Principals could deny their own liability for acts of the agent when the agent had acted contrary to the terms of the trust, leaving the agent exposed to face the consequences.

The behavioral theory used by the Common Law judges appears to be a conviction that when we are made accountable in public, our pride tends to keep us more scrupulous and diligent than when we can act in secret. Exposure and transparency were devices used to reduce agency problems.

Second, in its courts of Equity, English jurisprudence fashioned a number of rules that principals and beneficiaries could use. They could seek an accounting of monies had and received, with the burden on the agent to account for every penny received; principals could ask for the imposition of a constructive trust on money and property in the agent's possession and name when fraud and abuse had occurred; agents had to have acted with clean hands if they sought to recover from principals on their agency contracts; agents could be prevented (estopped) from entering claims and evidence in their favor if they had acted inequitably.

Use of self interest

A second basket of remedial responses to the "agency problem" lies in self-interest. It is in one's best interest to avoid faithless agents. Over time, therefore, faithless agents will not find employment as their reputation for negligence or disloyalty becomes generally known. This is why reference checks are so frequently relied upon. Generally, market based solutions to the "agency problem" rely on this mechanism of self-help. But it can be of limited utility where agents or those upon whom we rely for professional expertise have market power or are polished performers adept in the arts of lulling our suspicions with their smoke and mirrors – like Bernie Madoff to his investors.

Use of character

The third approach to minimizing the "agency problem" is to promote good character, the habits of living up to the virtues of trustworthiness, integrity, diligence, transparency and reliability. This agenda for securing better prospects for corporate social responsibility and business ethics – for avoiding asset bubbles and financial bubbles – and for putting in place the cultural foundation for specialization of function and division of labor operates at the level of the individual.

We must engage individuals to act as we would want if we want responsible and faithful agents. Such socialization, obviously, begins in the family, continues in school, and is finished in conditions of social engagement. We are concerned for the "presentation of self" in everyday life and Irving Goffman wrote about our dysfunctions in organizational settings. We want a good self to be presented, not a greedy, abusive, stupid or negligent one.

Having good character is one reliable ground for good steward-ship behaviors. The moral sense within us is a public good in that it promotes trust in our communities and reliance on our business performance. Trust and reliance form the substructure of success-ful modern capitalism.

That human persons possess a moral sense that distinguishes them from beasts and other earthly creatures is increasingly a pos-tulate of evolutionary studies, neuro-science, and brain research.

Thus, we must not presume that the "agency problem" is intrac-table and a permanent obstacle to responsible business decision-making. Rather, we should assume in us all an inherent capacity for reliable agency performance.

Set the bar higher and we will tend to jump higher; set it low and we will slack off and get away with poor performance.

道德

Tao Te 25 in Running Script © 2014 by Weiming Lu

CHAPTER SEVEN
SUSTAINING THE AGENCY PROBLEM

Organizations and Ethical Behaviors:
Anxiety has a Hundred Faces

Our global community of business leaders, politicians, regulators and commentators have not yet, I sense, fully digested intellectually the implications of the 2008 meltdown in global credit markets. But, after that in stunning succession, we have seen more failures in the delivery of responsible outcomes as we experienced the failure of General Motors as a going concern, the failure of Toyota to foresee, remedy, and explain failures in acceleration systems and brakes, and, perhaps most sadly, the failure of certain priests in the Roman Catholic Church in Ireland and elsewhere to maintain the standards incumbent upon those who would be God's vicars on earth and of their administrative superiors to quickly and efficiently deal with their wrongs and to comfort and heal their victims.

I could also suggest that the credit crisis failures of Bear Stearns, Lehman Brothers, and AIG, and the near failure of CitiGroup were similar failures of organizations to behave with due responsibility. And the recent US Congressional scrutiny of Goldman Sachs for being "net short" against the American housing market leaves more than a hint of corporate irresponsibility in the minds of some. When it comes out that employees of Moody's and Standard and Poors were apparently open to linking the quality of their ratings to the quantity of their fees – (low quality for higher fees), the pricing mechanism at the heart of financial capitalism was irresponsibly debased. And when a handful of bankers in London conspired to fix the LIBOR daily rates, they violated basic principles of integrity and professionalism. Drug companies have paid huge fines for unethical sales of drugs. Samsung stole intellectual property for cell phones from Apple.

Why is it then that so many such organizations, so blessed with talent, resources, and experienced leaders, fail so seriously?

I suggest that there is an unwholesome chemistry that brews such irresponsibility, a chemistry that works its mischief at the intersection of organizational realities and the individuals who work for these hierarchies.

The problem, I think, is inherent in every bureaucracy because every bureaucracy works through individuals. Put ordinary individuals into an ordinary bureaucracy and you increase the risk of something going rogue.

With the Wall Street firms that failed, with General Motors, with Toyota, even with the Catholic Church, there was at the wrong times a supine attitude towards confronting future risks and an unfortunate negligence in guarding against future negative externalities.

Some code of loyalty, some priority given to conforming to the immediate demands of the organization, froze decision-making within the ranks. Thoughtful, ethical leadership was prevented from happening when it was most needed. Some kind of ethical entropy was slowing things down from the assumption of responsibility to fear and avoidance.

This dysfunctional feature of bureaucracies feeds the Agency Problem. It accelerates individual propensities to be self-preserving and self-seeking, to put the short term interest over the long term common good, to ignore public goods and concentrated instead on private ones.

One part of bureaucratic dysfunction lies in constrained reporting. Bad news did not flow up these organizations with sufficient credibility to trigger responsible responses to potential trouble. Conventional wisdom was accepted as sufficient unto the day.

Second, there was inadequate tolerance of contrarians: of those who gave rise to cognitive dissonance within the ranks, who pointed to potential troubles, who tried to blow whistles or seek a change in organizational direction.

Third, organizational imperatives reward loyalty and team-players, those who get along and go along, because the organization does not to admit in public that it has short-comings. In protecting its reputation today it undermines that very reputation on the morrow.

While organizational failures, like fish, rot from the head; the deeper cause of the rot in organizations lies lower down the pecking order of power and authority..

Organizations are first and foremost formal structures of positions, each with duties and responsibilities, with reporting obligations and most with supervisory powers over other positions. Organizations are a system of coordination among roles mandated by the division of labor to promote the specialization of function.

From this perspective, organizations are best understood as flow charts of reporting relationships where superiors set tasks and goals for those who report to them. Organization and hierarchy seem to be one and the same under most circumstances.

But in each role or position is a person, an individual who brings individual skills and needs to the execution of his or her tasks. Much of the art of management is finding suitable matches between persons and job descriptions.

So, now if we look at the interaction of the self with the role, we can observe a powerful cause of ethical dysfunction in organizations.

The self of the person in the role has needs and those needs exercise great influence over how that person performs his or her duties and tasks as called for in the job description for that particular role. Most of us use our roles to advance our personal agendas. We are not necessarily loyal and studious agents of those who trust us with responsibility.

One set of personal needs can easily be associated with the kind of failure we have recently seen in major international companies and the Catholic Church.

Harry Stack Sullivan, MD, published his Interpersonal Theory of Psychiatry in 1953. Here Sullivan directed our attention to the presence in each of us of anxiety as a driver of our sense of self.

He suggested that, after birth, as each person develops his or her moral sense and becomes a citizen in society, we all experience - to a greater or a lesser degree – anxiety about who we are, what powers we have, and who cares for us. Such anxiety starts to arise in the interpersonal exchange of the baby with its mother and then with others who are bringing the new personality into full sociality. Anxiety is experienced as a falling away from security and acceptance.

The baby's response, naturally enough, is to minimize the level of felt anxiety and so return to security and acceptance.

As the baby learns to so minimize felt anxiety by manipulating the mother and other adults, a self-system arises in the young person that confirms its unique character and personality vis-à-vis others.

In his book Sullivan points out but does not dwell on the point that each adult person carries along such a self-system and uses it to reduce felt anxiety and seek security and acceptance. This dynamic of the presentation of self spreads throughout our interpersonal relations to any area where there is a chance that anxiety may be encountered.

If one had no protection against very severe anxiety, one would do practically nothing - says Sullivan – or if one still had to so something, it would take an intolerably long time to get it done. We must rise above anxiety if we are to live well and go far above it if we are to thrive. This resistance to anxiety is not just a shadow that follows us, but lives deep down inside our core sense of self. It doesn't just go away on sunny days.

Therefore, when I, for example, assume a position with an organization, I bring to that position my self-system, in particular, my ways of reducing anxiety. Not just my anxiety, but my need to reduce feelings of anxiety, come with me every day to the job.

A similar analysis of what happens when individuals engage in organized cooperation was offered by Erving Goffman in his noted 1959 book The Presentation of Self in Everyday Life. Goffman looks at people in social settings as performers, attempting to engender in others a perception of reality that is most advantageous to the self that is on the stage. We know each other by our respective "performances" and estimate others by the substance and quality of their "performances."

Combining the insights of Sullivan and Goffman, we can posit that my self "performance" is often scripted to reduce felt anxiety, anxiety that is engendered by being with others.

Now, I can reduce felt anxiety most directly by gaining a sense of security. My "performances" can be planned to gain access to security. This warming and reassuring perception of having power and control can come from the socially expressed approval of others, from having authority and positional power, from having discretionary wealth and money, from identification with the power and prestige of the organization, from avoiding risk, and from justifying my actions with non-contestable reasons prevalent in the organizational culture - like doing as I am told, following conventions, using math, science, professional expertise, or objective data.

In fact an organizational position would put me in a pretty good position to access all these forms of power to feed my need for security.

In my formal position in the organization – be it a company, a government, or a even church - I can command others; gain material reward by meeting the goals of my superiors; gain prestige in the minds of others from their perception of the power and prestige of my organization, avoid risk, go along with the conventional wisdom, and generally not rock the boat. With acts of demonstrable and unquestioned loyalty I can hope to move up the hierarchy and obtain more power over others and more of the worldly goods that work psychologically as a young child's security blanket.

Sullivan says that later in life many of us seek other persons and situations that replicate, or personify, our experienced learning of the good mother that once had reduced our anxiety as a young infant and child. Much organizational life has that very maternal quality of taking care of us and we respond with submission and reciprocal care. Our needs drive us to protect the organization in the here and now. Our vision of what is right narrows and our sense of self actually shrinks as we cling to our audience in giving a rewardable "performance".

In short, my self system primes me to act in all the wrong ways when my organization confronts poor risk management, failure, or potential embarrassment.

I cringe from genuine responsibility, which is determined by standards and needs outside the organization. I lower my standards and seek to reduce the anxiety through enhanced solidarity within the group. I shrink from being the bearer of bad news to my superiors or vigorously speak out to change group norms or ways of thinking.

My self-system is well trained to want to do best by myself, which quickly translates into doing what is best for me within the organization, which can easily become a course of conduct that gets me along by my going along, deferring responsibility to others or to the future.

In a conflict between two masters – my need to reduce anxiety and the best interests of the organization – I choose the path leading back to my psychological home. My master lies deep within myself.

We are easily pressured by our self-systems to obfuscate and delay, to minimize the bad news, to paper over what is uncomfortable or threatening. All this is merely human. We are mostly not bad people of bad intention seeking to cause harm, just vulnerable persons

The art of applied ethics and the introduction of social responsibility into organizations needs, I think, to take better account of anxiety in order to improve organizational outcomes.

Tao Te 25 in Running Script © 2014 by Weiming Lu

Chapter Eight

Exacerbating

the Agency Problem: Money

The cynical and sad musical Cabaret has it that "money makes the world go round." If so, then money must bear an awful responsibility for all the wrongdoing and misfortune that overtake humanity again and again.

On the other hand, St Paul wrote that "love of money is the root of all evil", implicating not money but ourselves as the proper cause of wrongfulness in the world.

On the other hand, Adam Smith proposed that seeking to make money need not be sheer malevolence when he said: "Man is never so innocently engaged as when he is making money."

Advocates for more corporate social responsibility, however, often point to profit – acquiring cash money – as the driving force behind business negligence, abuse of market power, and willful omission to correct harmful externalities. Greed, it is more often inferred than said outright, biases judgment and greed, it is also widely thought, is energized and encouraged towards its unrighteous ends by the ready availability of money to be made.

And the presence of money makes it easier for us to fall into the Agency Problem of being unfaithful to those who rely on us. Money is temptation. Money is also a very compelling way to measure the ups and downs of life even though it often leaves out of consideration many valuable dimensions of self-esteem, morality, ethics, reputation and honor.

Non monetized societies, as a rule however, do not enjoy much in the way of business activity or capitalism. At the same time, they are more prone to poverty than wealth with all the conceptual opportunity costs that come with living in poverty. Not having money also comes with a cost.

If we want the fruits of wealth, which are many, but we fear the effects of greed and avarice, what role should we give to money? Can we ever reach a positive moral assessment of those who strive for money?

Powerful ideas for thinking about money were given by Georg Simmel in his book The Philosophy of Money, written in 1900.

His first proposition is to accept the subjective theory of value. According to this understanding of human dispositions towards reality, the value of a thing is entirely determined by what we make of it. Value arises from our emotions and thoughts. Value, like beauty, is in the eye of the beholder, not in the flower or the painting. From this perspective, there are no absolute values to be imposed on us, only the partial and relative values that we impose on ourselves and, may from time to time, attempt to impose on others.

Consciousness, said Simmel, endows objects with significance, not the other way around. No object has intrinsic significance.

Accordingly, it is our natural right to value or not value money just as we may or may not value a cowrie shell, an emu, or The Rolling Stones.

When two or more minds converge on a single evaluation, then we have a common value. What has been subjective now becomes more objective in that it has acquired a post-individualistic meaning with social characteristics and implications. Any such valuation in common takes on tangible form and public appearance, gains resilience in the presence of time and space, and acquires an aura of respect, even prestige.

Simmel pointed out that a primary function of money is to facilitate the process whereby people can reach common valuations. When they agree on a monetary amount to fix on an object, or a promise, they have achieved something social, something more objective than their individual preferences. When many people with different subjective concerns all come to agreement on a monetary price, then a market price enters social reality and conditions subsequent behaviors. Money helps us live in community and mutuality.

Without money, it is more difficult to find easily expressed and sustainable equivalences. With money, agreements can be more easily reached, kept and memorialized and transactions can be undertaken with far greater confidence in their having real advantages. The philosophical role of money, therefore, is to convert the intangible and the merely subjective biases and prejudices of the individual into social truth. Money gives us more objective certainty, which is a goal of philosophy.

Money, which through exchange can bring us into conditions of social objectivity, can also be conducive to the removal of the personal element from relationships. In this way money can contribute to our distancing ourselves from others and in so doing to protect ourselves from them. Money is indifferent and objective; with it we can be aloof from the desires and manipulations of others. Money can bring about reassuring feelings of inner independence and individual self-sufficiency.

Money has the amazing capacity to make possible relationships between people but at the same time leaves them personally undisturbed. It balances out respect for different dimensions of human dignity by leaving people alone in their own subjective majesty while permitting them to respond to the values and preferences of others.

But to probe further into the dark side of human dynamics around money, we need to consider the complex mental process of valuation.

Abraham Maslow proposed a hierarchy of human needs where prior and more immediate needs associated with preservation of the self – responding to fears and threats, seeking food and shelter, etc. - are first attended to. Only after such necessities, as it were, were fully and satisfactorily addressed, would a person be likely to appreciate more abstract goals such as friendships, art, religious insight.

We can infer from Maslow's notion of a hierarchy that money easily associates itself with goods on the lower levels of the hierarchy. Food, shelter etc. are quite easily obtained with money. For most of us they are market goods which must be purchased from others. From Maslow's perspective, then, money would be less easily be associated with the more lofty, intangible desires and perceptions at the top of the hierarchy, giving money something of a debased quality.

Building on Maslow's arguments, a field of happiness studies has emerged. One point stressed by happiness research is that making more money does not reliably bring with it great happiness. The Kingdom of Butan suggested a measure of social success in "Gross National Happiness" which has triggered in recent years a movement rethinking the metrics of economic development. And the United Nation's General Assembly has instituted an annual "Day of Happiness".

Sigmund Freud associated money with his conception of an anal personality – someone fixated on retention and holding in. Anal personalities tend to be tight with money and stingy. They are also more comfortable as controlling personalities in their relationships with other people. Money for Freud took on a bad connotation of assisting anal personalities in their search for dominance over others.

Freud did not elaborate on the point at all but there is indeed an easily observed very strong link between money and having power. Since others need money to meet their own needs, we can use money to win their submission on a transaction basis. If we give them access to what they want - money, we can demand and receive in return some "price" paid by them for the goods or services we have at hand. That "price" could be money, but it could also be submission, labor, respect and public praise, help on a project, intimacy or some form of friendship.

Power offers another form of assurance as well; power provides means for risk reduction. Since many of us are risk averse – some of us all of the time and all of us some of the time – having power in our hands, under our sole control, brings emotional relief when thinking about what could go wrong or who could hurt us. Power leads us getting that which offsets life's contingencies. Having a stock of money readily at hand puts us in the driver's seat so to speak.

If our goal is indeed power, seeking money is a reasonable means to that end. What drives us, however, is not the money but the need for power. The need for power leads to the love of money.

And a need for power can be insatiable. When power is sought to make up for inadequacies, to fill a spiritual void of low self-confidence, to hold off fears of the infinite and the unknown, to make up for feelings of personal sinfulness and guilt or shame, then we can never enjoy enough power.

Correspondingly, such needy people can never have too much money. They are always on the hunt for what will make them feel more secure and less threatened.

At times, their approach to business can be to "cry havoc and let slip the dogs of war". It is dominance that they seek and power that they need at almost any cost. The premises of Social Darwinism, Herbert Spencer's theory of life and private freedom as constant rivalry and competition, fits comfortably with their understanding of who they are and what they need. Such strivers press for unconstrained competition and glory in making short term profits that they can appropriate personally not because they need the money, but because they would feel victimized without having the power that money can bring.

Avarice, as opposed to simple greed, is the will to power expressed through money where the power represented by money is experienced as the absolutely satisfying value.

Psychologists have studied motivations by using the "Ultimatum Game" where one player divides a pot of money between himself and another. The second player then gets to whether to accept the division or not. If the second player rejects the division, neither player gets any money. In this game, a stingy offer by player one to player two will usually be rejected – even though it will give player two some money. (The offers that get rejected are usually offer player two less than ¼ of the total pot.) Thus, game results imply that money in and of itself is not always a goal for human interaction. Other considerations come into play as well. The further implication is that people strive for relative, not absolute, prosperity, believing that it's not the money but the share that counts.

In one series of Ultimatum Games played among men only, men with high levels of testosterone were more likely to reject offers with low proceeds for themselves.

Higher up on Maslow's hierarchy of needs is having status in the eyes of others. Such status too confers a form of social protection, so it meets one's need for power. But it has, apparently, other attractions as well.

Adam Smith noticed this quite some years ago. In his 1759 book on human moral capacities, The Theory of the Moral Sentiments, Smith wrote: "… yet we cannot live long in the world without perceiving that the respect of our equals, our credit and our rank in the society we live in, depend very much upon the degree in which we possess, or are supposed to possess, 'the advantages of external fortune'. The desire of becoming the proper objects of this respect, of deserving and obtaining this credit and rank among our equals, is, perhaps, the strongest of all our desires, and our anxiety to obtain the advantages of fortune is accordingly much more excited and irritated by this desire, than by that of supplying all the necessities and "conveniences' of the body, which are always easily supplied." (p. 213)

In another recent experiment, volunteers were asked to take sips of what they were told were five different wines priced between US$5 and US$90 per bottle. But actually only three wines were used; two of them were served twice. Volunteers were monitored for brain functions. As they drank what they thought were more expensive wines, activity in their medial orbitofrontal cortices increased in tandem. What were thought to be more expensive wines triggered more engaged mental activity.

What costs more money is, pro-forma, most likely to be more exclusive, more rare, and more prestigious. Fewer people will have access to it. Participation in exclusivity generates perceptions of the value associated with being special, favored, above the rest; exclusivity is the reward that comes to wealth and status and most of us like it.

A dynamic money culture can indeed spawn cynicism and a blasé attitude in the face of tragedy and human need. This results, says Simmel, when the concrete values of life are reduced by our choices to the mediating value of money. What should be highly valued on moral or aesthetic grounds, is reduced to the lowest instrumental value, one completely relative at that.

Money is a servant of our desires. If the abusive desires motivating others have our concern, we might be wiser to tackle the problem directly by confronting the source of those desires rather than indirectly by reducing the means (money) used to temporarily assuage what will remain as an active command center in our psyches.

We are come to an ancient point of view: tranquilization of the passions should be uppermost in our minds. Character to govern desire removes the "love" that would and does turn money from a boon into an evil. Aristotle taught this as did Cicero and Marcus Aurelius and Confucius. In our time, an eloquent teacher of this perspective on business is the Dalai Lama.

Money in and of itself enters the world as a useful good. It is we who abuse it, as we abuse many other things in the physical world. It is a useful tool; it is an institution through which the individual concentrates his or her activity and possessions in order to attain goals that he or she could not attain directly says Simmel. Like any tool money is inert; it has no purpose of its own and functions impartially to all humanity.

Money is demonstrative of the truth that humans are the "tool-making animal", which infers, of course, that they are "purposive" animals with goals and desires. The tool incorporates into its use the aspirations of the human will.

Money reveals its indifferent and empty character, says Simmel, very clearly where the valuation process putting it to work is exclusively upon consumption. When desires are superficial, money facilitates the triumph of superficiality.

Simmel wrote that "the psychological structure of demand is such that in most cases it is focused upon the satisfaction itself and the object becomes a matter of indifference so long as it satisfies the need." If what we seek are status and power, and money is not available, will we not find other means to achieve our ends? And, the alternatives may be even more cruel or vindictive than making money.

Simmel notes perceptively that exchange – the transactions facilitated by money – are the highest form of interactions between people in that they are win – win, or non-zero. In a true exchange, which is voluntary and non-coerced by power or excessive need – each party is offered more than what he or she had before. So, the social work of exchanges is to increase the sum of value that is tangible.

As Adam Smith said in The Wealth of Nations, the butcher and the baker look to their subjective needs to supply us with meat and bread for our dinner and we look to our needs to supply them with money, which they value as a means to meet their needs. Their values and our values are both vindicated- simultaneously and separately. It is an alchemy that turns selfish reflections into social good.

Exchange presumes the scarcity of goods – that the goods available are not public goods made freely accessible to all upon use or demand. Exchange takes place through subjective valuations of that which is limited and so responds constructively to scarcity and fair exchange generates positive social enhancement enjoyed by the parties to the exchange.

Furthermore in making an exchange and paying for it with money, one is subordinated to an objective norm. We are socialized in the process and become less the wild beast or the imperious tyrant. Theft of what we desire – instead of purchase - stands distinctly apart from socialization and moral conduct.

Where there is pure subjectivity in the transfer and no exchange, we might have either robbery and theft, on the one side, or unilateral compassion and gift on the other.

Simmel warns that exchange with money reconciles opposites: relativism and society. Money perpetuates a relativistic world view where each can live with his or her own subjectivities. But at the same time through exchange, money permits individual relative things, as valued by individuals, to become something of social consequence and so to enter into history as objective phenomena.

Money as the expression of a concept of objective economic value brings forth, says Simmel, an interpretation of existence. Money can be a direct source of philosophic meaning as well as a means of exchange.

Money is no more than way stations in an endless series of cognitions. Cognition – valuation – is a free-floating process where elements determine their positions reciprocally and relative to one another. Truth here is relative like weight or price. Truth is an aesthetic more than a command. It works through induction far more surely than with deduction. Money thus tends to engender a cognitive culture of flux and change. Money has no respect for any eternal verities other that the process by which it is assigned to prices reflecting our values. As Simmel wrote, money corresponds to the "many-sidedness of our being and the onesidedness of any conceptual expression."

The ultimate principles of such a culture proposed Simmel become realized not in the form of mutual exclusion (I-It over I-Thou to borrow from Martin Buber) but in the form of mutual dependence, mutual evocation, and mutual complementation – just like in an exchange. The philosophical significance of money, then for Simmel, is that it is the clearest embodiment of the formula of all being, according to which things receive their meaning through each other, and have their being determined by their mutual relations.

Money interweaves all singularities and so creates reality among its users. Money could, Simmel affirms, thus play the role of God for a weak minded humanity. If we let it.

道德

Tao Te Ts in Running Script © 2014 by Weiming Lu

CHAPTER NINE
THE AGENCY PROBLEM
ADDS TO MORAL HAZARD

In American schools of business education, the discipline of business ethics began as, and largely remains, a school of moral philosophy. As such, its interface with finance and economics has been problematic. Moral propositions do not lend themselves so well to utilitarian calculations of prices, profits and losses. Often, moral propositions are taken to be alive in a parallel university to finance, one valid by its own terms but separate from, and perhaps in opposition to, run-of-the-mill business rationality.

Given this perceived separation, one often hears that a choice is necessary between ethics, on the one hand, and business success on the other. You can therefore have either but not both at the same time.

Considerations of Moral Hazard, on the other hand, sound in economics but resonate with ethics. Moral Hazard has more recently come to prominence with the failures of Bear Stearns and Lehman Brothers as part of the 2008 collapse of credit markets. Institutions "too big to fail" and so protected by government from the consequences of their bad decisions are considered by economists to be "moral hazards". Not held accountable for failure, they in fact aggressively court risk and chance failure.

Moral hazards occur when gains are privatized to actors and losses can be effectively socialized to non-actors. Those who are part of the Agency Problem like to privatize gains and socialize losses. Thus they are more likely than not to contribute to Moral Hazards. Largely oblivious to ethical and moral considerations, faithless agents see little harm in acting so that others will bear the risk of their mistakes or indulgences. One can even say that the behavior of Wall Street in the run up to the collapse of credit markets in 2008 was a giant exercise in Moral Hazard. They took the risks of issuing bad products at bad prices with too much leverage and left society to pick up the pieces when it all collapsed.

Morally hazardous environments promote unethical behaviors; they favor self-seeking and externalization of consequences to others. It is saying somewhat the same thing to state that moral hazards invoke higher odds of irresponsibly behavior. In conditions of Moral Hazard in which one is insulated from risk, one can be expected to behave differently than if fully exposed to suffering the consequences of taking risks. The party operating under conditions of Moral Hazard has a tendency or an incentive to behave inappropriately from the perspective of a party who will ultimately bear the risk of loss. The party operating under Moral Hazard takes excessive risks from the perspective of the party who may well pay for any resulting loss.

Moral Hazards convert private goods into public "bads". Moral Hazards reek with negative externalities of the kind that implicate others in our actions.

If there is to be no accountability for action, then no risk premium need be paid by the risk-taker in any way – financially, emotionally, psychologically – for taking risks. If good results happen, the benefits can be kept and if bad results occur, the losses will be borne by others. In morally hazardous environments, there is this asymmetry in the probable sharing of costs associated with risk. With this skewed distribution of outcomes, there is little incentive to be prudent and responsible for the consequences of one's actions. Such is precisely a condition where ethics has been marginalized in the minds of the decision-makers.

Knowledge of consequences coming home to roost provides encouragement for prudence. Dr. Samuel Johnson noted that "nothing so concentrates a man's mind as the prospect of hanging at noon."

Worry about moral hazard arose first in the infant insurance industry in England. It was thought that the taking out of insurance against loss might create a careless attitude on the part of the insured that would increase the chances that the contemplated losses would occur. For example, insuring one against loss from fire might encourage negligence in the insured with respect to living in incendiary conditions. The insured, feeling protected from paying the costs associated with more risky behaviors, would behave less responsibly and so bring about the very loss insured against. Moral hazard would thus redistribute risk more towards the insurance company.

Any environment where Moral Hazard is present favors irresponsibility and taking immoderate chances, shifting the risk of loss to others. In short, such environments cause one to favor self over others and predispose one to favor short term outcomes over longer term consequences. These environments then predispose people towards unethical behavior, behavior that imposes losses on others. Moral hazards implicate incentives. With no incentive to behave well towards others, it is presumed that many people will avoid behaving well.

Moral hazards challenge the moral sense. Moral Hazard is less of a problem with those who have a strong moral sense, a robust conscience, or a resolute ethical disposition to be concerned for others and for the greater good, even though they are not compensated socially for being so honorable. Internal volition to avoid harm overcomes the lassitude permitted in morally hazardous environments.

Moral hazards also implicate negative externalities. They foster consequences which may be negative that do not have to be internalized by those who cause the consequences. Taking a chance that pollution will occur when one has no need to worry about suffering from such pollution creates a negative externality in the pollution.

Moral Hazard shifts the distribution of likely outcomes away from a normal Gaussian bell shaped curve towards one where "fat tails" or unexpected disruptors at the outer edges of the curve are more likely to occur. In this way, they add to the overall social costs of activity.

This shift of probable outcomes away from a normal distribution creates situations where market failures are more likely. If there is Moral Hazard in the air in a market for goods or services, then such markets will have more difficulty equalizing sustainable outcomes for participants. Such markets will be subject to crashes as the risks they assume approach an outer limit and run into a "Black Swan" event which suddenly tanks prices.

Under market conditions of Moral Hazard there will be a distinct bias in the distribution of profits in the short run towards those participants operating at Moral Hazard. Losses will be systematically allocated through socialization more to those on the vulnerable side of transactions. If those who make profits under conditions of Moral Hazard can withdraw their earnings from the market before losses occur, they can securely benefit in the long run as well as having been fully protected from the risk of loss.

This is what happened with markets for financial intermediation in the run up to the collapse of credit in late 2008. The many factors which created that asset bubble in housing prices in the United States – lower credit standards, lack of due diligence by rating agencies, short term leverage used by financial intermediaries for trading on their own account, bonus compensation, lax public regulation – all had one thing in common: they accentuated a morally hazardous environment in financial services leading to the creating of large scale systemic risk in financial markets through excessive borrowing. Such financial intermediation was not sustainable and, in the end, produced more losses than wealth for society. It was not an example of Adam Smith's "invisible hand" at work.

Thus, market environments which grow morally hazardous are prime candidates for enhanced ethical oversight and even government regulation. A red line for legitimate interference in free markets is one between low Moral Hazard and high Moral Hazard. High Moral Hazard markets deserve strict scrutiny for warning signs of promoting negative externalities. High Moral Hazard market conditions increase social costs and inefficiencies.

By looking for situations of moral hazard and changing them, we can reduce inducements for irresponsibility and so promote sustainable business outcomes.

The law has acted in many ways to reduce moral hazards. Rules and regulations forbidding activities – thou shalt not steal; thou shall not sell adulterated food – are attempts to avoid negative externalities. The prospect of punishment is thought to enhance conduct protective of others.

Civil remedies in tort for negligent behavior let those who suffer from the acts of others transfer the cost back to the party who is at fault and responsible for the loss. The prospect of being held responsible for negative externalities is thought to heighten vigilance over one's actions to promote prudence and so lower losses.

In contract law, providing damages for breach of contract which are the plaintiff's expectation of what was to be gained from the bargain was adopted as a policy to encourage parties not to frivolously ignore their contract obligations. If they should breach, they would still have to internalize to themselves the full cost to the other party of such inconsiderate conduct. Facing the prospect of paying such damages was thought to lessen any Moral Hazards associated with the contract.

Further, in contract law, remedies for fraud and misrepresentation, for duress and unjust enrichment, are imposed to forestall morally hazardous environments from arising between the parties where one might otherwise be able to impose costs on the other with impunity.

Ethics per se operates beyond the law. It takes effect where the law permits the action but where there is still an asymmetry of outcomes between the parties. One party can legally get away with benefit leaving another to shoulder a loss. Ethics suggests that such negative externalities can and should be avoided through voluntary action of solicitude for others and by taking due care in consideration of how to make a profit. Sustainability or good stewardship of enterprise occurs where positive externalities are enhanced and negative ones removed, either through internalization of costs or avoidance of the questionable action itself. These morally unhazardous outcomes are the goals of business ethics and corporate social responsibility approaches to profit maximization.

A definition of good stewardship might be a frame of mind that minimizes moral hazards with respect to stakeholders. Imposition of personal fiduciary responsibility removes the temptations for selfish abuse of power that arise in morally hazardous environments. The contemporary movement to promote an oath of professionalism for MBA degree holders can thus be seen as an effort to contain Moral Hazard among business executives. The psychological dynamic of taking an oath has long been presumed to enhance self-awareness of one's opportunity to do harm along with encouraging a predisposition to refrain from so doing by invoking one's sense of honor and self-worth.

A number of circumstances seem more likely than not to foster Moral Hazard in business decision-making.

Bureaucracies promote moral hazards.

There seems to be natural laws of self-referential behaviors that come into play in hierarchical bureaucracies of every description – public and private. I think this happens because the chain of accountability between an individual and final outcomes becomes attenuated through what is euphemistically called "red tape", "office politics", "passing the buck", "getting along by going along", "not rocking the boat", "being a team player". These personal psychological concerns blur accountability within the organization.

On December 22, 2014 Pope Francis gave a speech in the Vatican wherein he drew attention to 15 "diseases" of attitude and performance on the part of members of the Curia of the Roman Catholic Church. While his immediate concern seems to have been the fidelity of his church as an organization to the spiritual presence of Jesus in our lives and, most especially, in the formal, institutional work of his church, his list of enervating "diseases" applies more widely across the scope of human endeavors.

In the theory of business organization and financial management, the so-called "Agency Problem" looms large. This problem, like the problem confronting Pope Francis, is lack of fidelity to higher purposes. The "Agency Problem" holds that, in general, people are not, and can't be expected to be, faithful agents of their principals, intensely loyal to them and studious in solicitude of their best interests. This is said to be true as well of fiduciaries towards their beneficiaries.

The corrosion of self-interest is said not only to intrude into agency and fiduciary efforts but also to so poison the minds of agents and fiduciaries that they constantly will abuse their powers for selfish gain.

The invidious workings of the bad Agency are not limited to for-profit businesses. All employees in bureaucracies are agents of their organization. They too, therefore, can be expected to succumb to the Agency Problem and in so doing create divergences between their ambitions and decisions and the needs and ideals of their organization. This leads to the well-known problems in bureaucracies of "red tape", "office politics", turf wars, silo-ism, lack of vision, and more.

Pope Francis's list of "diseases" therefore provides a description of how the "Agency Problem" works in practice in business and in government and all large organizations.

Here are some thoughts as to the more secular "presentations" as doctors say of these 15 diseases associated with the human condition:

1) thinking we are "immortal", "immune" or downright "indispensable"
   One of the most seductive ethical corruptions brought on by possession of power and authority is the conceit that we are better than others beneath us. Professional expertise – the cult that having academic credentials bestows unquestionable status – can similarly distort our sense of self in unhelpful ways.

2) excessive busy-ness.
   Being consumed by minutia turns us slavish and unfeeling. Constant puttering about distracts us from listening to others and from asking the right questions as to what is our vocation.

3) mental and spiritual "petrification".
   "It is found in those who have a heart of stone, the "stiff-necked" (Acts 7:51-60), in those who in the course of time lose their interior serenity, alertness and daring, and hide under a pile of papers, turning intopaper pushers ..." This is one of the stereotypes of the bureaucrat everywhere.

4) excessive planning.
   "When [one] plans everything down to the last detail and believes that with perfect planning things will fall into place, he becomes an accountant or an office manager."

5) poor coordination.
   An example of this was recently provided by the Valukas Report on the causes of General Motors being unable over a 10 year period to solve a small problem of faulty ignition switches in some vehicles.

6) "spiritual Alzheimer's disease".
   "... those who are completely caught up in the present moment, in their passions, whims and obsessions; in those

who build walls and routines around themselves, and thus become more and more the slaves of idols carved by their own hands." This is the loss of vocation, of alignment between self and higher purpose, of the potential for servant leadership. It is the appropriation of one's position for one's own purposes, the turning of a public good – the job to be done for others – into private property for the advancement of self.

7) rivalry and vainglory.

What more needs to be said of these woeful personal attributes?

8) existential schizophrenia.

This is the realm of hypocrisy, of not walking the talk., of being two-faced and using one set of standards for self and another for others. It is a loss of integrity which destroys one's trustworthiness, leading to a default work style of manipulation and command and control.

9) gossiping, grumbling and back-biting.

Again, what more needs to be said about these dysfunctions.

10) idolizing superiors.

"Those who court their superiors in the hope of gaining their favour. They are victims of careerism and opportunism; ... They serve thinking only of what they can get and not of what they should give. Small-minded persons, unhappy and inspired only by their own lethal selfishness (cf. Gal 5:16-25). Superiors themselves could be affected by this disease, when they court their collaborators in order to obtain their submission, loyalty and psychological dependency, but the end result is a real complicity." There has never been a bureaucracy where this pattern of patron-client rapprochement has not undermined the quality of outcomes and the idealism of the enterprise.

11) indifference to others.

Pope Francis said: "This is where each individual thinks only of himself and loses sincerity and warmth of human relationships. When the most knowledgeable person does not put that knowledge at the service of his less knowledge-able colleagues. When we learn something and then keep it to ourselves rather than sharing it in a helpful way with others. When out of jealousy or deceit we take joy in see-ing others fall instead of helping them up and encouraging them." These behaviors just kill the joy of working for an organization. They make having a sense of vocation impos-sible. They are the rotten substance of "office politics".

12) a lugubrious face

Being serious and judgmental with others, treating them with rigor, brusqueness and arrogance as if they don't count and have nothing to contribute to the common good.

13) hoarding.

Pope Francis commented: "filling an existential void in [one's] heart by accumulating material goods, not out of need but only in order to feel secure." Here is what scholars of organizations such as Max Weber and Francis Fukuyama call "patrimonialism". The organization becomes an exten-sion of the family, a patrimony there for exploitation. This gives rise to the great contradiction between self-interest and the common good. It is rejection of agency responsibil-ity to serve first and be rewarded for good service only.

14) closed circles

Forming factions and cliques. Placing personal networks at the center of one's concern. Not sharing information or lis-tening or reaching out to build wider coalitions.

15) disease of worldly profit, of forms of self-exhibition.

Turning "service into power, and ... power into a commod-ity in order to gain worldly profit or even greater power. This is the disease of persons who insatiably try to accumu-late power and to this end are ready to slander, defame and discredit others, even in newspapers and magazines." (Pope Francis) Self-exhibition is the disease of presenting oneself in public or within the organization as the savoir or messiah, the only one with the correct understanding and views to whom all others should defer. Or, perhaps, only that one is more capable than the others and so for that reason should be trusted with power and authority.

These are the serious diseases associated with the "Agency Problem" in every business. They need medical remediation, first for prevention, and then, when they present themselves, for surgical removal or medicinal shrinkage.

The need to coordinate across functional departments and so arrive at a joint decision dilutes the concentration of accountability. Where too many are in charge, no one is in charge. Decision by committee often leads to the least common denominator being chosen to keep all the players supportive of going forward. Then too, passing responsibility to higher levels who are not fully informed of consequences leads to the dilution of due care on the part of the entire organization.

Where decision-makers are isolated from accountability by nepotism, favoritism, or concentration of discretionary power with no oversight, the Moral Hazard surrounding them correspondingly increases. Holding a sinecure encourages acceptance of Moral Hazard.

The institution of intrusive compliance programs and internal audits by large organizations to minimize risks on the part of employees is one response to this coddling of Moral Hazard by bureaucracies. The setbacks for Toyota arising out of poor quality control and for BP out of poor safety practices were examples of such bureaucratic Moral Hazard at work.

Possessing "Other People's Money" promotes Moral Hazards

Tension over risk allocation between principals and agents is a well-known arena for Moral Hazard. The agent – any one who has responsibility for the assets and business interests of another – can act in such a way that risks are unfairly allocated to the principal. This again is what happened to many principals in the US housing bubble. Many who borrowed on home mortgages were not well used by the lenders, being given loans they could not afford on a sustainable basis. Many who were sold securitized mortgages and CDOs were given inferior products, not worth their face value, so that the probable risk of loss was fully passed on to them and not carried by the originators of the securities.

Paul Volcker's advocacy of a separation of commercial banking from proprietary trading using borrowed funds wisely proposes a regulation to reduce Moral Hazard in financial intermediation. The separation of a market function where prudence is a necessary public good – in other words, the absence of Moral Hazard is needed – from more self-referential assumption of risks makes sense in an the arena where "Other People's Money" – both of equity owners and creditors - is put to short-term, selfish use. Moral Hazard here puts at risk the stability of the important public good of financial intermediation in support of general economic growth across society.

Agents know more than their principals where risk lies and so have an asymmetric power over the principals in finalizing transactions. This imbalance in power can be abused by agents tempting them to be irresponsibly selfish as much as they can.

The law has sought to contain such Moral Hazard with rules of fiduciary responsibility imposing upon agents duties of loyalty and due care.

Compensation arrangements can promote moral hazards.

Methods of compensation can contribute to Moral Hazard or can reduce its temptations. Generally speaking, compensation in the form of fees and bonuses adds to the moral hazardness of a business environment. The incentive set by such forms of compensation is for the decision-maker to consider short-term outcomes over long-term effects. These incentives lay behind the collapse of Enron. Providing rewards for short-term results with no consequence for subsequent loss skews decision-making in self-promoting directions. This environment for Moral Hazard was seen both in the back dating of stock option scandals and in the accumulation of systemic risk which led to the financial crisis of 2008 and subsequent recession. Those who laid on risk in financial intermediation before the collapse of credit markets had no reason to worry about who would ultimately pay for any losses so incurred as they had taken out up front their compensation in cash through fees and bonuses.

Golden parachutes and immediately exercisable stock options were other forms of compensation for senior executives that have encouraged Moral Hazard.

Delayed compensation payments and liabilities for clawbacks would reduce Moral Hazard among employees.

Aggressively seeking short-term profitability promotes morally hazardous environments.

An extension of how Moral Hazard can be accentuated by certain compensation arrangements applies to business models that focus on short-term profitability. Sucking out short-term returns led to irresponsible ratings of securities dependent on sub-prime mortgages on the part of Moody's and Standard&Poors and irresponsibly high leverage ratios using overnight borrowings on the part of Bear Stearns and Lehman Brothers. Similar incentives were at the root of Enron's failure as misleading accounting was used to distort reporting of income so that earnings targets could be met, bonuses earned, and stock price increased.

A number of highly recommended CSR practices, however, can reduce the risks associated with Moral Hazard in firms.

CSR Mediation minimizes moral hazards.

Moral Hazard with respect to stakeholders happens when owners and managers do not sense any constraints of accountability to stakeholders. Tunnel vision seeking only what is best for shareholders gives rise to Moral Hazard where negative externalities are imposed on other stakeholders by company actions. A recommendation of many CSR professionals is for companies to engage with all their stakeholders. In the normal course of doing business smartly, management seeks to enhance the company's brand equity, which drives customer engagement through product planning, pricing, and investigation of customer preferences and concerns. Similarly, a smart company engages with its employees as another valuable, though intangible capital asset. Maintaining open and frank dialogue with equity ownership interests and providers of debt capital is a third way to constructively engage with key stakeholders. Following the lessons learned in the quality movement, working with suppliers as trusted partners enhances quality of product and service and can lower costs. Finally, listening to concerns from civil society reduces regulatory risk and enhances brand equity.

These forms of stakeholder engagement permit the company to minimize its negative externalities, reduce risk and become more sustainably profitable. The risks associated with Moral Hazard arising from short-sighted, thoughtless behaviors undertaken on the grounds that stakeholders will be unable to impose costs on the company are thus reduced.

Good corporate governance minimizes moral hazards

While corporate governance is designed in the first place to reduce the Moral Hazard associated with unfaithful agents (directors and corporate employees), it can extend its efficacious supervision to reduce the Moral Hazard of the firm with respect to a range of stakeholders. Good corporate governance provides for checks and balances so that thorough consideration of core values, risks and opportunities happens with regularity. Standards of governance enhance awareness and implementation of stewardship responsibilities in general. Proper application of fiduciary duties of due care at the board level bring about more sensitive consideration of stakeholder interests and of the risks of externalizing costs and/or negative consequences in ways that will hurt the firm in the long run. Good corporate governance practices make clear the mission and vision of the enterprise and open up channels of reporting and communication vertically and horizontally within the organization to de-bureaucratize it as much as possible. Good corporate governance practices reward responsible executive skills and attention to results. KPI's of the firm are aligned with its core values and accountability as a moral force within the company culture is rational and effective.

Transparency minimizes moral hazards

Secrecy promotes Moral Hazard. If what can be done can never be traced back to the instigator, accountability for the consequences evaporates. Once the connection between act and consequence is so severed, Moral Hazard is born. The temptation to act meanly and selfishly - to take no care for the consequences to others of one's actions - becomes stronger in such conditions. Only one possessing an offsetting strength of character can then remain responsible when acting in secret.

For this reason transparency is most efficacious when Moral Hazard is to be avoided. Public identification of decision-makers is required along with disclosure of the process used to reach the decision and the material considerations which were used to justify the action taken. In this way decision-makers will act under conditions of responsibility. They will be less likely to be arrogantly discretionary and will become more solicitous of good opinions. And, should the effects of their decisions go awry, they themselves will be at a foreseeable loss of at least reputation and prestige and possibly of position and fortune as well.

A famous instance of transparency at work was the 1776 signing of the Declaration of Independence by representatives of the British North American Colonies in Congress assembled. They put their names to a proclamation which was treasonous to the British Crown and pledged to the success of their effort their lives, fortunes and sacred honor, implicitly recognizing that defeat would deprive them of at least the first two. Benjamin Franklin then quipped that they must now all hang together or, most assuredly, they would all hang separately. Being transparent made them more effective politically as a committed leadership team.

To protect against Moral Hazard through the use of transparency, the profession of accounting was called upon. Providing public record of the results of transactions provides for accountability of decision-making. Measurement of results is foundational for evaluation of performance and inculcation of habits of responsible conduct. In securities law public audits are required and prudent investors always ask for copies of financial reports.

However, Moral Hazard can be promoted through technical manipulation of accounting conventions and rules. This was famously the case with Enron and its special purpose vehicles and so-called "sales" of energy to banks accompanied by a separate agreement to re-purchase the energy sold for a premium over the sales price. Both techniques, supposedly legal, allowed the company and its auditors to hide its true financial results of operations. Debt was removed from view and nominal profits could be publicly disclosed. These accounting entries encouraged Moral Hazard on the part of senior Enron executives as they undertook what was effective fraudulent misrepresentation on the public and their employees.

A similar use of accounting was used by Lehman Brothers in Repo 105 transactions where company debt could be offloaded for a few days just before and after public reporting of its financial position as required under American securities laws. The effect was 1) to delude the market as to the actual vulnerability of Lehman's business model and 2) permit its managers to continue reckless borrowing for speculative trading in financial instruments. Repo 105 accounting entries fostered additional Moral Hazard within Lehman in its last months. The continued ability to leverage the company at very high multiples of equity capital enabled its managers to avoid a responsible confrontation with the dangers of their strategy. The result was bankruptcy of the entity with great losses for its owners, employees, and creditors.

Facilitating Moral Hazard
does not always lead to happy endings.

It is important to note here the vital role of legal counsel in promoting some morally hazardous environments. Enron's special purpose vehicles, its contracts for the sale of energy, Lehman's Repo 105 transactions, and the SIV entities used by Wall Street firms before the 2008 credit crisis to hold debt off their balance sheets (debt incurred in speculation), were all made possible by the drafting skills of attorneys. Lawyers create the contracts which allocate risks under conditions of Moral Hazard so that accountants can then "helpfully" present financial results in ethically misleading ways. Without the lawyers, the degree of Moral Hazard would have been less.

One can also question how much of the morally hazardous environment that contributed to the speculation leading up to the 2008 credit collapse can be attributed to the complex legal contracts that made for opaque, hard-to-understand, ownership relationships that were behind securitized mortgages, CDOs, CDOs squared, synthetic CDOs. The blurring of responsibilities around sub-prime mortgages may well have enhanced Moral Hazard on the part of those who sold such financial instruments.

Perhaps the most important contribution to the environment of Moral Hazard that resulted in the 2008 collapse of credit markets was made by the rating agencies: Moody's, Standard&Poors, and Fitch. The most dangerous lack of transparency underlying the misallocation of capital investment to sub-prime mortgages occurred when securities supported by the prices of such sub-prime mortgages were rated higher than was justified by the normal probability of payment on such sub-prime mortgages. Individual mortgages with low probability of payment according to their terms were, when co-mingled into pools, given ratings that justified paying high prices for them.

Sub-prime mortgages with low or no interest teaser rates which would reset at higher rates later, with floating rates, with interest only or no interest, principal expanding terms, Alt-A loans, mortgages securing liar's loans, etc. were loans of money to borrowers most unlikely to pay in full and on time under their loan agreements. In giving investment grade ratings to securities derived from these risky loans, the rating agencies did not diligently investigate the individual mortgages supporting such securities. Thus the rating agencies contributed to unreasonable understandings in financial markets of the real value of such securities, misunderstandings that contributed to assumption of very risky investment prospects in such amounts as to destabilize the entire global financial system and the real economies dependent on its provision of financial capital and services.

Lack of transparency as to real values promoted Moral Hazard in global financial intermediation.

Given the failures of the rating agencies - and also of the sellers of rated securities who did not demand more exacting risk analysis of the securities to be sold - those who created the risks of financial loss – the lenders to sub-prime borrowers in the first instance – passed all of such risk on to largely unsuspecting investors in global financial markets.

When real risk is hidden, Moral Hazard increases as investors think more lightly about the consequences of their investment decisions. As asset bubbles grow, the real risk of each additional purchase increases while the nominal risk seems to shrink as the rising market price of asset value seems to provide increasing security for the incremental purchase. Until the collapse of the bubble that is. Then more stable values come to light. This divergence during the bubble between real risk and perceived risk generates Moral Hazard and so increases the chances of thoughtless investment.

In the sub-prime asset bubble and collapse, Moral Hazard encouraged the creation of short-term market realities that did not align with a normal statistical distribution of risk and pricing. Real risk was hidden, pricing was misleading and so investment decisions became foolish. Market participants acting under conditions of Moral Hazard thus brought upon themselves the sudden occurrence of a "fat tail" probability or, in other words, an unexpected "Black Swan" price collapse.

道德

CHAPTER TEN
OVERCOMING THE AGENCY
PROBLEM: SOURCES OF VALUE

Simply put, perhaps too simply but nonetheless with forceful clarity, the remedy for the Agency Problem is the Moral Sense. People with good character, with a sense of ethics, with strong moral fiber - people who can and do assume responsibility for others – are not problem agents, selfish and unfaithful, disloyal and negligent in their charges.

Adam Smith wrote a complex and dense book – The Theory of Moral Sentiments – to make this point. Smith here showed a way to avoiding Agency Problems through intentional socialization of habits of prudence and caring. Before Smith, John Calvin for the Protestants and Thomas Acquinas for the Catholics had similarly set forth belief systems in the public good, the social capital, that arose when people were encouraged to be moral and ethical. And before Calvin and Acquinas had been Marcus Aurelius, Cicero and the Stoics, not to mention Jesus Christ.

When we look for the sources of value that can set the Agency Problem aside and overcome its cynical teachings, we most often follow a trail of legitimation and personal meaning that lead to religions.

As a sample of the constructive role religion can play in promoting the public good of character that contributes to social capital, let us consider several examples.

First, contemporary Catholic social teachings. This will be followed by considerations of Buddhism, Chinese ethics, Taoism, Aristotle and Qur'an.

Aspirations and achievements aligned with papal encyclical *Caritas in Veritate*

Pope Benedict XVI's 2009 recent encyclical, Caritas In Veritate, from the point of view of Catholic social thought and teachings provides rather complete intellectual and spiritual support for moral capitalism and its efforts to promote more responsible global business practices. Catholic social thought presumes that people have the capacity to be moral and ethical, to live by higher standards of concern for others and the common good, to rise above the Agency Problem.

The Caux Round Table similarly believes that human actions and institutions are not condemned to the lowest levels of base and vulgar desires and motivations. Such a low level of intention and behavior cannot support robust economic growth and so must be continuously put in its place far away from the temple of social justice. The CRT's ethical Principles for Responsible Business, which are easily used in all business decisions, provide strategic leadership guidance for stakeholder relationships which embodies the high aspirational standard of Caritas. The CRT's risk management assessment platform, Arcturus, provides more day-to-day tactical analysis of stakeholder relationships from this aspirational perspective of Caritas.

The CRT's approach to free markets and private property and to the use of money and prices to stimulate wealth creation for humanity rests on three fundamental concerns. One is for human dignity; another is to apply the dynamic of Kyosei to decision-making; and the third is to serve as a steward of power and resources for purposes higher than one's own use and indulgence.

Importantly, in his encyclical Caritas In Veritate, Pope Benedict XVI concludes that financial profit is not the best measure of success and achievement. He writes as follows:

"Profit is useful if it serves as a means toward an end that provides a sense both of how to produce it and how to make good use of it. Once profit becomes the exclusive goal, if it is produced by improper means and without the common good as its ultimate end, it risks destroying wealth and creating poverty." (at paragraph 21)

The mismanagement of risk and pricing in technologically sophisticated global financial markets that produced the collapse of such markets in late 2008 and the current severe recession provides us with an immediately relevant example of how the wrong kind of profit seeking does indeed destroy wealth.

The Pope believes that this current economic crisis can become an opportunity for discernment, in which to share a new vision for the future, a process in which the world needs to "rediscover fundamental values." The CRT, it bears noting, was created to find such fundamental values from which a more responsible and sustainably profitable world business culture could grow and thrive. Our presentation of such fundamentals can be found in our sets of principles for business, government, NGOs and owners of wealth.

In line with the CRT's focus on human and social capital as the deep source of tangible wealth creation, the Pope notes that "the primary capital to be safeguarded and valued is man, the human person in his or her integrity." (at paragraph 25)

In an important part of his argument, the Pope continues:

"In a climate of mutual trust, the market is the economic institution that permits encounter between persons, inasmuch as they are economic subjects who make use of contracts to regulate their relations as they exchange goods and services of equivalent value between them, in order to satisfy their needs and desires. The market is subject to the principles of so-called commutative justice, which regulates the relations of giving and receiving between parties to a transaction. But the social doctrine of the Church has unceasingly highlighted the importance of distributive justice and social justice for the market economy, not only because it belongs within a broader social and political context, but also because of the wider network of relations within which it operates. In fact, if the market is governed solely by the principle of the equivalence in value of exchanged goods, it cannot produce the social cohesion that it requires in order to function well. Without internal forms of solidarity and mutual trust, the market cannot completely fulfill its proper economic function. And today it is this trust which has ceased to exist, and the loss of trust is a grave loss."

Like the CRT, the Pope recognizes that the market is not an intentional moral instrument; it only reflects the values brought to it by those who seek to buy and sell:

"Admittedly, the market can be a negative force, not because it is so by nature, but because a certain ideology can make it so. It must be remembered that the market does not exist in the pure state. It is shaped by the cultural configurations which define it and give it direction. Economy and finance, as instruments, can be used badly when those at the helm are motivated by purely selfish ends. Instruments that are good in themselves can thereby be transformed into harmful ones. But it is man's darkened reason that produces these consequences, not the instrument per se. Therefore it is not the instrument that must be called to account, but individuals, their moral conscience and their personal and social responsibility." (at paragraph 36)

The CRT's Principles for Responsible Business were designed to engage the "moral conscience and their personal and social responsibility" of those who make their living in the market economy, including financial markets of all types.

Economic development, believes the Pope, is impossible without upright men and women, without financiers and politicians whose consciences are finely attuned to the requirements of the common good. (at paragraph 71) The CRT hopes that its principles and their implementation can help attune consciences to such requirements of the common good in ways that can sustain justly profitable enterprises.

Precisely in order to help individual's link the "better angels of their natures" to their economic activity the CRT proposed its ethical principles for responsible business. James Madison in one of his Federalist Papers wrote that "if men were angels, there would be no need for government." The same thought applies just as well to markets and business as the Pope himself noted above: if all people were angels, markets would be perfect. But we are not angelic. To remediate that fault, we need guidance in forming our ideals, our standards of conduct, our modes of self-control, our concern for others. Such guidance, the CRT believes, does not come from within market exchanges but originates beyond them in culture and society. Thus, the CRT provides for general application its ethical principles and its Decision Style Inventory to assist individuals in coming to a more full appreciation of their ethical stance in decision-making.

The Pope acknowledges in his Encyclical that "Much in fact depends on the underlying system of morality." (at paragraph 45)

Ethics, the Pope writes, must apply to the system, to the core of business operations and financial intermediation. His scope for business ethics encounters no opposition from the CRT, which has long advocated principled decision-making for all in business and finance. The Pope argues that "Efforts are needed –and it is essential to say this – not only to create "ethical" sectors or segments of the economy or the world of finance, but to ensure that the whole economy – the whole of finance – is ethical, not merely by virtue of an external label, but by its respect for requirements intrinsic to its very nature." (at paragraph 45)

He adds later in his Encyclical the observation that "Finance, therefore — through the renewed structures and operating methods that have to be designed after its misuse, which wreaked such havoc on the real economy — now needs to go back to being an instrument directed towards improved wealth creation and development. Insofar as they are instruments, the entire economy and finance, not just certain sectors, must be used in an ethical way so as to create suitable conditions for human development and for the development of peoples. It is certainly useful, and in some circumstances imperative, to launch financial initiatives in which the humanitarian dimension predominates. However, this must not obscure the fact that the entire financial system has to be aimed at sustaining true development. Above all, the intention to do good must not be considered incompatible with the effective capacity to produce goods. Financiers must rediscover the genuinely ethical foundation of their activity, so as not to abuse the sophisticated instruments which can serve to betray the interests of savers. Right intention, transparency, and the search for positive results are mutually compatible and must never be detached from one another. If love is wise, it can find ways of working in accordance with provident and just expediency, as is illustrated in a significant way by much of the experience of credit unions." (at paragraph 65)

The Pope also requires of financial capitalism that: "What should be avoided is a speculative use of financial resources that yields to the temptation of seeking only short-term profit, without regard for the long-term sustainability of the enterprise, its benefit to the real economy and attention to the advancement, in suitable and appropriate ways, of further economic initiatives in countries in need of development." (at paragraph 40)

The Pope's recommendations on this point were anticipated by the CRT's Seven Points of reform, issued to focus remedial attention on improvements to financial markets in the wake of the 2008 crisis.

Just so, the CRT advances a program of "moral capitalism" that puts ethical considerations at the heart of business, not on the periphery. The CRT Principles uniquely integrate ethical aspects of stakeholder relationships with core financial requirements of business success.

In this very vein of analysis the Pope asserted:

"Locating resources, financing, production, consumption, and all the other phases in the economic cycle inevitable have moral implications. Thus every economic decision has a moral consequence." (at paragraph 37)

Thus the Pope concludes that:

"Yet there is also increasing awareness of the need for greater social responsibility on the part of business. Even if the ethical considerations that currently inform debate on the social responsibility of the corporate world are not all acceptable from the perspective of the Church's social doctrine, there is nevertheless a growing conviction that business management cannot concern itself only with the interests of the proprietors, but must also assume responsibility for all the other stakeholders who contribute to the life of the business: the workers, the clients, the suppliers of various elements of production, the community of reference." (at paragraph 40)

In 1994 the CRT first issued its principles for business calling attention to this very aspect of business decision-making – going beyond shareholders to stakeholders.

In what reads as a direct acknowledgment of CRT Principle for Business Number 2 on the obligation of multinational companies to contribute to the countries where they do business, the Pope wrote:

"It is true that the export of investments and skills can benefit the populations of the receiving country. Labour and technical knowledge are a universal good. Yet it is not right to export these things merely for the sake of obtaining advantageous conditions, or worse, for purposes of exploitation, without making a real contribution to local society by helping to bring about a robust productive and social system, an essential factor for stable development." (at paragraph 40)

In discussing his concern for environmental protections, the Pope in effect endorsed CRT Principle for Business Number 6 on taking action to preserve and enhance our natural environment. The Pope in paragraph 50 of his Encyclical refers to "a responsible stewardship over nature".

Part of the needed response to excessive technological expertise in our thinking, suggests Pope Benedict XVI in this Encyclical,
should be "a deeper critical evaluation of the category of relation."
(at paragraph 53) Isolated individualism gives rise to a profound
poverty of both spirit and understanding. It is a limiting constraint
on our use of human reason to properly balance our production
and consumption with the needs of both the human and the natural ecologies in which we must survive.

The Pope writes that: "As a spiritual being, the human creature
is defined through interpersonal relations. The more authentically
he or she lives these relations, the more his or her own personal
identity matures. It is not by isolation that man establishes his
worth, but by placing himself in relation with others and with God."
(at paragraph 53) Reciprocity, holds the Pope, must be considered
as the heart of what it is to be a human being. (at paragraph 57)

One of the core CRT values stances – Kyosei, a Japanese concept of symbiotic interdependence – provides just the kind of
relational thinking that the Pope recommends. Kyosei expressly
encourages non-zero or win/win decision-making where one's
own well-being depends on interactions with a wider set of forces
and resources.

Therefore, the task of preparing us for wise action the Pope
argues "cannot be undertaken by the social sciences alone, insofar
as the contribution of disciplines such as metaphysics and theology
is needed if man's transcendent dignity is to be properly understood." (at paragraph 35) Thus, the Pope worries that modern
technological thinking can only suggest that business investment
is merely a technical act, not a human and ethical one, which in
truth it is as well. He advises us that "Technologically advanced societies must not confuse their own technological development with
a presumed cultural superiority, but must rather rediscover within
themselves the oft forgotten virtues which made it possible for them
to flourish throughout their history." (at paragraph 59)

Technology, says the Pope, is a profoundly human reality, linked
to the autonomy and freedom of man; technology expresses and

confirms the hegemony of spirit over matter, and so must remember that it is never merely technology. Technology has its proper ends in expressing God's trust to humanity to keep and till the earth, an undertaking that should mirror God's creative love. (at paragraph 69) In short, technology is an expression of Caritas, a moral dimension that guides the use of numbers, algorithms, and practical theorems.

This inclusive approach to intellectual understanding of what makes for successful business is quite in keeping with the CRT's sensitivity to the "fit" of its ethical principles with many great world religious traditions.

One may not need theology to set a market-responsive price for goods or services, but one would be quite short-sighted and remiss to ignore higher purposes in seeking how best to sustain a profitable enterprise over time. Practically speaking, people are shaped in their behaviors by their cultures and religions. Thus, the CRT seeks not to ignore this dimension of global business reality.

In harmony with this CRT approach, the Pope observes in his encyclical that:

"Evolving societies must remain faithful to all that is truly human in their traditions, avoiding temptation to overlay them automatically with the mechanisms of a globalized technological civilization. In all cultures there are examples of ethical convergence, some isolated, some interrelated, as an expression of the one human nature, willed by the Creator: the tradition of ethical wisdom knows this as natural law. This universal moral law provides a sound basis for all cultural, religious, and political dialogue, and it ensures that the multi-faceted pluralism of cultural diversity does not detach itself from the common quest for truth, goodness and God." (at paragraph 59)

Pope Benedict's encyclical provides a well-thought out framework for providing not only private goods that enhance personal well-being but also keeping private goods situated in the context of quasi-private, quasi-public and fully public goods as well.

STEPHEN B. YOUNG
A Buddhist Philosophy for Corporate Social Responsibility

Buddhism most generally explained pertains to individuals and their confrontation with life's realities, both seen and unseen. Buddhism presents both an understanding of the transcendent, other-worldly, possible futures for all beings as well as specific guidance for optimal traversing of this world's circumstances.

A common-place understanding of Buddhism, especially Theravada Buddhism, is that it calls for renunciation of this world and its passions, attachments, and motivations and focuses our attention on transcending the norm of self-centrality.

And yet, an often overlooked reality of Buddhism is how much guidance the religion provides on how to live well in this world. Roughly speaking, Buddhism suggests the helpful role that right awareness can play in reducing our subjection to the vicissitudes of emotions and events. In this context, Buddhism provides advice for better decision-making. This decision-making – a "mindfulness practice" – opens a door to the full range of goods from fully private to fully public.

Corporate Social Responsibility ("CSR") similarly demands a certain level of awareness of the stakeholders who both influence a firm's success and who bear the consequences of decisions made by the firm. CSR, therefore, can be understood in simple terms as a decision-making framework for business.

The Buddhist paradigm for CSR brings Buddhist understandings of reality and guidance derived from those understandings to decisions made by the firm and its stakeholders.

The core of Buddhism is the law of Karma – a fixed connection between actions, reactions and interactions and resulting states of being. Karma puts emphasis on the power of actions, reactions and interactions to influence the quality of our being. A mind aware of the working of Karma seeks to become more and more sensitive to the range of actions, reactions and interactions that are possible so that wise choices can be made in the application of our conscious will to our circumstances. The "enlightened" mind in Buddhist terms has acquired full awareness of what is happening subject to the law of karma and so seeks behaviors that minimize tensions and frictions, stresses and strains, which arise out of life's complexities and contradictions.

Such an enlightened mind can bring the Dharma, or best practices of Buddhism, into this life through knowledge of oneself, faith in oneself, control of oneself, contentment of oneself with oneself, and respect of oneself. With the Dharma so internalized and not confined to external texts or limited to periods of mindfulness meditation, one can act wisely, react wisely, and interact with maximum good effect. Following the Dharma in thought and action permits one to take constructive advantage of the law of Karma.

When the self has understanding of where it is vis-à-vis others and the world around it, it gains an important form of wisdom. Self-confidence is needed to provide the will and courage to overcome doubt, ambiguity, uncertainty and confusion. Self-control is needed to move from understanding to action. Not to act is an affliction that arises in the mind. Contentment of the self comes from awareness that our understanding is firm and our acts are rightly directed. If we are not content, then we are falling short of our best efforts. Dint of effort leads to the experiencing of such contentment. Self-respect measures awareness that one can indeed make constructive efforts, that one has potential for the good, and that one's mind is indeed –right now – ready for deeper understanding

The application of the Dharma to one's life can be eased by the eight step path that takes advantage of Karma:

> Step One: right quality of awareness (wisdom and understanding) which eases one's way to:
> Step Two: right quality of thoughts, which eases one's way to:
> Step Three: quality speech (framing actions, reactions, and interactions) which eases one's way to:
> Step Four: quality action, quality reaction and quality interaction, which ease one's way to:
> Step Five: living in awareness of consequences, which eases one's way to:

Step Six: constraining effort within an ethical framework, which eases one's way to:

Step Seven: enhancing mindfulness, which eases one's way to:

Step Eight: deepening the power of concentration, which eases one's way to:

Step One: right quality of awareness, and so the cycle continues on and on.

The eight step path is a process of continual improvement in the Buddhist quality of one's living, making it easier and easier with experience and endeavor to have a proper quality of decision-making readily at hand at all times. Wisdom opens the door to conduct; conduct then facilitates acquisition of mental discipline; improved mental discipline brings new wisdom.

One can enter the progression of continuous improvement at any step and then move, step by step, towards a more enlightened state of thinking and acting. One, for example, could start with an action step: taking a leap of faith that acting with restraint of ego anxieties and desires will bring new insights that in turn will facilitate higher quality actions, reactions and interactions later on. Or one could start with a step towards heightened mental discipline, such as a meditative practice. This would lead to greater wisdom and so on to more enlightened actions, reactions and interactions.

The summit of the progression of continuous improvement is acquisition of ten excellent qualities, or Paramitas. These qualities of action are: generosity, giving of oneself; virtue, morality, proper conduct; renunciation; transcendental wisdom, insight; energy, diligence, vigor, effort; patience, tolerance, forbearance, acceptance, endurance; truthfulness, honesty; determination, resolution; loving-kindness; and equanimity, serenity. Such a person would appear to be emotionally and mentally released from so many of the trials and tribulations that come with living in the world. In addition, such a person would have capacity to enhance the lives of others without seeking recompense. Such a person could be easily trusted.

Buddhism and the Firm

The incorporation of this Buddhist approach into a firm's decision-making leads to corporate social responsibility. This paradigm of the business as following the eight step path in its decisions presumes that the firm also constitutes a repository of Karma just as an individual is. When the Dharma is then incorporated into the decision-making of the firm, Karma will lead to a higher quality of being for the business.

Any business beyond individual entrepreneurship is a collective effort. Under Buddhism, collectives too are subject to the law of Karma. An enterprise, then, is a locus of Karmic dynamics just as an individual person is.

Individuals constitute the collective. They include a sub-set of relevant stakeholders: those in governance, owners, employees of course. But also customers, whose values and behaviors shape firm operations in the marketplace, suppliers who feed into the firm's ability to deliver its goods or services, creditors and regulators who encourage or thwart firm actions. External demands on the firm from civil society activists or community leaderships trigger reactions and interactions which define the firm's Karma as being positive or negative. Seeking to accumulate positive Karma – or trying to avoid negative Karma – displays an enlightened self-interest that will facilitate sustainable profits and higher valuation of the business on a going concern basis.

Business Application of the Eight Step Path

The core of application of mindfulness under conditions of awareness of the law of Karma lies in choosing how best to act, how best to react, and how best to interact. Karma imposes a system perspective on decision-making. The self – the ego object of karma – is never isolated or alone; it is always in relationships – with natural forces and processes and with human purposing in surrounding social and cultural milieu. The karma of others impinges on the self; the intentions and emotions of others impinge on the self; the interests and ambitions of others impinge on the self – just as the self impinges on others. Actions of the self breed reactions from others; actions of others breed reactions from the self; self and others are in interactions every day.

Just so for a collective like a business. Initial wisdom leads to constructive conduct which turns Karma in favor of the enterprise which in turn enhances acquisition of more wisdom.

But not just any scope of awareness will enhance a firm's Karma. Narrowness in any form – the blinders imposed by selfish profit maximization, lack of technical knowledge, illusions of power or being in the right all the time – works against the acquisition of better Karma. Under the Dharma, wisdom variables should promote knowledge of firm, faith in the firm's vision, mission and strategy, control of its destiny, contentment with the firm's actions and prospects, and respect for the firm' values. Wisdom variables look upon the firm systemically, observing all its circumstances, its various salient stakeholders, and heighten awareness of the consequences of multiple firm interactions with stakeholders.

The wisdom of a firm – its equivalent to awareness and quality of thoughtfulness – resides in its culture – its sense of vision and mission, its business model and competitive strategy. And the wisdom of a firm also lies in the personalities of its decision-makers. Metaphorically, the firm revolves as a chariot wheel with the board of directors as the hub and the senior managers as the outer rim to contain the actions, reactions and interactions of those who act for the entity. The spokes are the stakeholders whose merits or demerits shape the karma of the firm.

Thus, a firm cannot benefit from application of the Dharma unless it engages with stakeholders. It needs to apply mindfulness to its customers, its employees, its owners, its investors, its suppliers, and its physical and social environments.

For example, a firm obtaining merit and avoiding demerit will not mislead or take advantage of customer ignorance, emotional insecurities, and excessive desires (greed, lust, anger, etc.). The mindful firm will be transparent as to the consequences of its products and services and will price them without seeking undo market power or using them as a means of unfair rent extraction.

With respect to its employees, the mindful firm will pay them fair compensation that will enhance their livelihoods, not subject them to degrading or harmful conditions of work. It will react to their reasonable needs with concern and constructive approaches. It will interact with employees as recommended by the quality movement to engage their best thinking on the firm's behalf and encourage their personal commitment to the firm's success.

The mindful firm will similarly be fair and transparent to owners, open and reasonable with creditors, solicitous of suppliers to obtain quality inputs, protective of the physical environment, and a steward of community progress. Obviously, such a firm will refrain from corrupt and illicit initiatives.

Having a vision, mission, and strategy which embrace stakeholders is the starting point of excellence in CSR management. If a firm ignores fundamental CSR perspectives, it cannot possess adequate wisdom about Karma. Where there is such poverty of wisdom, a firm cannot optimize Karma to its advantage in the rough and tumble of circumstances. The actions, reactions, and interactions it chooses will not meet the standard of wise conduct leading to more focused mental discipline as time flows on. Its unwise conduct will expose it to illusions, short-sightedness, regrets, untimely interventions, and failure to keep up with changes and new market opportunities.

A shortage of wisdom will lead to failure in stakeholder relationships. Actions taken, reactions to stakeholder interests and demands, interactions with the systemic drivers of firm profitability will all fall short of what is possible to promote sustainable firm success.

A Chinese Philosophy for Corporate Social Responsibility

Harmonious relationships have long been central to Chinese thinking about how best to live. At present, the goal of the Chinese Communist Party is to build a "harmonious society." Harmony as a goal of social justice embraces the non-adversarial interaction of public and private goods, with all gradations between the extremes. What is private has its time and place but whatever is a public good must also be respected and have its say in our decision-making. Finding the balance is the central problem for a society, a never-ending challenge that makes for a perpetual dynamic in our personal and communal lives.

Mencius advised: "Opportunities of time given by Heaven are not equal to the situational advantages afforded by Earth, which are not equal to the power that arises with the accord of men. (Bk II, Part II, Chapter 1,1) Success then arises when the time allotted by Heaven aligns with the conditions created by Earth and the willing agreement of others to cooperate. Being in harmony thus facilitates achievement.

But Chinese thinkers have differed widely in their understanding of how best to achieve harmony. For Taoists and believers in Five Element/Yin Yang energies, as are revealed in the Yi Ching for example, harmony is dynamic, ever fluid, ever changing. It is a natural order into which we must fit ourselves. The statesman QuanZi opted for state intervention in markets as a buyer or seller to take advantage of pricing preferences in order to advance public objectives. For example, he proposed that the state should buy grain when the price was low to help farmers but sell from its inventory of grain when the price was high to help those in the cities. In this way the state would harmonize the price of grain over time and so constructively stabilize the relationship between sellers and buyers.

For MoZi harmony was more static; it lay in personal submission to a chain of command running up to Heaven through Imperial officialdom. MoZi's recommended harmony was closer to a fixed order than to a perpetually spontaneously self-regenerating equilibrium of influences and tendencies. Confucius took a middle position where virtuous individuals willed themselves to harmonious relationships with others through self-mastery and by following the norms of proper conduct. For him there was both a non-directed openness to the process of finding harmony and the conformity of specified, set behaviors upholding a social hierarchy. But under the influence of later writers, the concept of filial piety, articulated by Confucius, became the mainstay of imperial social conformity where strict obedience to the male heads of families was proposed as the highest form of harmony among people.

Corporate Social Responsibility (CSR) seeks to promote worthwhile behaviors within free markets where owners of private property make decisions as they see fit. Thus, CSR needs to accommodate its recommendations to the fluid, open social and political architecture of market mechanisms. CSR presumes autonomy in decision-making and not directive allocation of market power and opportunities. Thus, CSR needs a philosophy which can be internalized by decision-makers as influencing their choices among market alternatives. CSR demands a philosophy which is horizontal across market participants, and those affected by markets, not a vertical jurisprudence of hierarchical command and control.

Such an ethic is easily found among certain notable ancient Chinese writers. It is a harmony of checks and balances, of reciprocity, of blending in with circumstances. The resulting harmony is a dynamic equilibrium that results from self-considered, autonomous interactions, not a static one imposed as a template by a power center on subordinates. The harmony achieved again and again through reaching such equilibria is always on the edge of chaos should individual decision-makers pull away from sensible cooperation and reciprocity.

Finding such horizontal harmony parallels the CSR endeavor to align a firm constructively and profitably with its various stakeholders. A firm with monopoly or other forms of market power (rent seeking) finds itself in horizontal relationships of reciprocity and mutual advantage with its customers, employers, those who provide it with capital - short term and long, equity and debt, its suppliers, its interactions with competitors and the introduction of new technologies, with the environment, with civil society and with regulatory public power. A philosophy that promotes optimal engagement with such stakeholders brings CSR perspectives to a firm.

Five Elements/Yin-Yang

A very ancient and culturally pervasive Chinese approach to harmony as a fundamental expectation was articulated in the various studies of Qi, the energizing power that sustains creation in all its manifestations. Qi was believed to express itself in two primary states – Yin and Yang. Yin and Yang would combine in various mixtures to provide for the variety of things present in creation. The name given to the most influential of these combinations was the Five Elements – wood, fire, metal, water, and earth. Such combinations, and changes thereto, occurred in patterns and systems according to formulae and repetitive sequences. The flow of Qi through Yin and Yang and all the intermediate combinations brought balance and harmony to creation. When Qi could not flow properly, or one of its forces was too intense and so out of balance, disequilibria would occur and harmony would be lost. It would then be important to restore balance by bringing in an opposing force – Yin to offset Yang and vice-versa.

The Chinese calendar was designed to chart the cyclical flow of Qi through time, with each year dominated by a particular combination of Yin and Yang constraints. A short cycle took 60 lunar years to complete and a great cycle 360 such years. The beginning of each new year ushered in a new set of possibilities and probabilities conforming to the relative balance of Yin and Yang for that year. So, for example, a Dragon year would be more favorable to certain eventualities than a Monkey year while the activities likely to prosper in a Monkey year would not be so favored in a Dragon year.

Chinese medicine, including acupuncture, was developed to harmonize the flow of Qi within the body. Qi Gong emerged as a set of physical exercises designed similarly to open up the channels of Qi within the body to promote good health through the attainment of balanced flows and harmonized states of Qi.

Experts concluded that human affairs would prosper more robustly if aligned with powerful flows of Qi. Thus astrology was developed to ascertain good fortune along with opposing frustrations and setbacks as destined for an individual according to the alignment of his or her birth with the directions and potentials of Qi present at that moment. Feng Shui studied the flows and concentrations of Yin and Yang in the earth so that houses and tombs could be auspiciously located to draw upon sustaining energy at such a site.

Securing a harmonious alignment with great power brought about, so it was and is thought by many Chinese, more felicity and prosperity. Studying the flows of Qi in all its forms showed the best way forward to mastery of time and circumstance. The Qi made a path or Tao through time and space which, if found and followed, lead to fulfillment.

The Doctrine of the Mean

Perhaps the most classic statement of pursuing horizontal harmony was presented by the text known as the Doctrine of the Mean. This work is attributed to the grandson of Confucius.

The operative concept for harmony in the Doctrine of the Mean is walking a path, one set out by Heaven itself. Keeping to the path provides a course of centering that avoids extremes, which lie off the path. In Chinese the path is called the Tao, or way. It appears in the Doctrine of the Mean as a natural reality existing prior to human intention and always impervious to human contriving. Finding harmony is the mindful following of a natural spontaneity that twists and turns of its own accord.

To find and then follow the Tao, it is recommended by the Doctrine of the Mean that there be "no stirrings of pleasure, anger, sorrow or joy" so that the mind may be in a state of equilibrium. But when feelings are stirred, they should be kept in due degree which is harmony. Equilibrium is the great root of good actions while harmony is the universal path within which action should be confined. The text affirms: "Let the states of equilibrium and harmony exist in perfection, and a happy order will prevail throughout heaven and earth, and all things will be nourished and flourish." (Chapter I, 5) Keeping to equilibrium and harmony is the path of the Mean.

Thus, autonomy, individualism, working through interactions under the influence of a balanced mind, arrives at order. For enterprises, CSR concerns give balance to the means of seeking profit and advantage in keeping with this recommendation.

Previously, Confucius had said "Perfect is the virtue which is according to the Mean. … The virtuous person embodies the course of the Mean; the petty person acts contrary to the course of the Mean." (Chapter II) "The Tao is not far from man. When men try to pursue a course which is far from the common indications of consciousness, this course cannot be considered that of the Tao." (Chapter XII,4) "When one cultivates to the utmost the principles of his nature and exercises them on the principle of reciprocity, he is not far from the Tao." (Chapter XIII, 3)

Attaining to the Mean in our actions saps our energies. Thus, it is a demanding course but suited for those who can access reserves of will and strength. Confucius noted that a virtuous person cultivates harmony without being weak. "How firm he is in his strength! He stands erect in the middle without inclining to either side. How firm he is in his strength!" (Chapter X, 5)

At a later point, the Text provides a description of one who has attained great mastery of the openness and ego-control that permits following the Mean. It is a description of an excellent leader, even one in private business:

> Quick in apprehension, clear in discernment, of far-reaching intelligence and all-embracing knowledge; magnanimous, generous, benign and mild; assertive, energetic, firm and enduring; self-adjusted, grave, never swerving from the Mean and correct; accomplished, distinctive, concentrative, and searching (Chapter XXXI, I)

As would be appropriate for the circumstance, such a person is fitted to exercise rule, to forbear, maintain a firm hold, command reverence, and exercise discrimination. (ibid)

Following the path of the Mean is quite practical: "The way of a person of virtue may be compared to what takes place in travelling, when to go a distance we must first traverse the space that is near, and in ascending a height, we must begin from the lower ground." (Chapter XV, I) Thus, finding harmony demands taking into account our immediate surroundings and responding to them. We do not impose ourselves upon conditions. One should harmonize with the times of heaven above and below conform to the earth and the waters. (Chapter XXX, I)

The Tao Te Ching

The text of the Tao Te Ching is as explicit as the Doctrine of the Mean on the necessity for harmony to be natural and not contrived as a form of imposed social order. The text argues for an open submissiveness of self, overcoming ego-intentionality, as the way to harmony. Thus the person finds harmony by being empty and receptive to what comes along. The Tao is like an empty bowl: it blunts sharp edges, unties all tangles, harmonizes all lights, unites the world into one whole. Harmony emerges not from exertion and force but from acceptance. (Tao Te Ching 4)

"Heaven lasts long, and Earth abides. What is the secret of their durability? Is it not because they do not live for themselves that they can live so long?" (Tao Te Ching 6) The inference here is that by taking care of others, one best takes care of oneself. That insight, applied to business, supports the CSR approach to sustainable profitability. Taking care of stakeholders leads to success for the business.

> Difficult and easy complement each other. Long and short exhibit each other. High and low set measure to each other. Voice and sound harmonize each other. Back and front follow each other. (Tao Te Ching 2) Bend and you will be whole. Curl and you will be straight. Keep empty and you will be filled. Have little and you will gain. Have much and you will be confused. (Tao Te Ching 22)

Differences are not inconsistent with harmony according to the Tao Te Ching; they make harmonious outcomes possible.

What we make should be useful to others: "We make a vessel from a lump of clay; It is the empty space within the vessel that makes it useful. We make doors and windows for a room; but it is these empty spaces that make the room livable. Thus while the tangible has advantages, it is the intangible that makes it useful." (Tao Te Ching 11) Form and emptiness reciprocate one with the other to bring forth advantage naturally and harmoniously.

When a leader is successful and things have been accomplished, all the people say "We ourselves have achieved it." (Tao Te Ching 17) A hidden hand did not interfere with spontaneity and the work was done to the satisfaction of all. Just so should businesses benefit from market freedoms. "To tamper with it is to spoil it, and to grasp it is to lose it." (Tao Te Ching 29) "The use of the Tao consists in softness." (Tao Te Ching 39)

Relying on timeliness leads to fitting outcomes without striving or ordering events to come to pass: "In fact for all this there is a time for going ahead and a time for following behind; a time for slow-breathing and a time for fast breathing; a time to grow in strength and a time to decay; a time to be up and a time to be down." (Tao Te Ching 29) "In handling affairs people often spoil them just at the point of success. With heedfulness in the beginning and patience at the end, nothing will be spoiled." (Tao Te Ching 64) Mindful concentration leads to success without imposing one's power on others, leaving social space for achieving equilibrium among interested parties.

Mencius

Mencius, who forcefully argued for the Confucian vision of virtue against rival schools of thought, was most explicit on the possibility of achieving horizontal harmony:

Mencius famously scolded King Hui of Wei-Liang for seeking "profit" for his kingdom. Mencius advocated that, rather than seek for himself, the King should instead dispense humane actions and encourage structured social interactions. Mencius' was promoting the accumulation of forms of social capital so that individuals would be more prone to find success in their endeavors. Mencius understood that open systems where equilibria must emerge from free interactions demanded more social capital than did closed systems of command and control. The social capital promoted by Mencius, and by Confucius before him, was known as virtue (te) and embraced a range of beliefs and behaviors, including propriety and the moralization of the self. Mencius rejected the order imposed by hierarch to favor more freely chosen outcomes. He affirmed that human actions brought forth peace and security and that social reciprocity brought forth correctness, a form of harmonious equilibrium. (Bk IV, Part I, Chapt X, 2)

Mencius urged the king to dispense a benevolent government to the people, sparing in the use of punishments and fines, and making taxes and levies light so that private activity could flourish and fields would be plowed deep and the weeding of them carefully attended to. (Bk I, Part I, Chapt V, 3) More prosperity would result from individual initiative than from directed state interference in private lives. Governing by humane actions secures the tranquility – a state of harmony – for all under Heaven. (BkIV, Part I, Chapter 1, 1) "The people turn to rule by humane actions as water flows downhill and as wild beasts fly to the wilderness." (BkIV, Part I, Chpt IX, 2)

Even kings were to be chosen by some form of popular choice where openness would bring forth the most suited person for the position. (Bk V, part I, Chapter V) Beneficial results flowed from allowing people to seek their own equilibrium through mutual thoughtfulness. "When one subdues men by virtue, in their hearts' core they are pleased and sincerely submit..." (Bk II, Part I, Chapt V, 2) Order and harmony result from the use of virtue rather than force. "He who finds the proper course has many to assist him. He who loses the proper course has few to assist him." (Bk II, Part II, Chapter 1, 4)

Regarding optimal economic outcomes, Mencius was clear that free exchange brought about an equilibrium between buyers and sellers, makers and purchasers: "The getting those various articles in exchange for grain is not oppressive to the potter and the founder, and the potter and the founder in their turn in exchanging their various articles for grain are not oppressive to the farmer." (Bk III, Part I, Chpt IV, 5) If you do not have an intercommunication of the productions of labor, and an interchange of services, so that one from his surplus may supply the deficiency of another, the farmers will have a superfluity of grain and women will have a superfluity of cloth. (Bk III, Part II, Chapt IV, 3) If large shoes and small shoes were of the same price, who would make them?" (Bk III, Part I, Chapt V, 18)

Confucius

The recommendations of Confucius as presented in the Analects do not expressly discuss harmony as a primary normative goal for the just social order. But indirectly we may easily conclude that a valued outcome expected from his recommendations and observations was indeed a harmonious society.

For Confucius smooth ordering of society was an inevitable result of his prescriptions for ethical behavior. He presented a role specific concept of correct behavior under which, if each person should properly live out the responsibilities and obligations of his or her social status, there would be harmony among all. He believed strongly that there would be orderliness and not chaos if "a lord should lord, a minister minister, a father father and a son son" (Bk XII, Chapter XI, 2). Accordingly, the first task of those in authority was to "rectify names". (Bk XIII, Chapter III, 2) Language and names shaped behavior through prescription of the correct and proper behaviors attached to each status and position. He believed that "when agreements are made according to what is proper for each status, what is spoken can be made good". (Bk I, chpt XIII) When language and so social conventions aligned with actions, society would avoid discord and dysfunction, self-seeking and abuse of one by another.

The requirements of a position – lord, minister, father, son, etc. – set a mean for behavior such that one should neither fall short nor go too far of what was proper.

Social positions were set in relation one to another. Behaving properly towards another function or office, such as filial piety or brotherly affection, created balance and harmony among individuals. Confucius said accordingly that "reciprocity" would serve as the one word needed as a rule of practice for all one's life, adding that what one did not want done to oneself should not be done to others. (Bk XV, Chpt XXIII)

Such a prescription for social harmony demanded rigorous self control. Possession of such self-control was the virtue he called for in righteous individuals. One who aspired to superior achievement in this regard should give thoughtful consideration to seeing clearly, hearing distinctly, keeping the countenance benign, speaking sincerely, being reverently careful in business, anxiously questioning others about doubts, thinking of the difficulties that come with getting angry, and thinking of righteousness when gain can be got. Such a person would not ruffle feathers or cause disputes or fall short in the performance of duty. (BK XVI, Chpt X) Confucius believed that it was advantageous to arrange relationships so that there would be no litigations. (Bk XII, chpt XIII)

The person with virtue could subdue the self and return to propriety. The power of virtue permits such a person to look not at what is contrary to propriety; listen not to what is contrary to propriety; speak not what is contrary to propriety; make no movement which is contrary to propriety. This course of disciplined conduct leads to humane actions where the love of superiority, boasting, resentments and covetousness are repressed. (Bk XII, Chpt I, 1; Bk XIV, Chpt II, 1) One capable of acting humanely wishing to establish himself seeks also to establish others; wishing to be enlarged himself, seeks also to enlarge others. (BkVI, Chpt XXVIII, 2)

Propriety contributes to harmony in that it prevents boldness from becoming insubordination and straightforwardness from becoming rudeness. (Bk VIII, chpt II,1) Society will become more harmonious with such paragons present and active Confucius believed, for inferiors would conform to the role responsibilities of the more virtuous as "the grass must bend when the wind blows across it." (Bk XII, chpt XIX) If people are led by the power of virtue, and common rules of behavior given them by the stipulated norms of propriety, they will have a sense of shame and will become good, leading to mutuality and social harmony. (Bk II, chpt III, 2)

Since what such a virtuous person seeks is in himself and not in others, virtue and propriety lead one to living in harmony with others. (BkXV, Chpt XX) Such a virtuous person cultivates himself so as to give rest to others. (BkXIV, chpt XLV) The man of virtue will consider righteousness to be essential and will not live at the expense of injuring his virtue. (Bk XV, ChptVIII; BkXV, Chpt XVII) The person animated by the power of virtue does not set his mind either for or against anything; what is his duty to others he will follow. (BkIV, chpt X) Not to be dutiful reflects a lack of courage. (Bk II, Chpt XXIV, 2)

Confucius accepted the proposition that sincerely holding fast to the Mean would forestall distress in society and that going beyond is as wrong as falling short. (Bk XX, chpt I, 1; Bk XI, chpt XV, 3)

MoZi

While the central thrust of MoZi's jurisprudence was a centralized hierarchy of command and control as necessary for order and peace in human affairs, he coupled this recommendation with a horizontal ethic he called jian ai or "universal love". Universal love was to be promoted, MoZi urged, in order that individuals would live in peace and harmony with one another. His assessment was that if selfish egoism were replaced by magnanimity, there would be no conflicts. The cause of disorder, Mo Zi wrote, was the want of mutual love. "As he loves himself and not his father, the son benefits himself to the disadvantage of his father. When the father loves only himself and not the son, he benefits himself to the disadvantage of the son." (Universal Love I) Mo Zi desired that everyone should love universally, without ego centricity, "loving others as oneself". "Now, since partiality against one another is the cause of the major calamities in the empire, then partiality is wrong." (Universal Love, III)

"When nobody in the world", he wrote, "loves any other, naturally the strong will overpower the weak, the many will oppress the few, the wealthy will mock the poor, the honored will disdain the humble, the cunning will deceive the simple." (Universal Love, II) But if Universal Love were to prevail, then, he concluded: states would not attach each other, houses would not disturb each other, thieves and robbers would become extinct; emperor and ministers, fathers and sons, all would become affectionate and filial.

Guan Zi

Guan Zi, a great minister in the feudal state of Qi, left a practical manual of statecraft. While his aim was to reinforce the power of the prince, he accepted the reality that a prince could not direct events and so had to ride along the ebbs and flows of circumstance, an echo of a Five Elements/Yin Yang approach to living.

"Of the former kings, those who used one Yin and two Yang became shogans, Those who used pure Yang became kings. Those who used one Yang and two Yin declined. And those who used nothing but pure Yin perished." (p.221)

So for example, the Guan Zi text note that social relationships are reciprocal in an echo of Confucius and cannot be commanded: "If the father and mother are unfailingly compassionate, the son and his wife will be obedient. ... If the father and mother are cruel and lacking in graciousness, the son and his wife will not treat them as parents." (p. 61)

Heaven maintains flourishing in the world through its constant activities – the successive states of Yin and Yang operative energies. "When activities are properly carried out, there is order; when they are neglected, there is disorder." (p. 63) So, for example, as long as Earth does not alter its regular activities, all things will have life." (ibid)

In line with Mencius, the Guan Zi text recognizes that a ruler may not impose himself on the people: hierarchy arises when people willingly submit in a process similar to that arising among horizontal relationships seeking mutual indulgence. "When the speech of

the ruler of men conforms to principle and accords with the sentiments of the people, the people will accept his instructions." (p.66)
"People follow after benefits just as water runs downhill. Therefore
those who wish to make the people come must first initiate benefits
for them. Then, even though not summoned, the people will arrive
by themselves." (p. 71) Order and harmony in the realm will spontaneously arise from the uncoordinated actions of people following
their natural instincts. "When the Tao is followed, the prince and
his ministers have a close relationship, fathers and sons feel secure,
and all living things are nurtured." (p.68) "When one adheres to
the way of Heaven, all his or her undertakings will appear to be
spontaneous." (p. 82) "Therefore, "contrived goodness is not goodness." (p.218)

The way is manifested in a person in the heart/mind. Thus,
obtaining order through spontaneous individual action demands
that each individual cultivate the fitting mental orientation to self
and life. (p. 216)

Han Feizi

Han Feizi wrote that "Tao is the beginning of the myriad things,
the standard of right and wrong... Therefore by resting empty and
reposed, one waits for the course of nature to enforce itself so that
all names will be defined of themselves and all affairs will be settled
of themselves." (Vol I, p. 31) "Let roosters herald the dawn and let
cats watch for rats." (Vol. p. 53)

Han Feizi advice was directed to rulers so that they could successfully use the workings of Tao to augment their power and control. He took a horizontal principle of spontaneity and used it to
enforce a vertical command structure centered on a ruler who followed the Tao and not his own pleasures and whims.

Han Feizi saw that the law functioned in imitation of the Tao
– standing above human partiality as a kind of Mean that should
not be abandoned to the left or to the right., neither unreached
nor overpassed. So, for example, he recommended to rulers that
"the intelligent sovereign makes the law select men and makes

no arbitrary promotion himself." (Vol I, p. 40) "Though he has a mouth of his own, he never speaks for his own advantage; though he has eyes of his own, he never sees for his private interest." (ibid)

The forms of Chinese ethical thought that seek to promote horizontal harmonizing through dynamic equilibriums of agreement and interest provide as well a philosophy for contemporary corporate social responsibility.

Strategic CSR understands that the profitability of any business turns on successful engagement with key stakeholders, especially with customers, employees, owners, creditors and suppliers. Putting those relationships on a basis of mutuality and interdependence enhances the reliability of firm profits over time. A dynamic harmony coordinating the firm with its stakeholders becomes a strategic goal for business success. Obligations of reciprocity with and respect towards others coincide with self-interest in making profits.

A Chinese framework for CSR of seeking harmony is suitable and will bring advantage to the enterprise.

Tao Te Ching and Sustainability

The Tao Te Ching text of philosophical Taoism is perhaps our most elegant statement of a fundamental approach to sustainability. It articulates a stance towards decision-making that is designed to enhance sustainability at every level of being. The translation I have used in this short commentary is that of Dr. John C. H. Wu. But I have used the concept of an "enlightened one" for my purposes in construing the teachings of the Tao Te Ching where Dr. Wu used as is traditional and literal the word "sage" to refer to the one who can act in alignment with the Tao.

The most current definition of sustainability is perhaps that found in ISO 26000 which advocates sustainability as the fundamental framework for all organizational endeavors, both public and private. Sustainable development is development that meets the needs of the present without compromising the ability of future generations to meet their own needs. Sustainable development is about integrating the goals of a high quality of life, health and prosperity with social justice and maintaining the earth's capacity to support life in all its diversity. These social, economic and environmental goals are interdependent and mutually reinforcing. Sustainable development can be treated as a way of expressing the broader expectations of society as a whole.

At the most cosmic the Tao Te Ching seeks to protect life itself from degradation and abuse at human hands. Optimal living should follow only the Tao, which is beyond human capacity to define, explain, or regulate. Most simply put, the Tao cannot be named; it cannot be subjugated to purposes formed by human cognition and the categories of human meaning. (The Tao that can be named is not the eternal Tao. Tao Te Ching 1 The eternal Tao has no name. ... When once the primal simplicity diversified, different names appeared. Are there not enough names now? Tao Te Ching 32) That which energizes and embodies the Tao persists to the maximum extent possible given that the Tao is the outmost limits of the possible. The the Tao itself is the ultimate in what can be sustained; in what goes on forever and ever; it what does not decay.

That which goes against the Tao meets resistance, generates friction, and suffers from entropy to find its way blocked and truncated, cut short and thwarted. Going against the Tao simply is not sustainable according to the assertions of the Tao Te Ching.

The Tao Te Ching text does not present an argument; it is not an essay nor an exposition of formal propositions linked through the logical connections of meaning in the words used. The Tao Te Ching seeks to educate us through metaphor. It gives us factuals and invites us to use insight and intuition to reach for an understanding of reality that corresponds with the factual presented. From the point of view of the author of the Tao Te Ching, truth is not propositional; it is not in words trying to express ideas and abstract conceptions; truth about reality is only in the mind of reader as he or she forms intuitive understandings of what is. Language in this Taoist tradition is only a sign pointing to reality. Its power to convey truth about ultimate truth should not be overestimated. It is much more

THE ROAD TO MORAL CAPITALISM

valuable when use for a more limited purpose – expressing human conceptions at the level of human culture and purpose.

A striking metaphor for not going against the Tao is provided by chapter of the Chuang Tzu Text, a companion to the Tao Te Ching. The example given is sustainability of a knife blade. By following the natural order by which an ox is constituted, a knife can carve an ox and never lose its edge. Not just one ox, but innumerable oxen without encountering dullness.

Keep on beating and sharpening a sword, and the edge cannot be preserved for long. (Tao Te Ching 9)

To be one with the Tao is to abide forever. (Tao Te Ching 16)

Individual

Many of the segments of the Tao Te Ching provide advice for sustaining the self, the individual person. Since the core of any human self is psychological, the Tao Te Ching is partly a text on psychological realities. It provides guidance as to how a person can be so mindful that no weariness comes on, no sense of ennui, no angst accumulates, and no afflicting emotions arise to wear down will and spirit, setting off depression, jealously, or other self-destructive propensities.

This is sustainability of the person.

A core conundrum in understanding sustainability of the self lies in the Taoist metaphor of emptiness. To be empty in the Taoist sense is, when properly understood, is to be resilient and survivable. So, it is not a literal emptiness where there would be no person at all, but a kind of emptiness that makes a person suitable for fitting in – as the emptiness of a cup or bowl gives it meaning and purpose and provides for its being a constant. It takes in and does not impose itself. (The Tao is like an empty bowl. Tao Te Ching 4)

Between Heaven and Earth there seems to be a bellows; It is empty and yet it is inexhaustible; the more it works, the more comes out of it. No amount of words can fathom it; Better look for it within you. (Tao Te Ching 5)

We make a vessel from a lump of clay; it is the empty space within the vessel that makes it useful. We make doors and windows for a room; but it is these empty spaces that make the room livable. Thus, while the tangible has advantages, it is the intangible that makes it useful. (Tao Te Ching 11)

He who keeps the Tao does not want to be full. But precisely because he is never full, he can always remain like a hidden sprout, and does not rush to early ripening. (Tao Te Ching 15) The Tao Te Ching assumes here that we will remember that early ripening leads to early harvesting. For to be over developed is to hasten decay, and this is against Tao, and what is against Tao will soon cease to be. (Tao Te Ching 30) When one is out of life, one is in death. (Tao Te Ching 50) The Tao Te Ching instructs us in how to sustain our living.

Attain to utmost emptiness. Cling single-heartedly to interior peace. (Tao Te Ching 16) The practice of Tao consists in daily diminishing. Keep on diminishing and diminishing until you reach the state of No-Ado. No-ado and yet nothing is left undone. (Tao Te Ching 48)

As for the Tao itself, it is nowhere in our world of sense: grasp it but you cannot get it. (Tao Te Ching 14) And yet it contains within itself a core of vitality, which is very real. (Tao Te Ching 21) Accessing that vitality opens the way to personal sustainability in life.

An individual whose mind is "empty" in this Taoist sense, does not contest, does not strive, but receives whatever there is to receive. It is a peaceful, symbiotic relationship with the surrounding environment, a relationship that gives rise to no tension or cause for alarm. It fears nothing and gives rise to no fear in others. It is sustainable in the flow of events and circumstances.

Such a mind sets no store by anything in particular; such a mind draws not discriminations and distinctions between "this" and "that" but, somehow, accepts all things as they are: just as the Tao itself does in its operations. Thus: Heaven and earth have no human sentimentality; they treat all things as straw dogs. (Tao Te Ching 5) Straw dogs were models of dogs made of straw to be burnt up in funeral ceremonies. A non-judging mind is an empty mind from the Taoist perspective but it is still an active mind, actively keeping itself from falling into temptation and making discriminations.

Closely following the metaphor of emptiness is the state of wu wei – or non action. Well not exactly a complete absence of action, a complete passivity, just as emptiness is still state of reality, a state of being. Emptiness is not nothingness. To wu wei is then to avoid a kind of intentionality, a confronting, a striving, an imposition of personal ideals and desires, an assertion of dominion over others and over things.

In gathering your vital energy to attain suppleness, have you reached the state of a new born babe? (Tao Te Ching 10)

The Tao Te Ching asserts that imposing yourself by not imposing yourself (wei wu wei) puts everything in regular order. (Tao Te Ching 3)

Therefore the enlightened one gets things done through wu wei and spreads his teachings without talking. He denies nothing to the teeming things. He rears them but lays no claim to them. He does his work, but sets no store by it. (Tao Te Ching 2)

Heaven lasts long and Earth abides. What is the secret of their durability? Is it not because they do not live for themselves that they can live so long? … Is it not because the enlightened one is selfless that he Self is realized? (Tao Te Ching 7)

This is achieving permanence for oneself through the use of Taoist accommodation. We ourselves become more sustainable by sustaining that around us in which we find ourselves. The self, according to this understanding of reality, is dependent on the non-self for its progress through life, space, and time. And at the ultimate essence of the non-self is the Tao. For the self to strive, to seek to overcome through greed and force, would be to cut short its life possibilities by putting it at odds with what it needs for sustainability.

The highest form of goodness is like water. Water knows how to benefit all things without striving with them. It stays in places loathes by all men. Therefore, it comes near the Tao. (Tao Te Ching 8) The great Tao is universal like a flood. How can it be turned to the right or to the left? All creatures depend on it. And it denies nothing to anyone. It does its work, but it makes no claim for itself. It clothes and fees all, but it does not lord it over them. ... All things return to it as to their home, but it does not lord it over them. ... It is just because it does not wish to be great that its greatness is fully realized. (Tao Te Ching 34)

An empty accommodating mind keeps its distance from wealth and power. Sustainability of self depends on keeping away from the means of imposing one's will on the Tao through acts of wei.

Fill your house with gold and jade, and it can no longer be guarded. Set store of your riches and honor, and you will only reap a crop of calamities. (Tao Te Ching 9).

What in the end is to be weakened, begins by being first made strong. What is in the end to be thrown down, begins by being first set on high. What is in the end to be despoiled, beings by being frint richly endowed. (Tao Te Ching 36)

The enlightened one prefers what is within to what is without. (Tao Te Ching 12) See the simple and embrace the primal, diminish the self and curb the desires. (Tao Te Ching 19) Have little and you will gain. Have much and you will be confused. (Tao Te Ching 22) He who knows when he has enough is rich. (Tao Te Ching 33)

An excessive love for anything will cost you dear in the end. The storing up of too much goods will entail a heavy loss. To know when you have enough is to be immune from disgrace. To know when to stop is to be preserved from perils. Only thus can you endure long. (Tao Te Ching 44) There is no calamity like not knowing what is enough. There is no evil like covetousness. Only he who knows what is enough will always have enough. (Tao Te Ching 46)

He who fusses over anything spoils it. He who grasps anything loses it. (Tao Te Ching 64)

The Natural World

The Tao Te Ching text provides for the sustainability of the natural world by implication. It was written at a time when human capacity could do little to change or effect the course of nature.

There was no industrialization, no mass consumption of consumer products, no electricity, no great release of greenhouse gases from human activity, no cutting away of vast forest acreages, no over-fishing of the oceans, no walking on the moon or splitting of atoms.

Its prescription for sustainability of our natural environment comes from extending its teachings for individuals as to how to sustain themselves and for rulers as to how to sustain the societies under their watchful eyes.

The doctrine of environmental sustainability to be drawn from the Tao Te Ching is one of keeping to the simple and to the sufficient. It is a doctrine of enough-ness, of not going too far in seeking possessions and enjoying consumption. The enlightened one avoids all extremes, excesses and extravagances. (Tao Te Ching 29) He who keeps the Tao does not want to be full. (Tao Te Ching 15)

The danger to nature foreseen by the Tao Te Ching comes from human striving and the application by humans to their actions of human distinctions and preferences. So: when all the world recognizes beauty as beauty, this in itself is ugliness. When all the world, recognizes good as good, this in itself is evil. (Tao Te Ching 2) Standards of beauty and good are human inventions. They do not come from the Tao which, of course, makes no distinctions and treats all things as "straw dogs". What people take to be beautiful, they seek to grab and possess and their greedy striving becomes something ugly. Just so, what people take for good, sets them at each other in exploitation and seeking of what they have defined as desirable and that activity contrary to Tao becomes evil.

By implication then, if humanity were to have no standards of beauty and good, it would be less intent on exploitation of the natural order of Heaven and Earth, which, in consequence, would be more sustainable.

The Tao Te Ching advises that humanity should follow the natural laws of Earth, which follow the natural laws of Heaven, which follow the Tao, which follows its own laws. (Tao Te Ching 25) Thus, it is not the place of humanity to upset or manipulate for its own purposes the natural ebb and flow of earthly creation.

The Taoist mind considering how to use the environment never loses its sense of wonder and repose.

The world is a sacred vessel, which must not be tampered with or grabbed after. To tamper with it is to spoil it, and to grasp it is to lose it. (Tao Te Ching 29)

When Tao prevails, Heaven and Earth are harmonized and send down sweet dew. (Tao Te Ching 32) In other words, when Tao prevails, the natural course of events is beneficial and nourishing, sustaining and providential. It would therefore behoove humanity not to tamper with the Tao, which demands self-restraint and timely moderation. In handling affairs, people often spoil them just at the point of success. With heedfulness in the beginning and patience at the end, nothing will be spoiled. (Tao Te Ching 64)

The Tao is hidden and nameless; yet it alone knows how to render help and to fulfill. (Tao Te Ching 41) The way of Heaven is to benefit. (Tao Te Ching 81) Too benefit is to make the other more sustainable, to empower and uplift. It is not to overly consume and hoard for personal satisfaction according to personal standards of right and wrong, beauty and melody, pride and honor. That is to wei and is the common error of humanity.

Subordinating nature to socialization, subjecting it to human vanity, would be contrary to Tao.

The enlightened one denies nothing to the teeming things. (Tao Te Ching 2) The highest form of goodness is like water. Water knows how to benefit all things without striving with them. (Tao Te Ching 8) Such intentionality would never have humanity striving with its natural environment but rather seeking to live in sustainable harmony with it. Humanity, if it followed the Tao, would contribute to the flourishing of nature and not be its enemy and its exploiter only.

The enlightened one is "always good at saving things, and therefore nothing is wasted.: (Tao Te Ching 27) Waste, a common by-product of human use of the environment, is misuse of nature and so contrary to the Tao. We should rather consume in ways that are moderate and cycled so that there is no waste on different uses that sustain other uses in a natural order of life.

Tao is to give life, not death. (Tao Te Ching 51) Through virtue it nurses, grows things, fosters them, shelters them, comforts them, nourishes them, and covers them with its wings. This set forth a maternal standard of caretaking that, when applied to the natural environment, would seek to achieve its continuous sustainability.

Aristotle

Aristotle's observations on the dynamics of what he considered to be the most natural political community for our species focus on the word "economy".

Aristotle essentially made the same disparaging distinction between the real economy and financial markets that is now in vogue after Wall Street's meltdown in 2008. What Aristotle called the "oikos" was management of the family's well-being; it was family management, a kind of entrepreneurial calling seeking better conditions for members of the entity through work and exchange.

Property is an instrument to living, says Aristotle and therefore necessary and desirable. A fair point for those of us who believe in free regimes of wealth creation. One can easily skip over his defense of slaves as legitimate property as that kind of subjugation is, thankfully, irrelevant to our current social and economic arrangements.

But then Aristotle makes a distinction between two kinds of property – one which we get from nature to sustain our lives and another which we create to facilitate our interpersonal relationships not from nature but from our promises to one another. The first includes things like wood, animals, tools, stones for houses, yarn for weaving, grapes for eating, etc., and the second is money.

There are limits to what we can get from nature, but, since money is created by society, there is no end to the amount of money we can aspire to collect. Aristotle doesn't like the impact of money.

Exchanges by barter, he notes, are limited by what nature provides and by what our labor and inventiveness can cull and stimulate from natural environments. Barter, however, he asserts, led to the invention of money. What is different about money Aristotle says is that its value is set by convention. It has no intrinsic use value;

only an exchange value and keeps that value only as long as people agree to accept it in payment for goods and services. It is a convention of human society.

Aristotle writes: "Money, then being established as the necessary medium of exchange, another species of money-getting soon took place, namely, by buying and selling, at probably first in a simple manner, afterwards with more skills and experience, where and how the greatest profits might be made. For which reason the art of money getting seems to be chiefly conversant about trade, and the business of it to be able to tell where the greatest profits can be made, being the means of procuring abundance of wealth and possessions; and thus wealth is very often supposed to consist in the quantity of money which any one possesses...."

Money, he says is the first principle and the end of trade; nor are there any bounds to be set to what is thereby acquired. "Thus in the art of acquiring riches, there are no limits, for the object of that is money and possessions; but economy has a boundary."

Economy, he writes, does require the possession of wealth, not for the hoarding of money but for the acquisition of other things. But money, on the other hand, seems to be an end in itself as many think the proper end of economy is to save and hoard money without end. Such people, says Aristotle seek to live, but they do not live well.

Such persons make everything subservient to money getting, as if this was the only end. Money getting is not necessary to the good life, says Aristotle, but economy is.

Aristotle's argument today seems unsophisticated but his insight into money nevertheless deserves attention. Where money is concerned as the end of human activity, a unique set of rules apply. There is no limit built into money or to money getting that tells us to stop, that our goal has been reached, that we have enough already. As a mega-millionaire recently responded to the question of whether or not he had enough money: "You can never have too much money."

With the invention of money, separate from economy of production and provision of services, hubris – that vicious appetite which drives our destinies to destruction - enters in to our pursuit of wealth and sound discretion beats a retreat.

This distinction between commodity trading markets in money and an economy constrained by factors of production such as land, labor and credit-worthiness raises an important policy question: can the confidence we have in self-regulation of economic markets be transferred to financial markets? Can a fixation on financial private goods lead to appropriate enjoyment of necessary and proper public goods?

I would say, no, it can't. Adam Smith's conceit of an invisible hand set in motion by self-interested private transactions but tending towards a public good seems more fit for the natural economy of Aristotle where there are limits and constraints than it does for financial markets where the socialized supply of money and credit is seemingly endless and the desire for the good of socially legitimated purchasing power pushes demand curves to irrational highs.

Thus, reflecting on Aristotle, we could imagine a less restrictive regulatory regime for the real economy and more controls on financial markets to confront the effects of hubris when it is really running wild with anticipation and imagination.

The efficient market hypothesis on the capacity of financial markets to find stable equilibriums of value does not seem to be accurate. Again and again, financial markets have not found themselves able to bring about a necessary equilibrium of prices at sustainable and reliable asset valuations. More than markets are needed to prevent major discontinuities in the amplitudes of price curves in financial trading.

Federal Reserve Chairman William McChesney Martin is famous for saying that the point of monetary and credit regulation is to "take away the punch bowl just as the party gets going". Aristotle would have approved.

Wall Street collapsed because it became obsessed with what Aristotle calls "money-getting". The punch bowl of earning very lucrative fees and bonuses kept getting topped-up. To think as many of the most highly educated and most highly compensated did on Wall Street that risk would just go away is true hubris.

Risk is, however, an Aristotelian phenomenon of the natural, "real" economy and sets limits on acquisitiveness. Risk can't be eliminated though social contrivances such as money or CDOs or CDSs. Reality is always the nemesis to human hubris.

The problem with markets for money is that they have no wise checks against hubris – a more classical term for what Alan Greenspan famously called "irrational exuberance." Hubris is also the core fault with people suffering from the Agency Problem. From the Tulip mania of 1636 to the 2008 meltdown of Wall Street, good old plain vanilla human hubris has upset financial markets again and again to the great loss of ordinary people who depend for their happiness on the natural "economy".

We would have been better off, I suggest, paying more attention to Aristotle in designing rules for Wall Street. We should have put a socially contrived nemesis in place to check the advance of our self-empowering hubris before it could do great damage by drawing upon itself a natural opposition to unending greed.

Qur'anic Guidance for Moral Decision-Making

The Qur'an teaches us that the power that we hold – personal, economic, political, cultural - is a trust that should not be abused. Giving in to the temptations that create the Agency Problem is against Qur'anic guidance.

The Qur'an reveals a proper destiny for humanity in that it should be wisely responsible in the use of power. It presents six inter-related aspects of that destiny, which are the nature of humanity, the assumption of trust responsibility, the office of khal fah, the necessity of wise discernment, the use of good counsel, and the seeking of justice.

First, the Qur'an teaches that each human is born possessing something of God's life force. According to the Qur'an, God provided humans with remarkable potential by breathing into the first created human some holy spirit. "We created man from dry clay, from black moulded loam, and before him Satan from smokeless fire. Your Lord said to the angels: 'I am creating man from dry clay, from black moulded loam. When I have fashioned him and breathed of My spirit into him, kneel down and prostrate yourselves before him." (Qur'an 15:29) "But He fashioned him in due proportion, and breathed into him something of His spirit. And He gave you the faculties of hearing and sight and feelings. Little thanks do you give!" (Qur'an 32:9) "We have honored the sons of Adam; provided them with transport on land and sea; given them for sustenance things good and pure; and conferred unto them special favors, above a great part of Our Creation." (Qur'an 17:70) "We created man in a most noble image ...." (Qur'an 95:4)

God therefore not just made human persons in the image of God but with some of his life force within each created human. Humans, according to the Qur'an are specially created by God to serve a divine purpose: "I am placing on the earth one that shall rule as my deputy" (Qur'an 2:30) Thus, all human persons are possessed with something of the Creator's energy, will, capacity and purpose. We have the possibility of being "godlings". But the gift of God's powers and spirit comes with a condition: such energies and capacities are to be used on a restricted basis for set, limited purposes. Our special status as possessing something of God's essence is not to be misconstrued as justification for our seeking to rival God as a master being. By no means. (Qur'an 59:12; 96:6)

Of course, the Qur'an is most explicit at how easily humanity turns from its higher potential to acts of unrighteousness because of temptation, or excessive pride, narrow fixations, lack of patience or too much sensuality. "Indeed, Man transgresses in thinking himself his own master" (Qur'an 96:7). "Man's soul is always prone to selfishness, but if you do good and are God-fearing, then surely God is aware of the things you do". (Qur'an, 4:128) "O David, We did indeed make you vicegerent on earth: so judge you between men in truth and justice and not follow the lusts of your heart, for they will mislead you from the Path of God: for those who wander astray from the Path of God, is a grievous penalty, for that they forget the Day of Judgment." (Qur'an, 38: 26)

Thus the Qur'an recognizes the probable emergence among people of the Agency Problem.

Second, the Qur'an relates that humanity accepted God's offer of executing a trust for the betterment of creation. The abilities and potentials that the Creator afforded to humanity and to each human being, the Qur'an teaches, are given in trust – am nah – so that God's purposes can be served on earth. "We offered this trust to the heavens and the earth and the mountains but they refused to bear it and were afraid of it, the but man undertook to bear it. Indeed, he is unjust and ignorant". (Qur'an, 33:72) "Believers! Do not be unfaithful to God and the Messenger, nor be knowingly unfaithful to your trusts." (Qur'an, 8:27) "God brought you out of your mothers' wombs in this state that you knew nothing: He gave you ears and eyes and thinking minds so that you may be grateful." (Qur'an, 16:78) "Do not follow that of which you have no knowledge for you shall be questioned for (the use) of your eyes, ears and minds." (Qur'an, 17:36)

Any concept of trust implicates goods of a mixed private/public quality. They might be quasi-private or quasi-public in character. They are private as they don't belong to any public entity, they are not part of the forma res publica, and they can be owned by private individuals with full rights to possess, use and dispose. But they must be used with a view to the interests of others who are dependent or beneficiaries or who must rely to their detriment on the wise use of such goods or services.

Of course, trust can be abused and many passages of the Qur'an discuss how humans do and most likely will abuse the various am nah given to them by God. According to Qur'an, evil doers are those who "break [God's] covenant after accepting it, and put asunder what He has bidden to be united, and perpetrate corruption in the land." (Qur'an 2:27) "If, after all the knowledge you have been given, you yield to their desires, then you will surely become an evil-doer" (Qur'an 2:145) "If you obeyed the greater part of those on earth, they would lead you away from God's path. They follow nothing but idle fancies and preach nothing but falsehoods." (Qur'an 6:116) "And there are some among them who twist their tongues when quoting the Scriptures so that you may think it is from the Scriptures, whereas it is not from the Scriptures." (Qur'an 3:78) "Do not devour one another's property by unjust means, nor bribe the judges with it in order that you may wrongfully and knowingly usurp the possessions of other men." (Qur'an 2:188) "Believers, do not live on usury, doubling your wealth many times over." (Qur'an 3:130) "God does not love aggressors". (Qur'an 2:190) "...vanity carries them off to sin ... do not walk in Satan's footsteps; ..." Qur'an 2:206, 2:208) "Do not make God, when you swear by Him, a means to prevent you from dealing justly, from guarding yourselves against evil, and from making peace among men." (Qur'an 2:224) "Men are tempted by the lure of women and offspring, of hoarded treasures of gold and silver, of splendid horses, cattle and plantations. These are the enjoyments of this life." (Qur'an 3:14) "God does not love arrogant and boastful men, who are themselves tight-fisted and enjoin others to be tight-fisted; who conceal the riches which God of His bounty has bestowed upon them ... and who spend their wealth for ostentation." (Qur'an 4:36,37) "Whoever recommends and helps in a good cause becomes a partner therein: and whoever recommends and helps an evil cause, shares in its burden." (Qur'an 4:85) "So do not be lead by passion, lest you swerve from the truth." (Qur'an 4:135) "Do not allow your hatred for other men to turn you away from justice." (Qur'an 5:8)

The goal of our amanah is to serve God as khalifah. We are here for God's purposes not only for our own. This precludes our selfish abuse of power or our acting haughtily from a warped sense of personal dominion.

God commands you to deliver trusts to those worthy of them; and when you judge between people, to judge with justice. (Qur'an, 4:5859)

Economic power, the power of ownership, of decision-making in business are noteworthy as capable of being held in trust. Under Anglo-American Common Law and corporate statutes, corporate directors and employees of companies are fiduciaries. In Qur'anic terms, they hold their powers as an amanah.

Third, the Qur'an reveals that the office holding the am nah given to humanity is that of khal fah, or vice-regent for God on earth. "Just recall the time when your Lord said to the angels, I am going to appoint a vicegerent on the Earth." (Qur'an, 2:30) The role and responsibilities of serving as khal fah are not to be under-stood as reserved for only one person seeking to govern the Muslim Ummah, but as expectations for each human to contribute to the achievement of God's right order. "O David, We did indeed make you vicegerent on earth: so judge you between men in truth and justice and not follow the lusts of your heart, for they will mislead you from the Path of God:" (Qur'an, 38: 26)

An important distinction can be made between the image of human persons as agents of God – as khalifah – and an image of human persons as masters in their own right as a challenge to God's dominion. Under Qur'anic guidance, each person is designed to be a true agent of a higher principal, not merely a selfish seeker of personal advantage and superiority. The role of khalifah, something more than beasts but yet less than God, is as subordinate as an appoin-tee and delegate who must turn for powers and direction to the prin-cipal and master. "Did you not know that God has sovereignty over the heavens and the earth?" (Qur'an 5:40) And, correspondingly, humanity is not to pick from within its own ranks those who will be given any such sovereign status. (Qur'an 96:9) "He is God besides whom there is no other deity." (Qur'an 59:21) Humanity was given its proportion and form by God alone. (Qur'an 82:7,8) Mankind was created only to worship God, not itself. (Qur'an 51:56)

The Qur'an instructs that if we succumb to the Agency Problem of being faithless agents due to our hubris and self-absorption, thinking that we can be God's equivalent in setting forth goals and purposes for the world, then we fail his command and do not live up to his expectations. In creating people, Qur'an reveals, God installed in us a capacity to rise about the Agency Problem. Whether we do or not is our existential challenge in this life.

Qur'an provides us with a suitable framework for so understanding the human person, and that is the fact of fitra, or our essential orientation towards life. That orientation is to be able to be moral, ethical and responsible; to listen and to cooperate; to be fair and just and control our worst instincts and passions. We were shaped by God, Qur'an instructs, to receive his teachings and have it in our power to live as we should. The operation of our fitra permits us to subordinate our will – appropriately – to a common authority, a public government.

Fourth, the Qur'an requires that, as each human executes his or her aminah and serves God as khalifah, he or she must use some of what has been given as part of the aminah – the capacity to observe, think, reason and judge – in order to take proper and correct action. One of the important capacities given to human persons by God is this faculty of ijtihad, or reasoning about reality and truth. Ijtihad is needed by human persons to distinguish between conjecture and truth. (Qur'an 10:36) "The meanest beasts in God's sight are those that are deaf, dumb, and devoid of reason." (Qur'an 8:22) Such beings have no capacity to discern truth or use ijtihad. How could they possibly serve God as a steward on earth, attending to his bounty and acting with moral purpose?

"We sent the former Messengers with clear Signs and Books, and now We have sent the Admonition to you (O Muhammad!), so that you should make plain and explain to the people the teachings of the Book which has been sent for them; and so that they (themselves) should ponder over it." (Qur'an, 16:44) "And We bestowed the same favour upon David and Solomon: Remember the occasion when the two were judging a case regarding a field into which the goats of other people had strayed at night, and We Ourself were watching their conduct of the case. At that time We guided Solomon to the right decision, though We had bestowed wisdom and knowledge upon both of them." (Qur'an, 21:78-79

The capacity of ijtihid, or practical application of the human mind to the events and circumstances of reality, was given, it seems,

in order that an individual's khalifahship can be successfully undertaken with wise use of all the various am nah held by that person.

Qur'an teaches that each individual person has the capacity
of ijtihad - reasoning from premises to conclusion, thinking wisely
about consequences, making ethical decisions, solving problems,
etc. As noted above, Qur'an warns us to beware of vanity, passion
and of hatred, precisely because such emotions have power to
turn us away from truth and justice. We reach truth through our
minds used rightly; we obtain justice when our reason keeps our
passions in check. Qur'an says: "Some there are who would indulge
in frivolous talk, so that they may without knowledge lead men
away from the path of God and hold it up to ridicule." (Qur'an
31:6) Knowledge, the capacity of our mind to seek and discern that
which is without us, that which is true and false, then is the path to
God. Without a capacity for reflection, comprehension, personal
judgment, how can we draw closer to God's will and purpose? What
would be the point of revealing a Qur'an if human persons had no
capacity to read and understand its words and its meaning? Qur'an
states that "God forgives those who commit evil in ignorance and
then quickly turn to Him in penitence." (Qur'an 4:17) Possession
of ijtihad enables us to become as God wants us to be, to rise from
ignorance and to learn when repentance is necessary. The capacity
of using right reason in restraint of our passions and desires and to
guide our wills according to known standards of right and wrong
enables us to become our best. "We have revealed it thus so that
We may sustain your heart. We have imparted it to you by grad-
ual revelation. No sooner will they come to you with an argument
than we shall reveal to you the truth, better expounded." (Qur'an
25:32) Qur'an was thus given to humanity in a process of dialectic
and response of one proposition to another, engaging humanity
in its capacity for understanding. "He that received wisdom is rich
indeed, but none will grasp the message except men of understanding." (Qur'an 2:269)

What would be the point of divine guidance if human persons
had no capacity to receive it, understand it, and, most importantly,

apply it to the conditions and circumstances of life as they change and unfold from day to day? It is our capacity for possessing and using wisdom and our mental faculties that is the receptacle that corresponds to the outpouring of guidance from God in Qur'an and in other signs from which humanity can learn the truth. "Indeed he that chooses Satan that than God for his protector ruins himself beyond redemption." (Qur'an 4:119) The choice between God and Satan is ours; what faculty shall we call upon to guide us in that choice if not our powers of ijtihad?

God has given us signs for our thoughtful mind to contemplate and to learn from: "In the creation o the heavens and the earth; in the alternation of night and day; in the ships that sail the ocean with cargoes beneficial to man; in the water which God sends down from the sky and with which He revives the earth after its death; dispensing over it all manner of beasts: in the disposal of the winds, and in the clouds that are driven between sky and earth: surely in these there are signs for rational men." (Qur'an 2:164; 6:99) "Those that hide the clear roofs and the guidance we have revealed after We had proclaimed them in the Scriptures shall be cursed by God." (Qur'an 2: 159)

Qur'an also teaches that "there shall be no compulsion in religion. Truth stands out clear from error", leaving us to use reason and faith as human capacities from which we can reach out to the Divine and learn of God's purposed and of right and wrong. (Qur'an 2:256) Compulsion would deny a person the free use of his or her reason as the grounds for conviction and moral conduct. God wants us to do the right things for the right reasons as he does on his exalted level of oversight. "Call men to the path of your Lord with wisdom and kindly exhortation. Reason with them in the most courteous manner." (Qur'an 16:125)

Qur'an makes a distinction between wrongful acts done without knowing intention but from carelessness and those done with knowledge. The latter acts only deserve retribution from God, thus placing an emphasis on right thinking as a guide to our conduct. "Your unintentional mistakes shall be forgiven, but not your

deliberate errors." (Qur'an 33:5) "But whoever is driven by necessity, intending neither to sin nor to transgress, shall incur no guilt."
(Qur'an 2:173) "Except those who are really weak and oppressed
– men, women, and children – who have no means in their power,
not a guide post to their way forward; for these there is hope that
God will forgive." (Qur'an 4:98,99)

Adam was given "names" or thought constructs by which to
serve God as Khalifah on earth. (Qur'an 2:31) In this way did God
empower Adam with the tools that opened up his capacity to use
ijtihad in his daily life. Similarly, Qur'an instructs that "you shall not
withhold testimony". Those hearing a case must know all the signs
and proofs of truth so that their minds can reach a right and just
conclusion. (Qur'an 2:282)

Qur'an, however, places some restrictions on our use of ijtihad.
First, like all our abilities it was given as an amanah or trust. It is,
therefore, a power to be used to attain higher purposes, not to be
selfishly abused. When we hold a power in trust, we become stewards or fiduciaries in order to achieve a future good that will benefit
more than ourselves. "On the Day when their tongues, their hands
and their feet will bear witness against them as to their actions. On
that Day God will pay them back all their just dues and they will
realize that God is the (very) truth, that makes all things manifest."
(Qur'an, 24:24-25)

Like all other powers, potentials, and opportunities that we
receive from God, ijtihad is subject to abuse in our hands. Abuse of
our use of ijtihad occurs when we treat it as a personal possession to
be used according to our selfish interests and passions. "Indeed, the
wrongdoers are led unwittingly by their own appetites." (Qur'an
30:29) "Many are those that are misled through ignorance by their
desires;" (Qur'an 6:119) When passions and appetites control our
behavior and not our right minds, then, use of ijtihad does not lead
us towards Islam, towards God and the right way, but, to the contrary, towards sin and wrong-doing. That is why, perhaps, building
up powers of mental acuity so that our minds are trained and strong
would be taking a necessary step towards living as God prefers.

When our use of ijtihad is persuasive to our hearts and the results of our thinking are compelling in our behaviors, we are more likely than not to do right. When we abuse our ijtihad we give in to the Agency Problem.

When we use ijtihad for our personal pleasure or other self-interest, we act like an owner of its powers and not like a trustee. An owner is entitled to selfish exploitation of a power for personal gain. A trustee is limited in the range of uses to which a power can be put. A trustee is bound to use the power, or the property, for the benefit of others. With powers received from God, we are bound to use them for God's purposes, which is to serve as Khalifah. Thus, ijtihad is subordinate to the moral ends of khalifahship.

Another way of putting this point about the wise use of reason, is to consider ijtihad as a special right belonging to human persons when every right comes with a corresponding responsibility. Our responsibility with respect to our use of ijtihad is to use it thoughtfully, upon due consideration, with an open mind, in the spirit of God's compassion and mercy.

For example, Qur'an instructs that "These are they who have bartered guidance for error: but their commerce is profitless, and they have lost true direction." (Qur'an 2:17) "Who is more wicked than the man who invents a falsehood about God or denies His revelations?" (Qur'an 10:17; 2:75) Here the person uses his or her human power to challenge God; a rebellious act inconsistent with holding a trust from God.

Qur'an teaches that wisdom is necessary to understand its revelations: "It is He who has revealed to you the Book. Some of its verses are precise in meaning – they are the foundation of the Book – and others ambiguous. Those whose hearts are infected with disbelief observe the ambiguous parts, so as to create dissention by seeking to explain it. ... Those who are well-grounded in knowledge say: We believe in it: it is all from our Lord. But only the wise take heed." (Qur'an 3:7) In this passage, disbelief – a failure in the good use of ijtihad, compromises a person's salvation hopes. The power of understanding is within us, but we must cultivate it and use it properly so that we may internalize its teachings.

So for example, we are not to use our right of ijtihad to twist scripture, to tamper with words out of their context (Qur'an 5:12), to charge an innocent person with one's own wrongdoing (Qur'an 4:112), to cheat in weights and measures, to ignore signs from God, to mediate in bad causes, to extract usury. It is a mistake to use knowledge to maliciously disagree with one another. (Qur'an 45:17) Hypocracy is another form of self-seeking and wrongful use of ijtihad. (Qur'an 9:73)

Repentance is a Godly use of ijtihad. "Those who seek to redress their wrongs will incur no guilt." (Qur'an 42:43; see also 9:104; 8:38) So is enjoining charity, justice, kindness, conciliation and peace among men. (Qur'an 4:114) Thus, Qur'an presumes that human persons in their right minds can accurately distinguish right from wrong. Such a faculty of judgment is part of our natures, given by God to be used as he enabled humanity to serve his Creation.

God knows that we will not always reach truth in our use of ijtihad; we are too impulsive and mischievous for that to happen all the time. Still, he expects us to make the attempt to live rightly, find truth, and obtain justice. It is our responsibility as a free moral agent to do so. "Your unintentional mistakes shall be forgiven, but not your deliberate errors." (Qur'an 33:5) He forgives us when we are under compulsion or are negligent or weak. "Indeed, in no way does God wrong mankind, but men wrong themselves." (Qur'an 10:44) "God does not change a people's lot unless they change with is in their hearts." (Qur'an 13:11) "If they accept your faith, they shall be rightly guided; if they turn back, it is they who will be in schism." (Qur'an 2:137)

Because we have been given the capacity for ijtihad to guide our path through life, God will not use his great powers to do for us what we will not do for ourselves. "Had I possessed knowledge of what is hidden, I would have availed myself of much that is good and no harm would have touched me." (Qur'an 7:188) He rewards right use and punishes wrong use of all powers given to humanity. We were not created, Qur'an says, to serve Satan. If we use our ijtihad for Satan's purposes, we turn away from God and will receive due retribution.

"Show forgiveness, speak for justice, and avoid the ignorant." (Qur'an 7:199) When tempted, it is our responsibility to be discerning and alert and to move towards God of our own will. He will not force us to move to him as there is no compulsion in religion. "Had the people of those cities believed and kept from evil, We would have showered upon them blessings from heaven and earth. But they disbelieved and We punished them for their misdeeds." (Qur'an 7:96) "Never have We destroyed a nation whom We did not warn and admonish beforehand." (Qur'an 296:210)"Had the truth followed their appetites, the Heavens, the Earth, and all who dwell in them, would have surely been corrupted." (Qur'an 23:71) Following God's guidance demands a critical faculty of mind to discern warnings and to find the right understanding. This is use of ijtihad as an amanah from God, as a blessing, and not as a tool of human arrogance, conceit and self-seeking.

"Some wrangle about God, though they have neither knowledge nor guidance nor divine revelation. They turn away in scorn, leading others astray from God's path." (Qur'an 22:8;9)

> Fifth, the Qur'an recommends use of institutions of consultation – shira – as a means for the application of individual ijtihad. "Those who listens to their Lord, and establish regular prayers; who conduct their affairs through consultation (shura), who spend out of what We bestow on them for sustenance..." (Qur'an 42:38) "It was thanks to God's mercy that you were gentle to them. Had you been rough, hardhearted, they would surely have scattered away from you. So pardon them, and pray for their forgiveness, and take counsel from them in matters of importance. (Qur'an 3: 159)
>
> The wisdom and thoughts of others function as a check on the possible corruption and selfish biases our own minds are prey to out of temptation and petty jealousies. As our own use of ijtihad may be imperfect or biased, we can

purify and correct our thinking by taking into account, as a responsible trustee does, the standards and conclusions of others. The Qur'an realizes only too well the limitations that may infect ijtihad with ignoble purpose or misunderstanding. We do not surrender our power of ijtihad to others in a process of shura; we only feed it with more raw materials of fact and opinion for thoughtful consideration as we assume personal responsibility for acting as God's agent - a dutiful and non-negligent khalifah.

Sixth, the purpose of the vice-regency, on the individual as well as on the collective level, is to achieve justice. "O you who believe! Stand up as a witness for God in all fairness, and do not let the hatred of a people deviate you from justice. Be just" (Qur'an, 5:8) "God commands justice, the doing of good, and generosity to relatives and near ones, and He forbids all shameful deeds, and injustice and disorder: He instructs you, that you will be reminded" (Qur'an 16:90) Indeed God wrongs none, not even as much as an atom's weight. Whenever a man does good, He multiplies it two-fold, and bestows out of His grace a mighty reward." (Qur'an, 4:40)

Justice requires fairness, honesty, transparency, compassion and mercy. Justice implies that humanity – both on the individual and the collective levels – will be empowered to carry out its office of khalifah and to execute its various amanah. Accordingly, tyranny was to be avoided in politics and the institution of zakah was recommended to provide powers of economic activity for all.

Justice is the ideal that demands overcoming the Agency Problem and the ample provision of goods both private and public so distributed that all can find their way to a meaningful life where virtue crowns our finding of happiness.

道

德

甲午年作氏于夢涌州

CHAPTER ELEVEN
OVERCOMING THE AGENCY
PROBLEM: I AND THOU

Some time ago now, when I was an undergraduate in the United States, the alienating intellectual pull of French Existentialism and The Beats was turning into the militancy of the New Left. Nonetheless, moral philosopher Martin Buber's distinction between the ethical actions attendant on "I-It" perceptions and those associated with "I-Thou" sensibilities was still in common usage.

Recently I finally actually read his short essay. The copy of I and Thou that I borrowed from a local college library had last been signed out in 1999. Buber's thought is far less current today, which is too bad as it still gives us a deep way of thinking about corporate social responsibility, private and public goods and the Agency Problem.

His "I-It" perceptions track our cynical sense for business and capitalism as self-centered manipulation of advantage while his

"I-Thou" perceptions of what really "is" far better track our aspirations for ethics and a transcendent moral sense. Buber's "I-It" places its self-esteem exclusively on private goods and fulfillment of the Agency Problem where there is no fundamental need to be faithful to others or live by norms of concern and duty. All is tactical, instrumental, exploitative with dominion as the goal of life. But Buber's stance of "I-Thou" brings in not only a perception of the legitimacy of the other, of goods beyond what can be held in personal dominion, but a firm rejection of the Agency Problem as permanent and inherent in human nature.

So, just as Buber believed that we can elevate ourselves from "I-It" exploitation of others to "I-Thou" respect and mutuality, the Caux Round Table proposes that business can be conducted on the basis of principled concerns for stakeholders.

For Buber "I-It" connotes the primary world of physicality and "I-Thou" establishes the world of relations, all that which takes on a moral dimension of justice and "ought".

To use the words of Jurgen Habermas, a philosopher on whose work much of the CRT's thinking about ethical action stands, the "I-It" perceptions focus on the realm of facticity and "I-Thou" sensibilities penetrate the realm of normativity.

According to Buber, the "Thou" that is there to meet us, comes to us through grace: "No system of ideas, no foreknowledge, and no fancy intervene between I and Thou. The memory itself is transformed, as it plunges out of its isolation into the unity of the whole. No aim, no lust and no anticipation intervene between I and Thou."

For Buber, it is relationship values that can exist a priori – sensed but not subject to proof, connections like beauty, love, and pity. By entering into relation, Buber asserts, our personality develops out of the primal, physical world.

In other words, then, while living in facticity, we aspire to the greater by becoming aware of normativity. From a business point of view, this is to say that while seeking a cash profit, we can do better for ourselves by being responsible in our relationships.

The person who is conscious only of his or her "I" in the face of all "It", stands before things, but not over against them. Such an "I" bends over particulars and objectifies them as scenery, isolating them in observation. The world of "It" is set in the context of space and time. This world offers us comfort, incitements, excitements, activity and knowledge. Our primary connection with the world of "It" is experiencing and using. It is doing business as usual, without much application of principle.

Institutions, such as governments and corporations, inhabit the world of "It". Buber says that institutions are where "all sorts of aims are pursued, where a man works, negotiates, bears influence, undertakes, concurs, organizes, conducts business, officiates, preaches. They are the tolerably well-ordered and to some extent harmonious structures, in which with the manifold help of men's brains and hands, the process of affairs in fulfilled."

Buber infers that "without "It" man cannot live. But he who lives with "It" alone is not a man."

This is because, according to Buber, "in times of sickness it comes about that the world of "It", no longer penetrated and fructified by the inflowing world of "Thou" as by living streams but separated and stagnant, a gigantic ghost of the fens, overpowers man." … "If a culture ceases to be centered in the living and continually renewed relational event, then it hardens into the world of "It"."

The world of "Thou" is a reality in which we share without being able to appropriate exclusively for ourselves. The self-willed person, unopened to relationships, cannot meet the "Thou" and is condemned to the doom issued by fateful powers driving the world of "It".

According to Buber, the principal advantage to be experienced in the world of "Thou" is confirmation of meaning, a sustenance which gives us courage and vitality while living amidst the world of "It".

Thus while the business of business may be business, the meaning of business – none other that the truly beneficial livelihood provided by business – must come from developing a sensibility to relation, from activation of the moral sense. It is here that some set of concerns such as those set forth in the CRT's Principles for Business, and not mere market rationality, provides that awareness of relation that leads to living in the world of "Thou" as well as in the world of "It".

Buber concludes: "Man can do justice to the relation with the Highest (God) in which he has come to share only if he realizes the Highest anew in the world according to his strength and to the measure of each day."

I rather like the affirmation provided by Buber's thought. His point seems to be, that while daily working within the world of "It", we can nevertheless escape the worst tendencies of that world, which are to reduce us to mere mechanism in the service of nothing redemptive. It is this optimism that I wanted to share with you.

道德

CHAPTER TWELVE

OVERCOMING THE AGENCY
PROBLEM: FRIENDSHIP IN BUSINESS

It is said that, in business, there can be no room for friendship. The effects of personal feelings can be inefficient in business transactions and, at worst, can even be dysfunctional in complex systems of cooperation that require predictable rational behaviors for achieving organizational goals.

Indeed, sometimes it is better that we play well our appointed professional roles and not just be our personal, emotional selves to let our feelings override our judgment.

US Secretary of State Dean Rusk once told my Father that to succeed in such high office he needed "ice water in my veins".

It is said that to succeed in business you need a calm, coldly calculating mind focused on self-advancement. No milk of human kindness advised for those who want to get rich.

Capitalism has been accused of needing only a "cash nexus" between people in order to meet its production objectives. Money – not friendship – therefore suitably mediates among people in free markets, binding them together through transactions based on the costs and gains of their respective utility preferences. Free market capitalism has, therefore, often been disparaged as being a cruel system, treating all things as "straw dogs" to be burnt in funeral pyres.

But, indeed, this may be going quite too far. Systems of cooperation and collaboration, simple or complex, thrive on relationships. Successful relationships cannot be only coldly calculating. Or at least this was the suggestion of Chester Barnard in his classic work, The Theory and Function of the Executive. Relationships in organizations and in organized networks of collaboration are not one-night stands of exploitation. Relationships, to bring about their advantages, can't be one-way streets. Nor can they survive a "My way or the Highway" attitude. They require mutuality, reciprocity, a balance of advantages and concern that can last longer than a June bug's life.

Power relationships indeed may be cold, calculating, and cruel. But the ability of such top down power relationships to sustain collaboration is problematic, depending on the sustainability of fear, other insecurities, or deeply ingrained greed in those who subject themselves to the use and abuse of power. Weakness in some leads them to submission and permits other-directed, power-based relationships to thrive.

Greed – so prevalent in business settings – also sustains relationships. But, in many cases, greed for money is only compensation seeking to offset other psycho-social wounds and insecurities. It is not so much the money but the power expressed through the money that drives this inter-personal dysfunction. Where greed is a factor in sustaining relationships, collaboration rests on feelings that are far from friendship, no matter how many smiles are given and nice words exchanged between the parties.

To be successful, business relationships need to be more organically constructed and less autocratic than power-driven, command and control hierarchies like to be.

One problem with adding friendly concerns and emotions to thinking about economic behaviors is that such human complications compromise the elegant simplicity of micro-economic formulas predicting price and other self-referential profit seeking behaviors. Economics and business finance as academic disciplines turn on the assumed anthropological construct known as homo economicus. People in the economy – investors, customers, employees, suppliers – are assumed to be without complicating emotions and hard-to-price feelings and aesthetic preferences. This concept lies at the heart of the Agency Problem.

But as any human life-cycle will reveal, we are not only homo economicus but also homo sapiens. Wisdom and knowing, not calculated efficiency, are keys to our character. Rational efficiency does not always dominate our decision-making. If it did, there would have been no thoughtless self-immolation on the part of Wall Street in the run up to the credit collapse of 2008.

As Aristotle famously noted, we are social/political creatures who live in communities. To realize ourselves, we therefore need relationships. In other words, it is hard to be "me" without some kind of "you". The dynamics of relationships can never be dismissed out of hand in any human endeavor and replaced with unfeeling, mechanistic logics of cause and effect. Martin Buber aligned with this understanding when he distinguished "I-Thou" settings from "I-It" settings.

CSR approaches claim that stakeholders are important to a firm's profitability. Stakeholders are in relationships with the firm. Managing a firm to enhance stakeholder relationships adds complications to simple formulas of supply and demand and marginal costs. Stakeholders bring to the table a wide set of relationship concerns. In the best of cases, the right kind of dependable stakeholders are in committed relationships with the firm. Customers have money and brand loyalty needed by the firm. Good employees work hard and make no mistakes. The best investors are patient and understanding of management's trials and tribulations. Is there no room at all in a successful firm for such non-cash aspects to stakeholder relationships, aspects which are filled with intangible advantages that are hard to price in terms of monetary units?

On the other side, dysfunctional relationships with stakeholders bring on intangible disadvantages to a firm. James Surowiecki commented in the New Yorker magazine (Sept 6, 2010) on the misuse by many firms of rationality in customer relations. He asked why firms spend so much money and are so solicitous when seeking new customers and take old or current customers more or less for granted? The old saw is that it is easier to get repeat business from a satisfied customer than it is to "win" over a new one. Surowiecki is saying that customers are not treated as friends should be. They are cultivated and then dropped in emotional importance – a bait and switch strategy. Is this really a wise business practice? His comment was: "But, because most companies are set up to focus on the first sale rather than on all the ones that might follow, they end up devoting all their energies to courting us, promising wonderful products and excellent service. Then, once they've got us, their attention wanders."

It might assist business management, then, to wonder a bit about friendship as a constructive business value.

Aristotle's other, less widely known discussion of ethics – is the Eudemian Ethics. His placement of friendship as an important branch of ethical accomplishment is very worthy of further reflection. Making and sustaining friendship would be another skill set honed by the ethical person, in addition to the practice of the prudence that seeks moderation and the development of the virtuous habits which lead to happiness. Friendship is a returning of purpose, so it is unique to humans who can discern another's purposes. It is possible among homo sapiens.

Friendship is a mental state, an orientation, a settled expectation, that works itself out in how we treat others. Friends receive more consideration than strangers. In conditioning our conduct, friendship is a source of considerate, ethical, behavior.

The special business of the political art, said Aristotle, was to produce friendships. This skill would seem to be appropriate, then, to any situation where cooperation must be put into place, as in a business, for example. What is politics other than contrived cooperation? What is business other than contrived cooperation in a monetary context?

Aristotle distinguishes between two levels, or even kinds, of friendship. First, there are "low octane" friendships which come into and fall out of favor according to our needs and short-term self-interests. Second, there are "high octane" friendships which move us to long term loyalty and altruism towards another.

Some find friends among those who are useful to them. These friendships said Aristotle are the majority of friendships but they end when the usefulness ends. They are conjunctions of "fair weather" friends. I suppose that, today, such friendships are the kind drawn out by Facebook, where you can "unfriend" someone just as easily as you once befriended them.

"Low octane" friends look on one another as objects, just as sellers and buyers do, Aristotle says. To use Martin Buber's more theological language, such "low octane" friendships are "I-it" relationships while "high octane" friendships are more like his "I-thou" relationships. In "I-thou" relationships the other has moral and spiritual possibility, reflecting life's deeper purposes. "I-it" friendships proceed through contract – deals of mutual advantage – says Aristotle. In contrast, a higher quality, more moral, friendship rests on virtue. Civic friendship ("I-it") looks to the agreement; moral friendship ("I-thou") to the deeper possibilities brought about by the relationship and, above all, to a sense of higher purpose in having such a friend.

Cicero commented that the generality of people have no conception of any other merit than what may be turned to interest. 'They love their friends upon the same principle and in the same proportion as they love their flocks and their herds; giving so much of their regard to each as is equal to the profits they respectively produce. (On Friendship) Jamie Dimon, CEO of JP Morgan Chase, one of the few survivors of the Wall Street crash of 2008, reportedly said: "Let's make friends with these guys before I eat them." (Andrew Ross Sorkin, Too Big To Fail, p. 437)

Here friendship, like commerce and exchange, can be said to take its rise from the wants and weaknesses of humankind and is cultivated solely in order to obtain by a mutual exchange of good offices those advantages which one could not otherwise acquire.

Adam Smith famously described how such temporary friendships, if you like, drive market capitalism. "It is not from the benevolence of the butcher, the brewer, or the baker, that we expect our dinner, but from their regard to their own interest." (Wealth of Nations, Chapter 2) Conversely, the butcher, the brewer, and the baker do not expect their livelihood from our benevolence but from our regard for meat, beer, and bread for our dinners. The exchange of mutual advantage without much regard for the deeper needs of whoever is on the other side of the exchange drives the world forward and creates wealth.

On this "low octane" level of friendship, Aristotle reminds us, can be found relationships resting on pleasantness or pleasure, which wane when pleasure changes. The dynamics of fashion or teen-age love reveal this level of faddish friendship. Time is said to show the true friend.

Yet we suspect that, as Cicero writes, nature has so disposed our hearts to engage in friendships upon a nobler and more generous inducement than acquisition of material advantage. He argued that the feelings of friendship, when in place, cannot be produced by the motive of interest alone. There is an instinct that draws congenial minds into union and not merely a cold calculation of advantage in doing so. As the American poet Robert Frost wrote in one of my favorite poems (Mending Wall): "something there is that does not love a wall."

Friendship may also be based on the virtue in another. Such friendships based on virtue are those practiced by the best people. Virtue is bringing one's personal good into alignment with a more profound good. Cicero agreed. In his essay On Friendship he stated that "true friendship can only subsist between those who are animated by the strictest principle of honor and virtue." But, being practical he added that this proposition "is altogether inapplicable to any useful purpose of society, as it supposes a degree of virtue to which no mortal was ever capable of rising."

Following Cicero, we may say that virtue is not an absolute standard of ideal perfection, but more usefully to business and commerce, an attainable degree of moral merit which is exemplified in practice.

Cicero adds that the more one looks for happiness within oneself, and the more firmly one stands supported by the consciousness of one's own intrinsic merit, the more desirous one becomes to cultivate friendships with others, and the better friend one proves to be.

Funny how this contrasts with our love of self. For the love which every person bears himself does not certainly flow from any expected recompense or reward but solely from that pure and innate regard which each individual feels for his own person. This is the stuff of "high octane" friendships.

To maximize the value from exchange, it would seem then, one would do better having "high octane" friendships. Such friendships demand more virtue from us and so have more ethical substance. An ironic interconnection: friendships help the self gain advantages emotional and material but an already strong and less needy self is more likely to find friends.

A friendship based upon the charms of virtue sits upon a firmer and more durable foundation than if it were raised upon a sense of human wants and weaknesses says Cicero. Weaknesses such as an immoderate desire for wealth or an inordinate thirst for fame and celebrity are the great enemies of friendship.

In "high octane" friendships, there is not artifice or duplicity; no deserting of a friend when times are tough or forgetting a friend when bad times turn prosperous and they are no longer useful. As the credit collapse of 2008 rolled towards reality, Gary Cohn, co-president of Goldman Sachs is quoted as saying when some of his customers took their money out of Goldman: "I have a long memory. Look, the one thing I'm doing is I'm learning who my friends are and who my enemies are, and I'm making lists." (Andrew Ross Sorkin, Too Big to Fail, p. 433)

One such client replied to Cohn: "I don't really give a shit; it's my money."

Cohn countered: "You can do whatever you want, but this will change our relationship for a long time."

Deeper friendships are an office. They come with duties, among which are to admonish and reprove; to give and receive advice. Solidly grounded friendships really do reduce risks and provide encouragement. They are a spiritual as well as a material resource and elide with our needs for religion, understanding, and love.

The bad person, who has no virtue inside, feels distrust and measures others by himself or herself, seeing everyone around them therefore as full of mistrust. Such persons without virtue then preemptively repay presumed mistrust with actual mistrust. They tend to prefer goods more than friends, since goods are beyond the pale of trust and mistrust. Goods by themselves will never intentionally let you down.

Which, parenthetically, may be one reason why possessing money is so important for some people. They can have no friends but still need a trusted resource. Others go for owning cats or dogs.

In terms of business social responsibility, those without virtue corrode and corrupt the implementation of high standards of conduct. They just take the money and run leaving the hindmost for the devil.

The behaviors of people without virtue are well described by Robert Greene in his bestselling book "The 48 Laws of Power." His Law 2 advises that "Never put too much trust in friends, learn how to use enemies" because "be wary of friends, they will betray you more quickly, for they are easily aroused to envy." He adds "If you have no enemies find a way to make them." Greene's Law 3 is "Conceal your intentions" to "keep people off balance and in the dark by never revealing the purpose behind your actions." His Law 7 advises to "Get others to do the work for you but always take the credit." Law 8 is a juicy one: "Make other people come to you – use bait if necessary." Greene says "Lure him with fabulous bait – then attack." In a similar vein, Greene recommends: "Use selective honesty and generosity to disarm your victim." (Law 12) He adds "One sincere and honest move will cover over dozens of dishonest ones. … Once our selective honesty opens a hole in their armor, you can deceive and manipulate then at will."

And again in the same vein, Greene's Law 14 holds that "Pose as friend, work as spy." Other Laws in Greene' manual of duplicity hold that "Play the perfect courtier", "Play to people's fantasies", "Discover each man's thumbscrew", "Think as you like, but behave like others", and finally "Assume formlessness."

To be a predator as Greene recommends is to fly in the face of almost all friendships, but especially any relationship based on virtue.

Aristotle also asserts that higher quality friendship and justice are very similar in effect, promoting balance and trust in relationships. The essence of Greene's approach to life is unfairness. No justice in his recommended uses of deceit to gain power.

Good friends need to be just with each other and just people are worthy of "high octane" friendship. Being just is a standard of conduct higher than the average "morals of the marketplace", to borrow a famous phrase that Justice Cardozo used in his opinion in Meinhardt v. Salmon on fiduciary duties. Being just prevents us from turning our backs on friends when fairness or compassion needs to guide our actions towards them. Justice asks more of us than self-interest alone. We may need to sacrifice some immediate self-interest in order to achieve a state of balance under all the circumstances. You cannot overreach in taking for yourself or exploiting others and still be just.

The justice practiced towards friends depends on ourselves alone. It flows from our values and behaviors. While public justice has rules and communal consequences, Aristotle points out, personal justice reflects our character.

Aristotle also pondered the impact of inequality on friendships. He saw that in many cases relationships are not between equals. One side has an economic, social, or political superiority. What kind of friendship possible in these conditions?

Those who are different can be friends says Aristotle. Opposites are friendly due mostly to usefulness and seek a mean between them. Both situations apply in business: those of similar aptitudes and habits more easily cooperate in joint ventures. But the opposite is perhaps more helpful to business: people with different skill sets and approaches who complement each other but are not rivals or fearful of one another leverage the firm's capabilities and give it resilience against changes in fortune.

Those who have superior power still need what others have: companies need workers; the wealthy need advice, the powerful need followers. "Low octane" friendships easy multiply in such relationships. Each seeks to take advantage of the other. The more powerful party is tempted to be nice when needy and to exploit when in firm control. The weaker is tempted to play the flatterer or be insincere in order to access a smallish share of material well-being, social status, or political influence. Many roads to success in organizations wind their convoluted ways through sycophancy, telling superiors what they want to hear, not what they should. Imbalance can be manipulated for self-advantage by the weaker, dependent, party as well as by the stronger.

Consider the quality of relationships around a monarch. As Shakespeare warned "uneasy lies the head that wears the crown." A king or queen has no true friends it would seem.

Here, in trade and business, do we find an intersection of market power and friendship. Having market power permits one to go thin on the office of friendship, shifting from a friendship of equals to one that is imbalanced. Power exerts an influence that can turn one deaf to the call of "higher octane" friendship. If power confers such an advantage, why not heed its siren call and friends be damned? Who needs virtue when power is readily at hand?

Lord Acton famously advised, did he not, that power corrupts and absolute power corrupts absolutely.

The "high octane" version of friendship in unequal power relationships is that of a fiduciary: one who cares about those dependent and seeks their good. Being a fiduciary demands inner character and personal virtue in order to withstand the temptations of power. One is not advised to select a bad person with no virtue to be a trustee of one's assets or minor children.

Fiduciary duties are required by the Common Law of all agents, partners, and corporate directors. Thus, aspects of "high octane" friendships as set forth by Aristotle and Cicero have long been imposed on business practices by the law. Every employee, from the CEO of a corporation on down, is an agent with fiduciary duties to the company and the company is in a moral relationship with them as their principal.

Fiduciary duties under the law don't run to customers or suppliers, the environment or the community. But does that imply that a business should look upon such stakeholders as beyond the pale of friendship considerations? Clearly not. "Low octane" friendships are a dime a dozen with customers, suppliers and communities. The questions then is should a business move up the quality continuum of friendships towards "high octane" relationship with these stakeholders?

One perspective to consider in this regard is the logic of the "Golden Rule". If you were in your friend's place, would you want you to make the relationship more virtuous, demonstrating your powers of higher character, or disengage from it?

Adam Smith gave us some sound advice on this point in his first great treatise: The Theory of the Moral Sentiments. There, he recommended stepping outside of ourselves when we must decide how far along the continuum of friendship we should go towards virtue, saying "We must here, as in all other cases, view ourselves not so much according to that light in which we may naturally appear to ourselves, as according to that in which we naturally appear to others." ... "Though [our] own happiness may be of more importance to [us] than that of all the world besides, to every other person it is of no more consequence than that of any other man." ... "If he would act so as that the impartial spectator may enter into the principles of his conduct, ... he must upon this as upon all occasions, humble the arrogance of his self-love, and bring it down to something which other men can go along with." ... "In the race for wealth, and honors, and preferments, he may run as hard as he can, and strain every nerve and muscle, in order to outstrip all his competitors. But if he should justle, or throw down any of them, the indulgence of the spectators is entirely at an end. It is a violation of fair play, which they cannot admit of." (at p. 83)

Third, we can apply the "Kew Gardens Principles" These considerations of how to act arose from the once notorious Kitty Genovese murder in New York City nearly 50 years ago now. One night in full view of people looking down from safety in their surrounding apartment buildings, Kitty Genovese was brutally and repeatedly attacked with a knife under the street lights below. She fought off her attacker. She ran and banged on doors to be let in. She screamed for help. No one who saw her being attacked or who heard her screams came to help her and not one of the onlookers even called the police from the safety and anonymity of their apartments. The resulting guidelines proposed by ethicists for action to intervene in a situation of unequal power – Kitty Genovese was vulnerable in her distress – are to do so 1) when a critical need exists – and the greater the need, the greater the obligation to act; 2) when there is proximity – knowledge of and access to the situation of vulnerability; 3) when you are capability; and 4) when you are the last resort for the person in distress – there are few others or no one else who can take constructive action.

Thus in friendships between unequals, the demands of friendship increase when the more vulnerable friend becomes more deeply in need of assistance. When, for example, customers are more dependent on the knowledge, skill, and care of the seller, say consumers of medical care, the seller, say a hospital, should adjust to a more "high octane" level of relationship.

Principles of corporate social responsibility would seem to support application of "high octane" friendships based on virtue in business settings. Optimizing stakeholder relationships cannot be accomplished with "low octane" friendships which is so subject to changes in the weather of life and so hard to distinguish from the power games played by those without virtue.

道

德

Tao Te 25 in Running Script © 2014 by Weiming Lu

CHAPTER THIRTEEN
DO WE NEED WALL STREET?

In the November 29th issue of The New Yorker John Cassidy asks in a commentary: "What good is Wall Street?" He ends his article with a quote from Paul Woolly: "There was a presumption that financial innovation is socially valuable. The first thing I discovered is that it wasn't backed by any empirical evidence. There's almost none."

Wall Street sustained losses of US$42.6 billion in 2008 but made US$55 billion in profits the very next year – when most people were coping, and many coping badly, with recession, unemployment, and declining asset prices. In the first quarter of 2010 traders at Goldman Sachs had their best quarter results ever –US$7.4 billion in net revenue. Since then, however, profits on Wall Street have fallen and firms, even Goldman, have taken to cost cutting and reduction in employment.

In securities trading these days, institutional fund managers and speculative high frequency traders are most of the market. Rarely do they provide capital for new or expanded business enterprise. Mostly they take cash out of the economy through the buying and selling of existing securities which represent the present value of past capital investment. The public offering of stock in Facebook was evidently designed not so much to raise money for the company but for early investors to "cash out" and transfer the risk of future success or loss to others who bought in to the gamble. Facebook has announced that it does not intend to pay dividends, so the only way an owner can make money from the purchase of Facebook stock is to sell it for a higher price. Such a purchase has little difference from the purchase of a lottery ticket or buying chips in a casino to place on a number at the roulette wheel. It is not an investment in the real economy only a wager on future financial happenings. Buying a cup of coffee would be a more substantial contribution to the real economy.

The investment in an existing, already issued financial contract – a stock or a bond, etc. – does help to set the market price for that contract. This provides investors with information. But how important to growth and prosperity is that information? I would argue not so much as prices of financial contracts can change every minute, even every second with high-frequency trading. One time price information in financial markets has some private utility for traders but little public utility for the rest of us. To put it another way, they are only moving the chips around among the poker players; total wealth is not increased in a trade of securities; cash just changes hands.

If someone buys at five and sells at six to pocket a one dollar profit, what value have they added? Some liquidity to the market for that security to be sure and there is a social good provided by liquid markets. But beyond that?

They took the dollar profit in exchange for a legal claim on future income and/or capital – a security. This is rent extraction, not wealth creation. Rents are paid for access to legal or political authority – as when we pay rent to a landlord, we buy a share of his or her legal title to real property. Patents and copyrights provide legal opportunities for rent extraction. Without legal title and the power of government to enforce those property rights, no rents could be charged.

If prices for securities rise, however, there is what is called a "wealth effect". People then feel a rising tide of economic prospects and their psychology encourages consumption and borrowing which do impact the real economy.

More realistic economic wealth creation through financial inter-mediation aggregates existing wealth from some to transfer its buying power to others to finance enterprise, innovation, and growth. This is most often done through new loans to business and new equity investment in companies, or through hybrid investments like warrants, preferred stock, and convertible bonds and debentures.

Traditional banking, investment banking, and venture capital provided these financial services. Insurance and other forms of risk protection and diversification also add real economic value in encouraging investment in enterprise.

But from 1991 to 2000 some 150 venture capital backed companies a year took in equity capital through Wall Street. But since 2000, such annual IPO offerings have averaged only about 50 per year.

Capital markets seem to have lost faith in new enterprises, and have become captivated by property, derivatives, bonds and every other asset class.

So where will the growth come from to hire workers and pay down national debts?

Lord Adair Turner, Chairman of the UK's Financial Services Authority, wrote recently that "It is possible for financial activity to extract rents from the real economy rather than deliver economic value."

If all financial innovation does is create new forms of rent extraction, what good does it do except to take money from the many and give it to the few?

In the United States, six firms – Bank of America, Citigroup, Goldman Sachs, JPMorgan Chase, Morgan Stanley, and Wells Fargo – have assets of US$9.2 trillion – 63% of national GDP.

John Maynard Keynes famously aligned securities exchanges with casinos in their social utility. Did he have a point? Casinos make a lot of money on millions of small transactions. They win every time you lose at their tables. What wealth do they create? They just take your money and move it to other pockets.

So does a poker game, or craps. Money moves among players but the total pot sees no growth in value. Some go home winners but others leave as losers to that extent.

The bets made by many securities traders are calculated by algorithms that measure a price as a deviation (higher or lower) from a statistical norm and plot the odds of deviation associated with that price. If you bet that the price will converge towards the norm, you can successfully arbitrage and make profits.

The algorithms that now control most trading in securities began as attempts to beat the odds in casinos. Our financial system's major profit seeking mechanism owes its life and its profits to the techniques of gambling.

Maybe Keynes had a point after all.

Gambling I would suggest is a form of extracting rents from the real economy. Gamblers seek rents associated with their legal rights. Gambling is all about getting power according to the rules. The rules of gambling – poker, black-jack, craps, chemin de fer, bridge if you will – create legal rights in players. Two of a kind in poker beats any single high card, etc. If the rules come down in your favor, you have a right to collect. You suddenly have a valuable property in how the cards or the dice fell. You can therefore trade in your property for some of the cash money put up by the other players, including the house.

Or, if you gain nothing to trade from the fall of cards or dice, you lose whatever price you paid to join the game. That entrance fee is also a form of rent, paid to those who "own" the game for access to their assets.

All the money that changes hands in gambling is brought into the casino or the game from the outside - from the real economy.

Rent extraction in gambling brings about a kind of "irrational exuberance" on the part of many players that does not exist in normal market transactions where pricing future returns is more realistic.

The more rent extraction is at work the less market mechanisms can do their job of providing economically efficient outcomes. Where rent extraction is at work, the elasticity of supply and demand curves tightens; free market checks and balances have less effect; prices don't signal true levels of demand or possible supply, they are artificially high. It is easier to make money through rent extraction than to be subject to market forces.

In the trading houses of New York and London, and their spin offs in Singapore, Hong Kong and elsewhere, rare is the month when they lose money. They beat the odds consistently, making money all the time. This is statistically improbable and gives rise to a suspicion that such trading using computers and high-frequency bids and asks is more rent extraction than getting paid a fair price for contributing capital or labor to the economy.

Monopolies and cartels create opportunities for rent extraction. Adam Smith in his book Wealth of Nations noted that business owners and managers love to get together and conspire against the public by setting up rigged markets to increase the returns to rent. The conspiracy among large banks in London to rig the daily cost of interest on loans – the LIBOR rate – was a cartel designed to facilitate rent extraction in financial markets. Prices were set to enable some traders to win their bets on the future prices of derivatives.

Corruption by officials and politicians is another form of rent extraction: use of state power for selfish gain comes at a price paid to those in charge of state authority. Here too market forces are too weak to control prices and economic outcomes.

If it is correct that financial intermediation has more and more become rent extraction, then it should also be correct that we need to give it less and less deference and government advantages.

The profits of financial houses should move back down in proportion to all profits roughly to the proportion that the financial industry contributes real wealth to national GDP.

Disproportionate rent extraction would appear to be highly unethical in any industry.

A fascinating set of issues, most germane to business ethics and corporate social responsibility, hovers around the proper role of highly liquid markets for equity securities ("Wall Street") with in an optimal structure of capitalist incentives.

Some – largely the efficiency conscious free market libertarians – would put Wall Street's needs as the distinctive measure of a good capitalism. Others – like Warren Buffet - are not so sure about making Wall Street's values a priority. They prefer to make a distinction between speculation and short-term profit taking, on the one hand, and fundamental company valuation on the other.

Many others from the standpoint of ethics and social responsibility object to the value set – not much more than greed and profit they say – dangled before us by stock market trading dynamics.

I once met with a very successful manager of equities who put this set of concerns in a very fruitful context. He runs his own investment firm in Minneapolis and now has nearly $2 billion in client funds under management. Like Warren Buffet, he makes a distinction between Wall Street values and the "real" values supporting a company's growth prospects.

His telling remark to me over lunch was about those in Wall Street who "rent" stocks for a time just to make a quick profit in trading or other short term activity.

"Renting" a stock as opposed to "owning" a stock – I thought that was a very helpful distinction for certain purposes.

Of course, a long-term "renter" often comes to act like an owner in terms of investment thoughtfulness, concern for the effects of depreciation, commitment to renewal and remediation, and using strategic foresight. Owners commit capital; renters pay current expenses. Owners take bigger risks associated with longer term time horizons.

Renters more typically are in and out of the property; exploiting it for a more narrow set of goals and moving on to the next opportunity.

In trading markets, like those for equity securities, the bright conceptual line between owning and renting gets dim. Owning a stock is subject to the temptations of just being a renter – paying a fee in order to play in a game of chance. We "buy" stocks it is said; and we commit our "capital" to the market. Yet even if we buy stocks to own, but things don't go our way, we just sell – turning ourselves retrospectively into renters of the security.

But what if this use of language – "owning shares in a company" - is out of date, created back in a time when stock holding was not a mass phenomenon and individuals were truly old fashioned, long-term owners in the style of today's Warren Buffet or in control of a family company. Now with so many shares in the market moving in and out of great funds on the command of computerized trading algorithms, what reality is left to the notion of share ownership?

When you "rent" a stock or other financial contract in order to trade on its future appreciation in financial markets, you play into shifting the character of the contract way over to a fully private good that has no respect for public concerns. The "renter" of a such a contract has a short-term interest and only in market perceptions. He or she most likely has no concern for the long term health of the enterprise that will pay on the contract and so gives it long-term value. If things go badly for the firm, the "renter" will just dump the contract as soon as possible.

The "renter" thus forgoes all the obligations, risks and rewards of actual economic ownership. The "renter" lives in a world of one-time, single-purpose, take-the-money and run, transactions, not commitment. Those who "rent" to trade have little need for trust or stakeholder relationships. They are only "fair-wealth" friends. They live the Agency Problem as they have no interest in stewardship.

Using the word "rent" to describe what is going on in Wall Street has another advantage other than being perhaps closer to economic reality. It points to a certain system of economic relations that is not fully in line with the requirements of a good capitalism.

"Rent seeking" for economists is not sound capital investment bringing new factors of production into the economy. In classical economics, it was long ago pointed out that paying rent for land does not bring the land into being; it is only a charge paid to the title holder to gain access to that asset. Opening up uncultivated land, on the other hand, really is an entrepreneurial activity that increases society's underlying capital assets. Renting land is like buying someone's already existing property: it moves money around and it sets up new legal rights to use the property. Humanity has been renting and buying and selling property rights for millennia in every part of the world long before modern industrial capitalism arose in Europe.

Rent is what an owner can charge for use of existing property. It is often non-free market in origin, made possible by rules of law or prerogatives of power. So, the premium available to monopolies and cartels over and above selling at marginal cost is often considered to be a rent premium and the practice of gaining monopoly market power to be one of rent seeking.

For example, when the City of New York limits by law the number of taxicabs, a price arises to "rent" the opportunity to make money by having permission to use one of those licenses. The most recent "rental" fee for a taxi medallion in New York City was $600,000, a nice price to pay for a legalism.

Rent seeking is the heart and soul of crony capitalism. It encourages irresponsibility, abuse of the power that is rented out for cash, having only limited time horizons for earning a return, taking risks with power or property while leaving the long-term consequences of rash behavior for others to bear, and minimizing reciprocally beneficial conduct.

"Renting" stocks for short-term exploitation of their legal powers gave rise to green mail pressures of yesterday and to the hedge fund pressures of today.

Having only such a "rentier" mentality was the focus of social criticism of classical landed aristocracies. Landlords then often prefered to rack rents and their tenants become more like indentured servants.

The incentives around renting for both lesser and lessee tend to cut off rights from corresponding responsibilities whereas ownership tends to bind property rights to responsibilities with its incentives to profit over time.

Renting can more easily become a license to be cavalier with money and property while enduring ownership is more likely to be a burden of care and concern.

Renting property is not, therefore, inherent in or essential for capitalism.

Renting stocks on Wall Street, therefore, is not necessarily a fundamental component of modern capitalism I would add.

Liquid equity markets for corporate control and a share of profits do have their justified place in modern capitalism. Better stock markets in developing countries indeed would contribute much to the economic growth of those countries.

The desirable functions of "Wall Street" financial institutions are: to permit companies to raise money, either to expand a business or to allow founders to realize the wealth they have created for society; two, to help retain staff with stock ownership and options as incentive to stay and build the company for future earnings; three, reputation assurance for customers, suppliers, creditors, and potential employees; and, four, pricing signals for the efficient investment of financial capital in one company or another, or one industry or another.

These functions are most associated with encouragement of ownership rights. That is their social office. These functions promote industry, thrift, and responsible management of corporate assets and opportunities.

Less constructive functions of "Wall Street" financial institutions, it seems to me, are those that encourage speculation, short-term – devil-take-the-hindmost – profit seeking, and illusory, unsustainable valuations of enterprise. These are more associated with "renting" stocks for a limited time and purpose.

Benjamin Franklin once noted that "The general foible of mankind is in the pursuit of wealth to no end."

This aspect of "Wall Street" set up the scandals of Enron and WorldCom. Playing to those who only "rent" stocks encourages earnings management and quarterly reporting of earnings. In high turnover trading activity around short-selling and options trading, money spent on "renting" shares in order to go short or to write a put options contract doesn't go to any company to help improve its balance sheet.

If today's Wall Street is more appropriately analogized to "renting" than to "owning" stocks, perhaps regulatory policy should take this into account in imposing costs, hurdles and consequences on those who are in the markets only to take from others and not to give of themselves.

High frequency trading: A Public Good?

I am increasingly drawn to the proposition that financial markets and capitalism are not soul-mates. They are more like fractious siblings competing for parental attention, or narcissistic partners in a rocky marriage, each needing the other but each fearful of the other's shortcomings.

There is a close tie between them which can't be totally severed. Traders in financial markets need real economic activity and growth in order to have financial contracts – stock, loans, options, derivatives, insurance guarantees, etc. - to buy and sell. Finance has no social purpose other than gambling unless there are related economic transactions to use the money which is bought and sold in financial markets.

And, reciprocally, productive capitalism needs cash and loans. You can't grow an economy without equity investment and credit. That was one of the big lessons learned by the Communists: government extractions, planned expenditures, and socialized property can't replicate the wealth creation potential of equity and credit markets responding to entrepreneurial initiatives.

But, trading in financial markets has its own gods and its own rules and they are not always wise and reasonable, tolerating "irrational exuberance" and other forms of hubris and ignorance.

For example, former Chairman of the US Federal Reserve System Paul Volcker has recommended a separation of proprietary trading for their own profit from service-oriented financial intermediation for large financial institutions, the very ones whose trading operations tanked the global credit system in the fall of 2008.

Big Wall Street trading houses are using new algorithms and super fast computers to spot price anomalies before other investors can even blink. This technology, available to a privileged few, gives them the equivalent of inside information in trading. Is such trading a public good so that its profits are respectable?

High frequency trading uses algorithms to trade at ultra-fast speeds, often 1,000 times faster than the blink of a human eye. Software programs decide when, how and where to trade financial instruments without human intervention.

Tobin Harshaw writes "powerful algorithms – algos in industry parlance – execute millions of trades in second and scan dozens of public and private marketplaces simultaneously. They can spot trends before others investors can blink, changing orders and strategies within milliseconds."

With so many such lightening fast trades, the average order size is falling and the number of separate trade orders is rising. On the NYSE the average order amount fell 67% from $19,400 in 2005 to only $6,400 recently. On the NASDAQ, the average order size dropped from $44,600 to $14,400 over those 5 years.

High frequency trading permits firms with massive computer capacity to track momentum moves in the prices of financial assets, buying and selling quickly to capitalize on the likely very small movement of a price up or down towards an expected equilibrium price.

High frequency traders can issue and the cancel orders almost simultaneously, confusing others as to what prices are real. And, placing orders first can get a tiny premium – but tiny premiums aggregated over millions of trades become handsome profits.

Tradebot in Kansas City said in 2008 that, on average, it holds a stock for 11 seconds. Many high frequency traders end each day with no position in the market, having sold off all buys. They thus provide no sustaining support to the prices of the financial instruments in which they trade. They assume no equity risk of enterprise. They are merely parasitic profiteers and not owners.

Computers detecting via their flash orders that there is an interest in a stock issue tiny orders at a price below a buyers limit price. If that tiny offer to sell is accepted, the computer issues additional tiny offers at incrementally higher prices until the buyer's limit is reached. Now knowing what the buyer's limit price is, the computer offers a large lot for sale just under that limit, taking for itself the margin between the lower price – which the buyer would have loved to get – and the limit price.

Up to half of all stock market volume consists of such algorithmic trades. The company Tradeworx runs computers that buy and sell 80 million shares a day. Some of the biggest high frequency traders make billions of trades a day. Tradeworx computers get prices from exchanges, decide how to trade, complete a risk analysis, and generate a buy or sell order in 20 microseconds. Last month the US firm of Algo Technologies unveiled a system that can trade in 16 microseconds.

On May 6, 2010, the mysterious "flash crash" in the NYSE may well have been both caused by and exacerbated by high frequency trading. During the ten minutes of price collapse, some 19 billion shares were traded. When prices began to plunge, operators of the Tradeworx computers entered a command to sell everything and shut down. Several of their competitors issued similar commands to their computers. Trading went into meltdown, sending chills through the financial world.

With the advent of high frequency trading, technology has created a new financial market place, one perhaps less fair to those without access to massive computing power. The new market demands new thinking as to its ways of operating responsibly in support of the economy.

THE ROAD TO MORAL CAPITALISM

There are other objections to high frequency trading.

First, it provides low quality liquidity. Unlike NYSE specialists who were required to maintain a fair and orderly market, high frequency traders can drop out at any time. Recently the Financial Times reported that among one thousand orders, some 99% were quickly cancelled.

SEC Chair Mary Shapiro spoke on the "illusion" of liquidity that happens when trading is too fast and automated. She noted that in periods of high volatility investors can find it difficult to buy and sell shares. In times of market stress, liquidity can be ephemeral as retail investors become scared and cautious and flee to higher quality assets. So it is debatable that high frequency traders are proving liquidity to the general public. If they are not providing a needed intangible asset for market capitalism, what do thay do that deserves compensation?

Michael Goldstein, professor of finance at Babson College, has suggested that "speed limits" might be necessary on the highways of institutional trading. The response from high frequency traders is that "speed reduces risk" by more quickly finding equilibrium prices. But with such reflexive trading, when does the market "equilibrium" price reflect the actual value of the underlying financial asset?

Second, high frequency trading can generate false trading signals. A spike in such trading can attract momentum investors when there is really no substantive demand for the security. Such a spike then attracts options traders who start to build positions. These positions then attract risk arbitrage traders who believe there is potential news that could affect the stock to exploit.

High frequency trading determines overall market direction without fundamental or technical reasons. The defense of high frequency trading that it accelerates finding equilibrium prices strikes me as questionable. Trades executed in microseconds respond not so much to foundational reasons for valuing economic activity but more to "friction" and marginal "transaction costs" in the movement of information in financial markets. Momentary equilibrium prices that reflect miniscule adjustments don't strike me as that important for markets to serve the needs of capital allocation in society at large.

When word of high frequency trading appeared in the New York Times on July 24th, 2009, people reacted. Two of the three US equity exchanges said they would end "flash orders" by the end of September. This came after Mary Shapiro, chair of the US Securities and Exchange Commission, said the Commission would clamp down on flash trading. After the May 6th "Flash Crash" the SEC is introducing "circuit breakers" to stop trading on the NYSE when prices move too quickly, too fast.

It is hard for me to square high frequency trading and its profitability with the equilibrium needs of a fair market that will produce prices with integrity to permit capitalism to avoid irrationality. That being so, rules and regulations to limit the market freedoms of traders may very well be in order so that private interest can't too easily trump the common good.

If much of what Wall Street gives us is "renting" financial instruments and "high speed" trading, why is it needed? This side of Wall Street is dedicated to pursuit of very private goods and not to the provision of public goods in sustaining what capitalism needs in viable and robust financial markets to funnel savings into productive investment in the real economy. So why should we have a legal regime that exposes the entire global economy to losses and recession when such "renting" and trading create imprudent asset bubbles that burst?

Financial reform in the UK has proposed "ring fencing" within financial houses to separate the trading operations from those that support the real economy. The policy goal is to permit money making through trading, but at the sole risk of those who spend their money in trading.

道

德

Tao Te Ei in Running Script © 2014 by Weiming Lu

CHAPTER FOURTEEN
DODD FRANK REFORMS:
NOT ENOUGH

The official American response to the 2008 collapse of credit markets was the Dodd-Frank legislation, a long complicated set of rules. The legislation proposals of the Obama Administration which were limited in scope.

In keeping with traditional responses to market failures, these proposed reforms first look to non-market decision-makers to countermand the preferences of market makers that would seem to introduce excessive risk to the public good. Thus the Federal Reserve System would become a "super regulator" of systemic risk in financial markets.

The concept behind the proposed reforms is to monitor and contain "systemic risks" to the financial system. The goal is not to prevent future asset bubbles and resulting collapses in asset prices, but to isolate such market volatility from public bailouts.

Second, financial products sold to consumers be vetted and approved by a public agency just as pricing and capital investment decisions of public utilities have long been vetoed or ratified by public utility commissions.

Third, more information about derivatives be made public when they are bought and sold.

But the central thrust of the reform proposals seems to be enhancing the power of the Federal Reserve System to forestall the accumulation of systemic risks which might lead to another sudden collapse of confidence in financial markets.

The goal behind such supervision seems to be separation of private risk from public remediation. The cost of private risk should be born only by private risk takers. If private investors seek higher returns by running higher risks, then they should absorb the losses associated with such risks as well. Whenever there is market failure, private investors should take all the losses. There should be no public bailouts and rescues of for-profit financial firms. The losses will hit only the pockets of those who signed up to shoulder the risks thereof.

A just ethical comment on last fall's massive deployment of public funds and credit to offset the deflationary effects of the Great Panic was that in the run up to and the bursting of the asset bubble in securitized consumer debt and home mortgages, CDOs and CDSs, the "gains were privatized and the losses were socialized." Many who took profits out of the system in return for providing faulty financial intermediation were able to keep their gains while the Federal Reserve System and the US Federal Government had to pay for many of the losses they had caused with their imprudent business strategies.

This "socialization of the losses" is not the entire story. Many – owners of Bear Stearns, Lehman Brothers, and other failed firms, for example – lost the value of their ownership interests. But the reality of recession caused by the asset bubble was such that governments had to spend funds to clean up a mess made by private financial markets in order to protect standards of living for ordinary citizens and asset prices in general.

The common weal of the global economy was put at hazard by certain leaders in financial markets. Governments had an obligation to contain that hazard as best they could. Now they want to prevent a recurrence of such expenditures on their parts and such dangerous and thoughtless behaviors on the part of private markets. The proposition that we can isolate private financial markets and let them alone to do whatever they please because government can prevent the accumulation of systemic risks in the future rests on a premise about the nature of private markets. That premise is known as the "efficient market thesis".

Believers in efficient markets hold that all the information needed to make sound pricing decisions is available to market participants and they buy and sell back and forth until prices of goods and services reach contingent equilibria between the opposing forces of supply and demand. Under conditions of efficiency, no one can be wiser than a market for very long. Its prices are assumed to be the most correct possible under the circumstances. The efficient markets thesis is a version of the "wisdom of crowds" convention.

Systemic risk, it is argued, undermines the desired conditions of efficiency in markets. A few players have such market power that their decisions overwhelm a market's capacity for self correction. They can impose their biases on prices. Their risks, then, become socialized to affect the outcomes experienced by others who had no intention to participate in such risky undertakings. This seems to have been the case, for example, with AIG, which had sold so many guarantees of the borrowings of others (CDSs) that its bankruptcy would crash collateral values and balance sheet viability for thousands of other companies and transactions. AIG posed a risk to the system. It was too big. It created an inefficient market by accumulating excessive risk for itself and so, for others as well.

So, it would seem probable then that prevention of systemic risk accumulation would allow us to leave markets to themselves to buy and sell as they see fit. This would be the logic behind the Dodd Frank reforms.

But there is a flaw in the efficient market hypothesis, one exposed by John Maynard Keynes in Chapter 12 of his famous General Theory of Employment Interest and Money. In this Chapter 12, Keynes explained how markets for financial instruments function. He wrote about stock markets and any other market for financial contract rights where traders buy and sell contracts for future shares of income and capital appreciation, in the form of debt, equity, warrants, options, futures, derivatives, etc.

Keynes asserted that in any such market something he called the "state of confidence" directed its energies in the setting of prices. The "state of confidence" in any financial market was that socialized state of belief about what prices should be that had a disproportionate effect on reaching outcomes in efficient markets. The "state of confidence" was more powerful in the aggregate, according to Keynes, than the independent decisions of particular buyers and sellers.

No financial market, argued Keynes, could escape the directing influence of the "state of confidence."

Now, the "state of confidence of any financial market was the sum of two subordinate conditions. One was "a speculative convention" peculiar to that market and the second was the "state of credit".

The "speculative convention" is the variance from a mean of various ideas and conjectures about the future in the minds of buyers and sellers. A wide variance from a mean point of view, or a broad consensus, produces a stable speculative convention. On the other hand, a narrow variance with resulting lack of consensus indicates unsettled intentions among buyers and sellers and so more volatile pricing movements.

Now, much buying in financial markets is done with credit, or leverage. For example, at its fall, Lehman Brothers had leveraged its capital 44 times in order to buy financial products. Without access to credit, most market makers fail. Thus, the "state of credit" is vital to the activity level of financial markets. The "state of credit" according to Keynes is "the confidence of lending institutions towards those who seek to borrow from them". The 2008 meltdown in Wall Street occurred due to a sudden collapse in the confidence level of lenders. There was a "flight to quality" as those with cash refused to lend it for any purchase except for purchase of the most secure and highly valued assets, such as US Treasuries.

Thus the pricing outcomes of any efficient financial market will reflect the equilibrium "state of confidence" in that market, which in turn will reflect the nature of any "speculative conventions" and the intensity, positive or negative, of the "state of credit".

Dysfunctions such as asset bubbles in financial markets occur due to shifts in "speculative conventions" and the "state of credit". Firmly held "speculative conventions" and intensely positive "states of credit" will produce a "state of confidence" leading to asset bubbles. Changes in "speculative conventions" and collapses in positive "states of credit" will end asset bubbles and trigger rapid declines in asset prices, leading to financial crises.

"Speculative conventions" are co-determinative of the "state of credit". As long as a "speculative convention" holds the imagination of buyers and sellers, the prices determined by than convention will have the respect of lenders into those financial markets. But when the terms of a convention lose their persuasive appeal, lenders choke, worry suddenly about risk and seek more security for or higher returns on money lent. When faith in a convention collapses completely, lenders pull out from credit markets and the "state of credit" turns abusively negative.

This is another way of saying that financial markets don't always get asset prices right. They price assets according to "speculative conventions" only. If the conventions become excessively irrational, then, as night follows the day, prices will be excessively irrational as well.

As Keynes noted, there is no necessary conformity of "speculative conventions" to fundamental economic realities. Such conventions are first, only conventions; they are not an external objective truth but only the mental inventions of buyers and sellers. Second, they are speculative in two senses: they are merely guesses – theoretical speculations - as to what will happen and they incorporate taking a chance on the future.

There is a necessary disconnect between speculative conventions and future reality just as there is a necessary disconnect between illusion and truth. Speculative conventions can be no more than approximations of the future; they can never be guarantees of what will be. Conventions are subjective, formed as much by emotions and prejudice as by common sense, and may or may not fully align with objective reality.

This fact applies with particular force to valuations. The holy grail of any financial investment, its summum bonum, the sanctum sanctorum of a financial contract, is its value. The perceived value of the instrument relative to its market price drives its market. A perfect market would always price an instrument - a share of General Motors, a CDO, etc. – at its "true' value. And, its "true"value would reflect justly and fairly the money returns in capital and income that its owner will receive.

Asset bubbles, for example, occur when prices wildly exceed realistic values; and panics occur when prices wildly underestimate longer term values.

And when faith in a convention so collapses, even equity investors are hard to come by, even though asset prices are dropping and long-term bargains become more and more available.

The presence of speculative conventions inside efficient markets holds those markets in permanent slavery to occasional outbursts of "irrational exuberance".

Financial markets have a casino-like aspect as they are driven by traders who think only for the moment. As Keynes said: "When the capital development of a country becomes a by-product of the activities of a casino, then the job is likely to be ill-done."

If financial markets were only casinos isolated from society like the casinos in Macao or on remote Native American reservations in Minnesota and Wisconsin and off-limits to all but gamblers who like to lose their money on a regular basis, then we could ignore them and their capacity to take our money. Keynes even noted in his chapter 12 that "it is usually agreed that casinos should, in the public interest, be inaccessible and expensive. And perhaps the same is true of stock exchanges."

Thus the Dodd-Frank reforms seek to isolate irrationally exuberant market outbursts from drawing on the public fisc when irrational exuberance collapses into irrational panic.

This is a notable goal but a minimal one. Why can't modern capitalism so balance markets that speculative conventions themselves are brought within the bounds of rationality? In other words, why can't we have financial markets that actually get prices right with minimal destabilizing volatility?

The need to get such prices right is important. Correctly pricing assets is necessary for sound economic growth and the provision of finance for business enterprise. Whether we like it or not, however, financial markets are necessary for capitalism. Funds are needed to run real economies and liquid markets perform the wonderful function of collecting funds from some to pay over on condition to others who will put them to work in creating real economic wealth.

No modern economy can afford to over isolate its financial markets and confine them only to gamblers who love to bet on future prices of assets. Where one gambler wins, another loses and cash changes hands. But an economy needs access to the cash to invest in production and doesn't want to be at risk of paying too much for assets, or not having access to cash when the gamblers panic and asset prices collapse.

Thus the Dodd-Frank reforms did not go far enough. They left global capitalism too exposed to "immoral" greed and irrational pricing.

To save ourselves from harm, we must confront Grendel's mother in her watery den, not just kill her bloodthirsty son; we must take on the operations of "speculative conventions".

The problem posed by "speculative conventions" is that they can't be regulated, or dictated for markets. They arise in freedom and have complete intellectual randomness. No one can force a convention on either a buyer or seller. Their own individual thinking, ambitions, emotions, insights, fears, calculations, knowledge guides their acceptance or rejection of conventional wisdom. Their personal self-interest and self-regard drives their behaviors.

Now, here Keynes had a brilliant insight into investors which is the heart of his Chapter 12. He noted that experience and common sense has taught most investors in financial markets that they are best rewarded in the short-term not by making superior long-term forecasts of the probable yield of an investment over its whole life. No, as traders in financial markets, they are more likely to profit if they can foresee "changes in the conventional basis of valuation a short time ahead of the general public." Keynes adds: "They are concerned, not with what an investment is really worth to a man who buys it "for keeps", but with what the market will value it at, under the influence of mass psychology, three months or a year hence."

The battle of wits among buyers and sellers, therefore, is to "anticipate the basis of conventional valuation a few months hence, rather than the prospective yield of an investment over a long term of years." For, as Keynes said, "it is not sensible to pay 25 for an investment of which you believe the prospective yield to justify a value of 30, if you also believe that the market will value it at 20 three months hence."

In a most famous paragraph, Keynes described as would a social-science researcher the workings of financial pricing: "professional investment may be likened to those newspaper competitions in which the competitors have to pick out the six prettiest faces from a hundred photographs, the prize being awarded to competitor whose choice most nearly corresponds to the average preferences of the competitors as a whole; so that each competitor has to pick, not those faces which he himself finds prettiest, but those which he thinks likeliest to catch the fancy of the other competitors, all of whom are looking at the problem from the same point of view. It is not a case of those which, to the best of one's judgment, are really the prettiest, nor even those which average opinion genuinely thinks the prettiest. We have reached the third degree where we devote our intelligences to anticipating what average opinion expects the average opinion to be."

The prudently risk-averse investor, therefore, just as much as the overconfident, greedy investor, seeks to know not where the market should be but where, in the minds of other investors, it most likely will be.

To make financial markets for capital more moral and less dysfunctional to the harm of the common weal, we need to influence this process of formation of speculative conventions. We need to better tie the process to long-term valuations that reflect the dynamics of the real economy more than to the speculations that run rampant in the traders' casinos. In short, we need speculative conventions that are less volatile and better align with fundamentals of wealth creation.

Keynes made a distinction which should inform our thinking today and our reform efforts between the activity of forecasting the psychology of the market, which he called "speculation" and the activity of forecasting the prospective yield of assets over their entire life, which he called "enterprise". He worried that in very liquid investment markets, there was a tendency for speculation to predominate over enterprise.

It is enterprise, we must never forget, that drives the wheels of wealth creation and so ameliorates conditions of social injustice. Speculation just moves cash from one gambler to another.

Keynes noted that: "Speculators may do no harm as bubbles on a steady stream of enterprise. But the position is serious when enterprise becomes the bubble on a whirlpool of speculation. ... The measure of success attained by Wall Street, regarded as an institution of which the proper social purpose is to direct new investment into the most profitable channels in terms of future yield, cannot be claimed as one of the outstanding triumphs of laissez-faire capitalism, which is not surprising, if I am right in thinking that the best brains of Wall Street have been in fact directed towards a different object."

And, if we can constructively reform the process of making and unmaking speculative conventions in financial markets, we will reap the additional benefit of moving the "state of credit" to a higher and more sustainable level of confidence.

Thus, we can influence the over-all "state of confidence" in financial markets to keep them running smoothly consistent and profitable for all.

More challenging dynamics than containing systemic risks still await thoughtful reform efforts.

The CRT has proposed the following reforms:

Imprudent decisions on the part of investment banks, banks, mortgage brokers, insurance companies, and consumers - all seeking profitable advantage - brought the financial network that sustains global capitalism to crisis. Great American financial houses – even Lehman Brothers that survived the Great Depression of the 1930s - are no more; banks in America and Europe have been propped up by governments; massive amounts of liquidity have been injected into the financial system by the US Federal Reserve System and other central banks.

Trillions of dollars in private wealth was destroyed in a matter of weeks, some of it never to be regained. There is no trust or confidence in financial markets. Credit is becoming scarce although capitalism cannot function without it. The losses and uncertainties have spread from the collapse of the subprime mortgage market in the United States to the global community.

This is not business as usual. The state in major financial centers has stepped in to protect the economically vulnerable where markets have failed. Yet, ironically, government policies also contributed in various ways to the evolution of an environment where risk was negligently addressed by financial markets, paving the way for the current crisis.

Financial institutions upon which all business success depends for its well-being have not met their fundamental responsibilities. Even with their failures to be prudent, in some form financial intermediation must be facilitated as a matter of first importance for the global economy. The role of financial institutions – including stock markets, banks, and insurance companies - in supporting a successful free market is uniquely necessary.

The causes of this crisis were a lack of rigor in valuations, of prudence in the extension of credit, and of transparency in management. This failure was not of individuals only, but reflected, in addition, profound shortcomings in the structures of private sector governance both as prescribed and as applied. In short, risk was not managed well; it was not even properly understood both by those creating it and by those bound to mitigate it.

Driving this lack of prudent management - this failure to take into account the full range of risks inherent in massive extensions of credit in American sub-prime mortgages, in the sale and purchase of collateral debt obligations, and in the guarantee of payment by those structured financial products through credit default swaps - was a shortsighted and dysfunctional system of incentives and personal remuneration.

Compensation of senior company officers and fund managers was decoupled from long-term wealth creation and was misaligned with the interests of stakeholders. Compensation based on fees earned and other incentive-based benchmarks blinded many otherwise intelligent managers to the long-term consequences of their decisions.

Compensation provided rewards even when excessive risk was undertaken and was provided in ways that shielded senior corporate officers and fund managers from liability for their decisions.

As a result, the best interests of customers, owners, employees and communities were systematically overlooked. Decision-makers were so focused on the short-term that little attention was paid to finding exit strategies for risk accumulation. Demand for immediate returns at high rates from a few key stakeholders, in part, drove these compensation arrangements.

Financial intermediation was decoupled from long-term wealth creation and re-focused on short-term speculation in financial instruments such as CDOs. Systemic risk for the global economy was accumulated through excessive leverage leading to unsustainable asset valuations.

Regulation failed to halt this growth in systemic risk, though to be fair, it must be noted that many aspects of the failed business activities were subject to inadequate regulation.

But, in a larger sense, the current crisis results from deeper social trends that belittle the importance of ethics and responsibility in business decision-making. Ideological commitments to "neo-liberalism", Social Darwinism, shareholder returns, free market fundamentalism, divorced business leadership from standards of good faith and wise stewardship.

Thus, the crisis has further exacerbated the low levels of trust which the global community places in business, with profits privatized to those who created the crisis and losses socialized to taxpayers, employees, customers, and communities. Though justly perhaps, owners of the financial institutions responsible for the crisis have lost most of their ownership wealth when their firms failed or were bought out.

Interestingly, the recent movement promoting corporate social responsibility – prominently featuring the United Nations Global Compact and the Global Reporting Initiative - was also ineffective. CSR standards and monitoring NGOs did not provide checks and balances that might have mitigated to this failure of capitalism to advance the common good. It is now apparent that much of the CSR movement was not closely connected to core business risk management.

Compounding the problem have been institutions of business education that have not integrated standards of corporate responsibility into the financial metrics that reward thoughtless short-term market behaviors, such as the enthusiastic accumulation of debt and reliance on rising asset prices.

Uniquely, the CRT Principles for Business did provide strategic ethical guidance, which, had it been followed, would have kept those institutions more faithful to their obligations of stewardship and out of crisis. The CRT Principles seek to drive constructive behaviors that will enhance bottom-line valuations of business success and so sustain responsible long-term wealth creation for society.

This is not the first time that market capitalism has so failed. Less than a decade ago, global markets lived through the bust of the dot-com and telecom bubble in equities and the accounting scandals of Enron and World-Com. Before that, world financial markets were upset by currency collapses in Thailand, Malaysia, Indonesia and Russia. And before that, the United States lived through the savings and loan/junk bond bubble and bust.

There is indeed a cancer deep within capitalism which causes these crises of excess self-seeking but which, fortunately, does go into remission from time to time. Every so often, capitalism's immune system of market discipline fails so that this cancer of "irrational exuberance" metastasizes once again but through the use of new investment vehicles. The object of reform, obviously, should be either to eliminate the cancer once and for all or to boost society's market immune system of accurate pricing and valuations in order to keep the cancer in longterm remission.

With respect to the current crisis in financial markets, there are no clear remedies on the table. Business leaders are largely silent; academics have little to say; and politicians are putting out fires, not designing a sustainable future that removes once and for all the underlying problem.

The way forward to free markets that are consistently reliable in their capacity for robust wealth creation is through the imposition of higher standards of transparency. Lack of transparency, again and again, leads market capitalism down wrong roads. Such opacity has long been a fundamental flaw in institutions of private enterprise.

At the core of these recent shortcomings were the boards of directors of the corporations involved. They were not sufficiently encased in an environment of accountability and transparency. The market failure, therefore, was ultimately a failure of governance.

The following remedial steps deserve priority attention:

- First, internal procedures for thorough risk management and fully adequate disclosure must be specified and required of companies at the board level and below. Boards should assure risk consideration across this range of concerns. The CRT risk assessment process of Arcturus provides an example of what can be required of companies.

- Second, members of corporate boards should be trained and certified as skilled in the assessment and management of social and business risks, broadly speaking. Business is not without consequence for society and should, therefore, be attentive to the demands for responsible execution of its private office of trust and profit.

- Third, boards should delegate such strategic risk consideration of stakeholder interests to a special committee that is supported by a designated senior corporate officer.

- Fourth, boards should make annual disclosures of the results of risk assessment across the full range of stakeholders in form and content that convey material information and comments in easily understood prose that is meaningful to those stakeholders.

- Fifth, disclosure of risk factors and concerns should be subject to evaluation by rating agencies and third party assurance.

- Sixth, executive compensation should reflect success in the prudent management of risk with alignment of incentives to achievement of long-term wealth creation.

- Seventh, opportunities for companies and individuals to hide income by utilizing tax havens and secrecy jurisdictions should be eliminated.

These reforms will not only address the causes of the current crisis, they will have a salutary effect on a broader and longer basis. Such reforms to eliminate the underlying, systemic flaws in the system should have as an objective promotion of global social responsibility on the part of all companies.

道德

Tao Te 55 in Running Script © 2014 by Weiming Lu

CHAPTER FIFTEEN
THE EXISTENTIAL GROUNDS OF
MORAL CAPITALISM

What can advocates of business ethics and corporate social responsibility do constructively to advance the sustainable economic growth which supports human happiness in this world? Is their role only that of by-standers? I argue that thought-leadership is a foundational contribution to better practical outcomes. Being a professional implies action, as well as the accumulation of expertise through scholarship, fact-finding, insightful consideration, and communication of suggestions and conclusions to the community at large.

A starting point for thinking about the existential grounds for Moral Capitalism examines private rights. Use of private rights is the basis of free markets and capitalism. But when rights are taken to their fullest extent, they always run the risk of trespassing on the rights of others who don't think the way we do about ourselves and our claims on the world. Many instances of market failures occur when one party simple exercises rights to the legal maximum. Non-legal arguments –ethics and morality - are then called upon to provide restraints where the law is silent.

The common good melts away under pressure from individuals demanding special treatment.

Such is the critique of brute, free markets, where the struggle for market power among individuals asserting personal rights to property and profit does not guarantee the greatest good for the greatest number. Rights logic in free market conditions seeks to impose costs on others, while obtaining benefits for the self alone. Raw, self-interest conceptualized as personal rights does not provide an invisible hand promoting the common weal.

If it is "my way or the highway," usually, we end up on the highway looking for a ride.

Self-restraint, then, is more likely to produce the common good than aggressive self-seeking and exploitation of claims of right. Self-restraint is ethics applied in action. With ethics, compromise becomes possible and overreaching brinkmanship avoided. Ethics, or the capacity to act with virtue, opens the door to higher levels of prosperity, civil order and happiness for a community.

With ethical thinking the interests of stakeholders can more easily come into consideration in decision-making. With ethics, the self-interested "I/It" approach to life becomes the more transcendent "I/Thou" engagement between self and other.

Simply put, ethics arises out of concern for the consequences of our actions on others. Ethics places restraint on selfishness; it keeps us from going to the extreme.

Aristotle famously described ethics as moderation – keeping to the middle, avoiding extremes.

Buddhism teaches us the wisdom of following the middle path.

Taoism and the Confucian text, The Doctrine of the Mean, find justice in keeping to the Mean or the Tao, which never flow too far away from accommodation with reality. We expect the discipline of morality and ethics to constrain our behaviors, placing the self in

some serving relationship to other sources of value. Morality – rules
for conduct – and ethics – consideration of consequences – provide
for some level of transcendence over selfish autonomy and isolation. Morality and ethics constructively unite an individual living in
time and space with what lies beyond both his or her physical person and his or her psychological homestead. In our time, the most
effective challenges to morality and ethics arise from various forms
of relativism; a denial that standards of conduct do, can, or should
exist that might constrain our self-seeking. Relativism leaves each
person a sovereign authority ruling over a minuscule state with no
duties to foreign powers. Relativism legitimates the self in not going
along with the moral and ethical standards of others. Relativism
also de-legitimates telling others how they should think and act.

The most pervasive form of relativism is psychological abso-
lutism, the claim that each person is autonomous, unique, and
need only respond to internal concerns bounded by that separate
autonomy. This is an idolatry of the self, where the single person is
privileged above all things in the cosmos. The ideal here is self-actualization in separation from all contexts and contingencies spoken
of as "self esteem," a psyche freed from guilt and shame, and thus,
cut loose from social obligations.

From this perspective arises the argument that nothing should
constrain the person other than individually and willfully chosen
beliefs and standards. Respect and deference to individual distinctions is then the necessary moral and ethical stance for others.

Any common good must arise from the voluntary assent of individuals, who are completely free in their feelings and thinking to
adopt any value or behavior that extends their personality as they
see fit.

A second pervasive form of relativism arises from the claims
of Reason as a personal thought process to critique every possible
proposition, and in so doing, to have the last word in our minds.
This flows from the claim of every individual to be enlightened,
to challenge convention, authority, the reasoning of others, and
to have freedom of conscience. In an enlightened age, there can

be no convention, no tradition, no authority, no canon, which can demand the acquiescence of an individual self. Everything is subject to dis-establishment, deconstruction, and possible rejection.

The third pervasive form of relativism arises from the observation that our use of Reason is often conditioned by our religion, our race, our gender or sexual orientation, our social class, our ethnic culture. Thus, the conclusions reached by Reason in only one such social or cultural context, it is said, cannot be taken as giving rise to authoritative thinking for any other culture or social setting. Given this necessary parochialism in our thinking, we are said to be intellectually precluded from offering insights into anything functionally transcendental.

Further, it has been argued that our beliefs are conditioned by self-interest to defend and protect our social and cultural privileges and practices. Thus, assertions of right and wrong, of good and bad, can be deconstructed to reveal nothing more than self-interest at work, a revelation that permits us to dismiss and disdain such assertions by others when selecting our own perspectives on life. All arguments can thus be undermined by an ad hominem critique.

Thus, today, we are equipped with a variety of compelling points of view that marginalize the workings of morality and ethics. We are, consequently, left mostly with the self-referential pursuit of power as our guide through life.

This understanding of the human condition has been made fundamental in financial theory and economic analysis through an assumption called the "agency problem." This is an assumption that people are only self-interested and so cannot bring themselves to be faithful agents or trustworthy partners. Dynamics of fear and greed are therefore sufficient to optimize cooperative undertakings. In such a context, any strenuous call for business ethics or corporate social responsibility has to be laughable.

Relativism gives us a dark and depressing vision indeed, but one often supported by observations of human conduct. Thomas Hobbes spoke of the life of man as "solitary, poor, nasty, brutish and short."

The influential, but now overlooked Chinese jurist MoZi (470-391 BC), insisted that "everyone approved of his own views and disapproved the views of others, and so arose mutual disapproval among men. Everyone worked for the disadvantage of the others with water, fire and poison. Surplus energy was not spent on mutual aid; surplus goods were allowed to rot without sharing; learning about the Tao was kept secret. The disorder in the human world could be compared to that among birds and beasts" ("Identification with the Superior I," Y.P. Mei, The Works of Motze, 55).

Napoleon Bonaparte quipped that, "Men are moved by two levers only – fear and self-interest."

Freud once complained that, "the problem before us is how to get rid of the greatest hindrance to civilization – namely, the constitutional inclination of human beings to be aggressive towards one another." Thus for him, the "fateful question for the human species" was to what extent its "cultural development will succeed in mastering the disturbance of [its] communal life by the human instinct of aggression and self-destruction" (Civilization and its Discontents, 89, 92). In short, Freud tied the future of humanity to its capacity to effectively realize morality and ethics without showing us how to walk that road towards justice.

But if there were to be truth that could compel our acceptance of its certainty, morality and ethics would be empowered. The possibility of collectively distinguishing between right and wrong, good and bad, would seem more feasible. The alignment of self with something more transcendent would become more cogent, undercutting resistance to reaching out for such alignment within each person.

Might there, then, be such a truth function discoverable in our age of relativism?

By truth function here I mean something different from many philosophical speculations and religious teachings on what conceptions are true.

First, I do not include in my concept of a truth function any so-called truth revealed in an act of religious insight. I put into a separate category of propositions all truths that we may or may not accept, but which we can come to accept through a personal act of willing belief of a revelation to us. It could be a belief in the Christian God, in the Prophet-hood of Joseph Smith, the charisma of a political leader, or that our spouse is intelligent and charming, etc. Each of these propositions is open for acceptance or rejection on our part, as well as on the part of others. Our belief in its truth has no compelling force on the need for others to agree with us.

And, if we choose not to believe, the idea in question loses its importance as to how we live our lives. Our perception of the world simply evolves in a contrary direction. If we choose not to accept the revelation, it carries no truth value for us.

Such revealed truths are consistent with relativism – each to his or her own way in religion and philosophy, and similarly, with judgments about taste.

No, for a truth function I am searching for something more collectively compelling than mere revelation.

I would like to suggest that actually, there are propositions or beliefs, facts so to speak, that lie beyond our powers to eliminate from life. They constrain our willfulness in thinking and feeling. They can pinch our selfishness and intrude into our psyches, confronting us with that which we cannot change, even though we would like to. We may want to run from them, but, given their nature, we can't secure such separation. We are in their thrall, just as we are subject to gravity.

I am referring now to what was once called "Natural Law" by writers in international law and politics. So-called "Natural Law" thinkers were seeking a basis for common justice after uncompromisable sectarian warfare broke out between Catholic and Protestant Christians in Europe in the 16th century. With Protestant revelation at odds with the separately revealed Magisterium of the Catholic Church, neither set of insights and beliefs needed to admit its inferiority to the other. Each stood on its own ground of presumed truth. Compulsion by one party was met with resistance by the other.

Since the intellectual claims to authority of revealed religion were no longer compelling, writers such as Hugo Grotius, Samuel Pufendorf, and John Locke turned to more secular observations in order to find legitimacy for laws making distinctions between right and wrong. They moved away from revelation.

They pointed to circumstances that did not vary with human preferences and desires, to conditions that transcended individual willfulness. From this transcendence of certain conditions, they argued that belief in such circumstances and in what could be rationally deduced or intuited from their existence provided a basis for the superiority of some obligations over other, more self-referential behaviors. From the superiority of these obligations a common culture could be conceptualized and placed into institutional arrangements. Our lives would gain structured limitations from conventions derived from natural conditions beyond our control. We could be social in mind, as well as in fact. An interesting case for moral and ethical certainty was made by James Wilson, a member of the Constitutional Convention of 1789. He wrote: "Order, proportion, and fitness pervade the universe. Around us we see, within us, we feel; above us, we admire a rule, from which a deviation cannot, or should not, or will not be made . . . In every period of our existence, in every situation in which we can be placed, much is to be known, much is to be done, much is to be enjoyed. But all that is to be known, all that is to be done, all that is to be enjoyed, depends upon the proper exertion and direction of our numerous powers. In this immense ocean of intelligence and action, are we left without a compass and without a chart? Is there no pole star, by which we may regulate our course?" (The Works of James Wilson, Belknap Press, 1967, 97).

Wilson suggested in his 1790 lectures on law that everyone has a faculty which enables them to "trace the connection between actions and their effects, and our actions are nothing else but the steps which we take, or the means which we employ, to carry into execution the effects which we intend" (100).

Here, Wilson was following the observation earlier proffered by Cicero in De Officis: "Now there is this special difference between men and brutes: that the latter are governed by nothing but their senses, never look any farther than just to what strikes and affects them at present, and have a very little or hardly any concern for what is past or to come; but the former are creatures endowed with reason, which gives them a power to carry their thoughts to the consequences of things, to discover causes before they have yet produced their effects" (De Officis, London, Dent and Sons, 1953, 6).

A second faculty noted by Wilson was conscience. Following Adam Smith, another Scot moral philosopher, Wilson calls this faculty a monitor within us or over our conduct. He was pointing to a dynamic of constraint whereby some part of our nature evaluates and judges other parts of our liveliness.

Yet, "the science or morals is founded on truths that cannot be discovered or proved by reasoning." Reason begins with truths already known on which arguments can be grounded. Morality and ethics have their intuitive truths, one of which is the power of moral perception (133). What in particular we consider to be right or wrong, admirable or despicable, is less important than the fact that we each have a capacity to make such distinctions.

Whether or not we accept the fact that we possess a moral sense, it is still there, working away within us, willy-nilly. We can disacknowledge the fact that we have such an internal capacity only at some loss to ourselves of happiness accompanied by an inward perception of alienation from our most workable self.

We can close our minds to the process of morality and ethics, but our natures do not thereby abandon the capacity to do so. James Wilson noted that, "without this controlling faculty, endowed as we are with such a variety of senses and interfering desires, we should appear a fabric destitute of order out of joint with the order and proportion surrounding us" (136).

But, possessed of the moral sense, "all our powers may be harmonious and consistent; they may all combine in one uniform and regular direction" (136). Then, we can consider ourselves to have a life of meaning and fitness for our times and circumstances. This, then, provides grounds for happiness and fulfillment. Once we accept that we have the capacity, it remains but to use it. With its use we turn towards a more moral and ethical way of living.

This possession of a moral sense implements a law of nature – one immutable, not by the cause of an arbitrary proof proceeding from linguistic conventions, but because it has its foundations in the nature, constitution, and mutual relations of men and things (145).

In one of his works – The Whole Duty of Man According to the Law of Nature (Liberty Fund, 2003) – considered immutable circumstances as a living truth for all persons, giving rise to constraint on our will in line with the requirements of morality and ethics. He found natural law to be "that which is so agreeable with the rational and social nature of man that honest and peaceable society could not be kept up amongst Mankind without it" (52). Pufendorf argued that, whether we like it or not, one, we each have a social nature transcending a haughty individualism and, two, a social order embraces and succors individuals. It is, therefore, truthful to believe in the moral sense. He noted that, "it must follow then, that whatsoever advantages accompany human life, are all owing to that mutual help men afford one another" (53).

When asked to provide one word only which might serve as a rule of practice for one's entire life, Confucius answered as Pufendorf might have, "Is not reciprocity such a word?" (Analects, Bk XV, Ch XXIII). Yet, Pufendorf wrote sharply of all the circumstances in which people do not behave morally or ethically, but as wolves to one another (homo homini lupus), from which he infers that for any to prosper in society, it is necessary that all be sociable. This, he says, gives rise to laws of human society whereby men are directed how to render themselves useful members thereof, and without which it falls to pieces. These necessary rules of fellowship he calls the "laws of nature," or more appropriately, the moral and ethical requirements brought on by human nature (56).

These laws are laid upon men by their natures as a means not invented by the wit or imposed by the will of men, nor capable of being changed by their humors and inclinations, to accomplish the end of promoting sociable living (57).

For Pufendorf, "So to him who has well studied the common nature and condition of man, it will be easy to discover those laws which are necessary for the safety and common benefit of Mankind" (52). In short, individually, each of us has the power to be anti-social, to be deviant, selfish, and cruel, but such power can be authoritatively constrained by morality and ethics on behalf of a common good, the presence of which reaches into our hearts through the moral sense.

It is most important to note in passing that the moral sense does not invalidate the value associated with the self. Our personal dignity and well-being carry moral and ethical weight, as well.

In 1758, Emmerich de Vattel published his treatise on the law of nations, which afterwards has been substantially ratified by international legal practice among nations. Vattel, too, began his argument for international law with reference to a law of nature, which he describes as immutable. This law, or really a set of facts, he sets down as: "Man is so formed by nature that he cannot supply all his own wants, but necessarily stands in need of the intercourse and assistance of his fellow-creatures, whether for his immediate preservation, or for the sake of perfecting his nature and enjoying such a life as is suitable to a rational being" (The Law of Nations, J. Chitty, editor, Philadelphia, 1863, lix). From this observation, Vattel deduces a proposition that "the general law of society is that each individual should do for the others everything which their necessities require, and which he can perform without neglecting the duty that he owes to himself" (ibid).

Following upon this truth of individual dependency on society, reason would lead us to the conclusion that we cannot disentangle ourselves from morality, ethics, society, and consideration of our actions. We are constrained by being who we are. We have no choice about having or not having that fundamental condition, though we can put ourselves in opposition to its inclinations and willfully impose ourselves onothers and on society.

Knowing that we can be just right for our place in life and that such a sense of rightness is natural and does not arise from our selfish desires alone seems close to the insights given by early Chinese Taoist writings, such as:

> Silent and boundless, standing alone without change, yet pervading all without fail, it may be regarded as the Mother of the world. I do not know its name. I style it Tao, and in the absence of a better word, call it "The Great" (Tao Te Jing 25).

> When the great Tao was abandoned, there appeared humanness and justice.

> When intelligence and wit arose, there appeared great hypocrites.

> When the six formalities lost their orderliness, there appeared filial piety and paternal kindness.

> When darkness and disorder began to appear in a kingdom, there appeared the loyal ministers (Tao Te Jing 18).

> Failing Tao, man resorts to Virtue.

> Failing Virtue, man resorts to humanness.

> Failing humanness, man resorts to morality.

> Failing morality, man resorts to ceremony.

> Now ceremony is the merest husk of faith and loyalty; it is the beginning of all confusion and disorder (Tao Te Jing 38).

The Tao may be abandoned, but it does not go away. In its place, we humans place inferior cultural inventions of our own. The more substantial and eternal truth is contained in the Tao, not in our fashioning. The Tao is presented as the most superior reality, the most completely natural of all presences, as that which is timeless and endless, which never changes, which only is.

Thirty spokes converge upon a single hub; it is on the hone in the center that the use of the cart hinges.

We make a vessel from a lump of clay. It is the empty space within the vessel that makes it useful.

We make doors and windows for a room; but it is the empty spaces that make the room livable (Tao Te Jing 11).

We may not see the emptiness, but it is always there to serve more than itself. The Tao is like that.

In the Confucian tradition, The Doctrine of the Mean affirms that what Heaven has bestowed is Natural. Accordance with this nature is the Way (Tao); the following of this path comes from learning. Confucian recommendations for personal propriety and humanness flow from accepting the truth of a moral sense.

Buddhism, in the initial teachings of the Buddha, takes a similar stance. Beyond our wills, in nature, lie various realities which we can appropriate for ourselves that can change the way we relate to what is around us. This is the noble eightfold way of conforming our efforts, to that which is beyond us.

The noble eightfold way was presented to us as part of the Dharma, or law of nature. Our disbelief does not make the Tao, or the noble eightfold path, or the moral sense disappear. They are and they abide without any dependence on our discovery of them or our mentally voting for their continuation. We cannot shape them to fit our predilections. We can align with them, struggle against them, or ignore them, but their operations will not leave us alone. Thus, they are true in my sense of the term. They transcend our will and all our fits pique. Transcendent in being real on their own terms, they are untouched by the three arguments for relativism noted above.

We may ignore such truth. That choice is part of our human freedom. We always have the options of ignoring morality and ethics or of intentionally acting contrary to their best advice. The question for each of us is: should we accept this truth and live with it, or challenge it? The argument for acceptance, I suggest only briefly, is the appropriateness, the beauty, of seeking to perfect our selves within reality.

Christian beliefs resonate with this truth about morality and ethics, as well. Martin Luther, in his 1520 essay on The Freedom of the Christian argued that a Christian, first, needed to incorporate faith in God's redemptive grace in his or her spiritual nature in order to become righteous. But from the perspective of having a moral sense, Luther, second, affirmed that a Christian in his or her mortal, worldly nature was a servant called to perform works that offset his or her selfish will to seek one's own advantage in the world. For Luther, personal rejections of this understanding of how a Christian should live would not, and could not, destroy the existential reality he described. For Luther, this truth was not merely natural, but natural as having been established by God in his wisdom and compassion with God's actions and intentions revealed through Scripture.

Pope Benedict XVI, in his Encyclical Caritas in Veritate, proposed one understanding of truth very similar to mine: "Truth, by enabling men and women to let go of their subjective opinions and impressions, allows them to move beyond cultural and historical limitations and to come together in the assessment of the value and substance of things" (at paragraph 4). (Though the Holy Father also speaks in this Encyclical of truth in another sense, one that I do not use in this essay: truth as Logos, intelligible formal linguistic propositions arising from somewhere beyond human invention and conceit). In line with my suppositions about the role of truth in our lives, Pope Benedict concluded that "Without truth, without trust and love for what is true, there is no social conscience and responsibility, and social action ends up serving private interests and the logic of power" (at paragraph 5). Without truth, Benedict warns, "cultures can no longer define themselves within a nature that transcends them, and man ends up being reduced to a mere cultural statistic" (at paragraph 26).

The encyclical Caritas in Veritate asserts as a matter of knowable fact that "As a spiritual being, the human person is defined through interpersonal relations. The more authentically he or she lives these relations, the more his or her own personal identity matures. It is not by isolation that man establishes his worth, but by placing himself in relation with others and with God" (at paragraph 53). Correspondingly, Pope Benedict XVI noted "reciprocity as the heart of what it is to be a human being" (at paragraph 57).

Pope John Paul II, in his Encyclical Centesimus Annus of 1991, has similarly affirmed about the human condition: "All human activity takes place within a culture and interacts with culture. For an adequate formation of a culture, the involvement of the whole man is required, whereby he exercises his creativity, intelligence, and knowledge of the world and of people. Furthermore, he displays his capacity for self-control, personal sacrifice, solidarity and readiness to promote the common good. Thus, the first and most important task is accomplished within man's heart" (at paragraph 51). Pope John Paul II here can be understood as affirming the existence of and the importance of the moral sense in each of us.

I read the Qur'an to confirm the truth about human nature that there is a fit place for each of us in an enveloping order discovered through exercise of the moral sense. The Qur'an, however, presents this truth as a revelation from a Creator God, which so provided for humanity out of mercy and compassion.

We read in Qur'an 16:78: "God brought you out of your mothers' wombs devoid of all knowledge, and gave you ears and eyes and hearts, so that you may give thanks." The human person, accordingly, grows in capacity to appreciate what is greater than his or her isolated set of feelings and interests. Qur'an further instructs us in 15:19 that humanity was created by God with an infusion of his spirit, giving to each person something of God's intent and capacity to judge right from wrong. This capacity of acting with responsibility was given to each person so that he or she could serve as God's steward (khalifa) in creation, doing good and avoiding unrighteousness (2:28). In 76:1, Qur'an reveals to us that we were created by God to be put to the proof of our moral nature. Finally, we are instructed by Qur'an that God created persons who could observe and learn from their surroundings: "in the alternation of night and day, and in all that God has created in the heavens and the earth, there are signs for righteous men" (10:5). And in 16:9, we learn: "It is he who sends down water from the sky, which provides you with your drink and brings forth your pasturage on which your cattle feed. And with it He brings forth corn and olives, dates and grapes and fruits of every kind. Surely in this there is a sign for thinking men."

In the books of the Old Testament, which contain much of the Jewish religious tradition, I find in the books of the Wisdom tradition such as the Proverbs, Ecclesiastes, and the Book of Wisdom, incorporation of the truth I assert here as a reliable compass for morality and ethics. These books speak to a more universal understanding of the human condition and the human person that those that relate historical events or, like the writings of the prophets, reveal the purposes of the Lord God of Israel.

The core truth that I suggest emerges from this presentation of our dependence on a natural order, which has given each of us a moral sense, is that the self has no unquestioned, absolute sovereignty. It has no imperium over others. Its operations – even its intuitions and reasoning – are not fully autonomous, but rather, contingent on a context and intertwined with externalities. In fact, we are more like partners in joint ventures than tyrants able to rule all we see at will.

All arguments for such imperium and all self-serving intuitions that guide us towards exercise of such imperium run up against the moral sense as a real presence in life. Such conflict alienates us from where we are supposed to be in life and leaves us less well off. The individual self is, therefore, rightly understood always to be, in one degree or another, faithful to others either as fiduciary or as beneficiary. From conception to death, the human person is constrained by this truth. Morality and ethics are natural to us, though we may, from time to time, seek to avoid this truth.

Consistent, then, with this truth is the admonition of Jesus Christ that to love God above all else and to love others as we do ourselves get us very near the Kingdom of Heaven (Mark 12:34).

Knowing that we are in some sense without complete self-sovereignty opens the mind to consider what duties are owed to whom. Here is the realm of discourse on morality and ethics wherein we may graciously tolerate a range of differences in degree of opinion as to what actions are preferable. But no degree of difference should be willingly accepted that denies the need for morality and ethics as shaped by the natural tendencies of our moral sense towards sociability and responsibility.

Moral Capitalism and Human Flourishing

The goal of moral capitalism is promoting human flourishing. Those who profit from capitalism should earn their rewards as a consequence of contributions to the system of wealth creation and the good and wise use of wealth for betterment and worthy purpose.

Stewardship and accountability for one's deeds convert personal gain into vocations which fuse personal uniqueness with awareness of larger, more significant accomplishments.

We can graph the possibilities of capitalism using two axes. One axis is a continuum from sadness at the bottom of the graph to happiness at the top. The other axis is a continuum from lack of material possessions and wealth on the left to plenty and wealth on the right.

HAPPINESS

Spiritual Piety &
Transcendence

Best Case

NO-MATERIAL
POSSESIONS
(ECONOMIC POVERTY)

WEALTH

Worst Case

Greed;
Social Darwinism

SADNESS

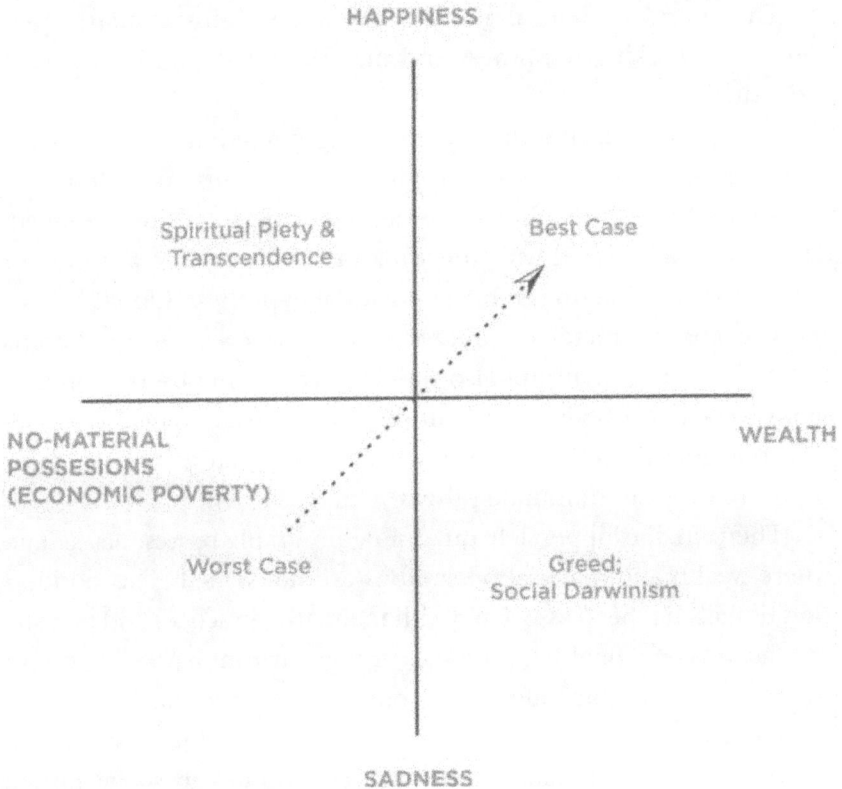

The trajectory of Moral Capitalism is from poverty and sadness on the lower left quadrant to happiness with wealth in the upper right quadrant.

The graph presumes that happiness and wealth are positive enhancers of human flourishing in everyday life.

There are strong arguments from wisdom traditions that, on the individual level, happiness can be superficial and illusory and material possessions a source of worry and a distraction from spiritual and psychological well-being.

But, from the perspective of engagement with the vicissitudes of living, material possessions support the activation of efficacious human dignity and so the experience of self-actualization, a form of happiness.

The moral and legal motifs of human rights similarly presumes that seeking happiness and material well-being is due each
individual.

The graph indicates that the lower right hand quadrant - where
wealth is not associated with happiness - represents an undesirable
outcome of raw greed and some degree of personal unhappiness.
The insight associated with this quadrant is that there are ways of
gaining wealth that do not bring personal happiness. One thinks of
the Dickens' character Ebeneezer Scrooge who has his gold coins
but no love. The quadrant also reflects a common observation that
many seek and obtain wealth under some psychological compulsion that identifies wealth with selfish urges such as the need for
power in order to dominate others.

Then, in the upper left quadrant the graph represents a state
where wealth and material possessions are not valued. This position
traditionally has been associated with meditative practices and pietistic
satisfactions. Personal happiness is, in this environment, sought and
found in intra-psychic states of awareness and appreciation of reality.

Finally, the upper right quadrant represents the desired outcome of a good capitalism, one that contributes to social justice
and human flourishing. The graph assumes that for happiness to
be associated with wealth, the way that such wealth is earned must
be congruent with the better angels of human nature. It must be a
pursuit of wealth that is ethical, responsible, and sensitive to stakeholder concerns and interests.

Markets and the Intangible of Beauty

Can capitalism measure the value of artistic creation. Should
artists be subsidized or should they be subjected to the power of
consumers?

If no one buys their works – consider Van Gogh – do they have
a claim for mistreatment at the hands of boorish, vulgar philistines?

Or do all of us have some moral duty to buy what we don't like?
To attend concerts that give us no pleasure? To buy books or poems
which don't speak to us at all?

To what extent might artists of all genres have a claim on society to provide them with a living in order that they can freely produce what they please?

Who should set value on art – its creators or its consumers?

Selling entertainment to mass markets made many artists very well-to-do. Giving customers what they were willing to pay for worked fine for consumers and for such artists gifted with the ability to read what their audiences desired.

But highbrow formats don't thrive under free market conditions. They need sponsorship. The market for their products is limited to a small range of customers. The value proposition brought forth by sophistication is subtle and ineffable, beyond the scope of rational concepts to capture and domesticate.

Should the artists who produce such expressions of limited "value" in the sense of commercial acceptance and in the sense of rare insight and skill be subsidized? What value do they bring to the common weal? Do they produce public goods of sufficient specificity and importance that they can claim a share of society's wealth?

What about Van Gogh? Would we be worse off without his paintings? Should he have just given up when no one wanted to buy his oils?

What about architecture? Who should pay for an architect to reach for the sublime?

Can art as a public good be reconciled with capitalism and its harsh demands for customer satisfaction?

Markets, as a rule, do not perform at their best where public goods are needed. Individual buyers and sellers who drive markets with their decisions to buy or sell are best at pricing that which is immediately before them, immediately gratifying, tangible and of obvious utility. They are less willing, in the normal case, to price with assurance that which is distant, not easily used, intangible and of no immediate emotional attraction. Private goods fall into the first category of what can be priced and public goods into the second. Because it is more difficult to price public goods, markets don't allocate them well. Buyers and sellers don't show up for transactions in public goods. Intervention by society – mostly by government – is necessary to promote the supply of public goods.

Some non-market form of financing – subsidy or the imposition of regulatory burdens on public "bads" – is most often turned to when the public interest is to be enhanced.

Where art partakes of a public good, therefore, it moves beyond markets towards alternative venues for production. Those interested in the production of such public goods for their inherent aesthetic or cultural impacts and advantages must set up non-market criteria for subsidy and patronage. This is a cultural/political process of compromising different tastes and points of view where price is only part of the decision to finance what markets will not.

Public goods have a claim on corporate social responsibilities ("CSR"). Corporate social responsibility is the business function which negotiates the relationships between business, society and government. It presides over the arena of goods, which are hard to price. It is the decision-making metric which values for business externalities to market prices, intangibles and stakeholder relationships.

Business should, therefore, as a matter of best CSR practices, place a value on highbrow art which can't sustain itself through normal market dynamics, but which elevates our souls, brings beauty to our lives and promotes goodness in our sensibilities.

道

德

CONCLUSION
LOOKING OUT FOR A
BETTER FUTURE

"If we could first know where we are and whither we are tending, we could better judge what to do and how to do it."
- A. Lincoln, June 16, 1858

The preceding chapters have pointed out both serious failures in modern capitalism and remedies for those shortcomings. Capitalism is here to stay; it has no rival proceeding from contrary principles. The experiment in "public ownership of the means of production" was a repressive and often fratricidal failure that produced no good at all. Free markets, private property, material incentives rewarding human desires and ingenuity, each and all manifest the deepest drives of human cognition and aspiration incarnated in each and every person.

But capitalism does have its shortcomings, to say the least. The system provides no guarantees of prosperity; it facilitates inequalities of income and wealth; it shortchanges the cost of externalities; it is not fully rational but subject to many human ethical and intellectual failings.

Our global future is being threatened by large and unsustainable imbalances in the outcomes of global financial intermediation and market dynamics. Despite significant recent progress in promoting corporate responsibility and better governance, unacceptably high levels of debt, unemployment, inequality, and environmental degradation still prevail in the global marketplace.

Poor governance, with its tolerance of crony capitalism and even profiteering from corruption, along with short-term strategic thinking and a serious vacuum in real leadership across all sectors continues to work against achieving a sustainable and prosperous world for us all. These shortcomings must be offset and the imbalances they cause corrected if our longer-term prosperity and wellbeing are to be secured.

Even Adam Smith recognized that free markets do not automatically deliver effective mechanisms of good governance and accountability. Put simply, free markets by and in themselves do not always serve the common good, nor prevent corrupt behavior. But the best solution to these shortcomings is not to jettison the modern free market economy itself; it is to re-institutionalize the values that made this system successful in the first place. Wise stewardship, good governance, and concern for stakeholders are the necessary core values of any sustainable market economy.

What then must be done? What steps must be taken? How do we fully capture the proven and unique capacity of free and fair markets to create wealth, deliver fulfilling employment, promote true justice, and lift the level of prosperity for all? How can we inform, energize and support policy and community efforts to bring about this positive change?

How might the system be improved?

For one, its responses to checks and balances can be strength-
ened to minimize extremes and reduce volatility in outcomes.
Better intellectual understandings of value and valuation can help
in this. Rejection of cronyism and corruption can also put up bar-
ricades against injustice and dysfunction.

First and foremost, government, business and civil society must
fully embrace the reality that their prospects are fundamentally
interrelated and mutually dependent. Business, for example, can't
be a power unto itself - autonomous from considerations of ecological and community well-being. And ethical and moral values cannot
simply be subordinated to short-term interests and profits.

For another, recognition of the importance of the moral sense
and its contributions to sustainability and profitability would
enlighten capitalist decision-making.

Humanity's moral sense speaks through many religions. It is
the "golden rule." It resides in the Catholic social teachings of
human dignity, subsidiarity, solidarity, and goods encumbered
with a moral lien in favor of society. It justifies reformed Christians
in their ministry of seeking God's grace. It is expressed in Islamic
guidance that humanity is a steward for the Lord, holding his
bounty in trust. It motivates Confucian concern for virtuous self-
restraint. It lies within Buddhist mindfulness that the self is always
in transition.

Respect for human dignity now constrains the autonomy of institutions – cultural, social, political and economic. Rights of dominion, once acceptable and legitimated by law and state practices,
are being circumscribed. In the arena of capitalism, the evolution
has been and continues to be towards a new, more complex, law of
property. Decision makers are less and less tolerated when they seek
to internalize positive advantages and externalize to society negative consequences. Property rights now come with encumbrances to
take into account the needs and interests of stakeholders. It is as if
the law of nuisance – sic utere tuo ut alienam no laedas: "so use your
own so as not to injure another's" – is expanding both at the hand
of state regulation and through consumer advocacy on the part of

civil society. The resulting practice is corporate social responsibility ("CSR").

From the dawn of time, economic activity that brought improving living conditions for our ancestors promoted divisions of labor and mutual cooperative engagements with the greatest gains occurring when tasks are divided among workers demanding trust in others and reliance on their capacities for performance and their good intentions. Violence, exploitation, oppression, deceit – all undermine economic achievement.

The successful quest for better livelihoods only takes place within systems of cooperation and production: systems set within the order of nature and within social and cultural institutions. Systems have their dynamic ecological realities of taking in and giving out, of exchanging resources consumed for outputs dispensed, of consuming and producing. System ecologies evolve to adapt to change, always seeking some higher of efficiency, satisfaction or equilibrium.

Social justice implies human flourishing. For social justice to occur individuals need supportive communities and communities need reciprocal commitments of participant and cooperation from individuals. Mutuality lies at the heart of social justice. Recent advances in neuroscience and evolutional biology establish with near certainly that all persons come into the world with a capacity for moral engagement with others. Fostering such moral engagement, then, can only promote social justice.

To assist the system steer away from destructive self-interested and short-term thinking, incentives must be re-aligning so more enlightened and long-term thinking prevails. This means that the interests of all stakeholders, in the broadest societal and environmental sense, must be factored into policy, decision-making, and performance scorecard. Additionally, the relentless and ultimately unsustainable pursuit of compound growth for growth's sake needs to be offset with other considerations of value. Political, business and community mindsets must therefore shift from a near total preoccupation with quantitative growth to one equally concerned over the quality and sustainability of growth.

As part of the needed rebalancing, the full spectrum of long-term risks and impacts that flow from current activities and actions must be recognized and managed. The true present value and real prospects of a company incorporate not just tangible assets and liabilities but also intangible ones – such as customer loyalty, employee productivity, supplier quality, credit worthiness, community approval, and environmental externalities. A total value view of a company's long-term, true 'sustainability' balance sheet consequentially needs to be embraced and managed – not just a narrow financial view.

If this happens, then a new capitalism can emerge that, under this nuanced, more restricted understanding of ownership, puts stakeholder considerations front and center in business enterprise. This is a capitalism more and more guided by the innate moral sense of humanity. A capitalism that not only can survive, but that can – and will – help the entire world thrive in the coming century.

1 See *Global Public Goods*, Inge Kaul, Isabelle Grunberg, Marc A. Stern, editors; Wikipedia at "public goods")
2 Habermas, Jurgen Theory of Communicative Action; From Fact to Norm
3 Goldman, Daniel *Social Intelligence*; Pinker, Steven, The Blank Slate;
4 Dawkins, Richard, *The Selfish Gene*; Dennett, Daniel, The Intentional Stance
5 Hamilton, William, "Innate Social Aptiitudes of Man". *Biosocial Anthropology* 1975
6 Dobbs, David, "A revealing reflection" in *Scientific American Mind* April/May 2006, 22-27
7 Gazzanniga, Michael. *The Ethical Brain*, 2005; Hauser, Marc, Moral Minds, 2006;
8 Fukuyama, Francis, Trust
9 Harrison, Lawrence and Huntington, Samuel, *Culture Matters*, 2000
10 Berger, Peter, and Luckmann, Thomas, *The Social Construction of Reality*, Doubleday, 1966
11 ibid, p. 60
12 ibid. p. 91
13 Lonely Crowd, p. 3
14 ibid, p. 5
15 ibid, p.47
16 ibid, pp 47-48
17 ibid, p.73.
18 Salinger, J.D., *Catcher in the Rye*
19 Bell, Daniel, The Cultural Contradictions of Capitalism, p.12
20 ibid, p. 37
21 ibid, p. 46

22 ibid, p. 55
23 ibid, p 67-69
24 ibid, p 71
25 Brookhiser, Richard, The Way of the WASP
26 ibid p. 130
27 Mailer, Norman, "The White Negro"
28 Weber, Max, The theory of Social and Economic Organization, p. 332
29 ibid, p. 328
30 Saul, John Ralston, *Voltaire's Bastards*, 1991, p. 77
31 ibid, p. 260
32 ibid
33 Parsons, Talcott, and Shils, Edward, editors, *Towards a General Theory of Action* 1951
34 ibid, p.76
35 Bell, Daniel, *The Coming of Post Industrial Society*, 1976
36 ibid, p. 126
37 ibid, p. 127
38 Mills, C. Wright, White Collar, chapt 8
39 Miller, Perry *Errand into the Wilderness,*
40 Jefferson, Thomas, *Notes on the State of VIrginia*
41 Roosevelt, Franklin, Inaugural Address. March 1931
42 John F. Kennedy, Inaugural Address, Jan 21, 1961

www.ingramcontent.com/pod-product-compliance
Lightning Source LLC
Chambersburg PA
CBHW031921190326
41519CB00007B/376